Notes
from the
Hyena's Belly

Notes
from the
Hyena's Belly

AN ETHIOPIAN BOYHOOD

Nega Mezlekia

PICADOR USA

NEW YORK

We gratefully acknowledge the support of Webcom's Unpublished Authors Sweepstakes Programme.

Library of Congress Cataloging-in-Publication Data

Mezlekia, Nega.
    Notes from the Hyena's belly : an Ethiopian boyhood / Nega Mezlekia—
1st Picador USA ed.
        p. cm.
    Originally published: Toronto; New York : Penguin, 2000.
    ISBN 0-312-26988-9
    1. Mezlekia, Nega, 1958– —Childhood and youth. 2. Jijiga
(Ethiopia)—Biography. 3. Ethiopia—History—1974– . I. Title.
DT390.J54 M48 2001
963'.2—dc21   00-050126

First published in Canada by Penguin Books under the title *Notes from the Hyena's Belly: Memories of My Ethiopian Boyhood*

10 9 8 7 6 5 4 3 2

To Mam and Wondwossen

መሽ በሩን ዝጉት ከቀሪ ልማይ፤
ተከፍቶ ማደሩን ሲየወደውም ሆይ።

TABLE OF CONTENTS

Notes
from the
Hyena's Belly

BOOK ONE: SUNRISE

SAINTS AND SINNERS

I WAS BORN IN the year of the paradox, in the labyrinthine city of Jijiga. After a three-year absence, the rains had come, swelling the rivers and streams. The clay desert, as dry as the skin of a drum, became green once more. Queen Menen, wife of King Haile Selassie, lay dying. She was as reluctant to leave this world as I was to leave the womb.

My father sent for the neighbour, a nun who also practised as a midwife, to assist my mother in this difficult birth. Queen Menen, far off in her palace, sent for fortune-tellers and Devil-tamers—modern medicine was failing to cure her. In our small home, lost somewhere in the tangled paths of domestic Jijiga, the midwife pronounced her certainty that there was not one child, but two—with golden crowns on their heads—fighting against their own birth. This nun could interpret the language of the unborn and the dreams of the dead, and had heard the twins whisper their belief that they had been delivered to the wrong universe.

The nun needed help. She asked for the assistance of another midwife, Mrs. Tsege Kebede, who was found at a local bar celebrating the deliveries of six children just the day before. Tsege was already quite drunk when she walked in, and bragged about her legendary success in delivering the unexpected. Tsege had once helped a passing angel, caught between the two worlds, with the agony of childbirth, successfully delivering her young with wings intact.

Now, as the two women bickered over how to convince the twins to be born, how to assure them that they had, indeed, been sent to the right universe and that, though this world might be tarnished, violent and rife with pestilence, it was nothing one couldn't get used to, in time, my father stubbed out his last cigarette and came indoors to announce the dawn of a new day. As he pronounced his sentence, I slipped into this strange bickering world that smelt of incense and *ood*.

"The sun has risen," my father said. I was named for his words: *Nega*.

With sunrise the farmers' market on the other side of the city came alive. Somali women balanced fragile pots of milk and butter on the crowns of their heads—each vase a necessary and natural extension of the bearer, as if a second head had appeared over each woman at dawn. On their backs they carried sacks of grain to sell at the market. The Somali men led caravans of camels into the city, loaded with sacks of sorghum, corn or charcoal. Some camels bore stacks of firewood that reached far into the sky—each camel dragged forward savagely by a rope tied to its upper lip, splitting it in two.

In our home, my mother's eyes reflected the two bickering midwives as they peered down at my emerging head and fell strangely silent. Shaking their heads in disappointment, they told my mother that her new son had a head big enough to give the illusion of twins. They told her that her son would lead the life of a rebel, as he had refused to be born wearing his golden crown. Tsege went back to the tavern to have another drink. The nun went home to her morning prayers. Looking back, I am relieved that my father came in when he did. Had it not been for his announcement of dawn, the two disappointed midwives might have convinced my exhausted mother to name me for the size of my head.

Meanwhile, somewhere far away, the Devil-tamer pronounced his cure for Queen Menen: the sacrifice of the young. "Candidates must be free of any form of body piercing; they must have no wounds or scars that would compromise the quality of the blood," he announced. Countless messengers were dispatched from the palace to scour the countryside looking for children who had neither bruises nor scars.

In 1958, the year of the paradox, I was born in Ethiopia, in a hot and dusty city called Jijiga, which destroyed its young.

J IJIGA IS BUILT on a vast, unmitigated plain, with no greenery in sight except for the occasional cactus bush used as shelter by the wandering hyena, and the inevitable sacred tree in every compound. The city is surrounded by rocky mountains on all sides save the north, which is open as far as the eye can see. The northern horizon is curtailed only by the sun's mirages and the eternal dusty winds of the dry season. Jijiga is in an arid part of Ethiopia, a dry, sandless desert where even the smallest wind creates devils—whirlwinds of dust that rise high into the heavens and are visible from miles away.

By day we children chased wind devils, poking holes in their bellies with knives. By night we huddled in bed, remembering our mothers' warning to tell all strangers that our ears were pierced so that we would not be snatched up and sacrificed for the ever-dying Queen. We could hear the wild howls of hyenas from the desolate mountains and knew that any cow or donkey left outside the gates of the compounds would spend its night in the hyena's belly.

THERE IS A story about the donkey and the hyena called "The Donkey Who Sinned."

Once upon a time a lion, a leopard, a hyena and a donkey got together to solve a riddle, to discuss the bad conditions that plagued the land, to discover why the rains had stopped coming and why food was so scarce.

"Why do we have to suffer like this? How long do we have to go on without food?" they asked, over and over.

"Maybe one of us has sinned and God is punishing us," one of them suggested.

"Perhaps we should confess our sins out loud, and ask God for forgiveness," another added.

To this all of them agreed, and the lion began:

"I am sorry, for I committed a very terrible sin. I once found a young bull in a village, broke his back and ate him."

The other animals looked at the lion, whom they all feared because of his strength, and shook their heads.

"No, no," they protested, "that is not a sin! That is exactly what God would have liked you to do."

The leopard followed:

"I am very, very sorry, for I committed an awful sin. I once found a goat in a valley that had wandered from the herd. I hid behind a bush, caught him and ate him."

The other animals looked at the leopard, whose skill at hunting they all admired, and protested:

"No, no, that is not a sin! In fact, if you hadn't eaten that goat, God would have been angry with you."

The hyena then spoke:

"Well, I think I am the sinner. I once snuck into a village, caught a chicken by surprise, and ate it all at once."

"No, no," the animals protested, "that isn't a sin. God would have liked it if you ate two of them."

Then the donkey spoke:

"Once, when my master was driving me along a trail, he met a friend and stopped to talk. While they were talking, I went to the edge of the trail and nibbled at a few blades of grass."

The other animals looked at the donkey, whom no one feared or admired. After a moment of silence, they shook their heads sadly and said:

"That is a *sin*! A very terrible sin! You are the cause of all our misery!"

And so the lion, the leopard and the hyena jumped on the donkey, cut him up into pieces and devoured him.

We children lived like the donkey, careful not to wander off the beaten trail and end up in the hyena's belly.

JIJIGA IS A divided city—by common, though unspoken, consent. The northern half is inhabited by Christians, mostly Amharas, and the southern by Muslims, mainly Somalis.

The Somali man is easy to identify: he is almost always dressed in a *sherit*, a long multicoloured garment stitched like a sack, which is tied about the waist, hanging loose at the bottom. Most carry a cane in one hand, and a piece of twig in their mouth, with which they brush their teeth if they happen to have nothing better to do. The nomads who venture into town may wear huge daggers at their waists. They are usually barefoot, though they may carry sandals to wear in town—balanced carefully over the shoulder, hanging from the end of their canes.

The women wear colourful, loose-fitting dresses that fall to their feet. As the woman walks, she holds her dress with one hand so it doesn't drag on the ground. She might drape a vibrantly coloured shawl over her shoulder and head, and wear sandals on her feet. I do not recall once seeing a Somali woman outdoors in the company of her husband or a male friend, even on major social occasions, like Ramadan, or at weddings or funerals.

The northern half of town appears to have consulted with a different fashion designer. The men dress in various forms of Western jackets and pants. The women signify the different phases in their lives by the colour and make of the dresses they wear. A girl invariably picks colourful outfits, cut according to the style of the time—though always hanging well below the knee. She might even indulge herself and wear a T-shirt and a pair of jeans. After marriage, however, her wardrobe will undergo a drastic transformation. It is as though the monotony of day-to-day life, of kitchen duties and the rearing of children, slowly bleaches all colour from her life. A woman who is wife and mother wears a traditional white dress and head-wear, and a *netela*—a white, lightweight shawl with colourful trim.

Although I was born and raised in the northern part of town, the excitement and intrigue of the other half was not lost on me. A family friend, Mustafa, brought home everything I needed to know.

Mustafa was one of two permanent house guests at our residence. He occupied one of the service rooms. Our other perpetual guest was Ms. Yetaferu, who stayed in the other service room, and was constantly at odds with Mustafa. The two were seldom on speaking terms, and when they were it wasn't because peace reigned in the compound.

Mustafa was barely five feet tall, a squat man who often sported a couple of days' growth of beard. He had a great sense of humour; an unpredictable, often contradictory character; and an insatiable passion for crime. I don't recall ever wondering how he came to be in our household. I do recall that Mustafa's father was a family friend who, on his deathbed, made my father promise to watch over his young and reckless son despite the fact that Mustafa had an array of uncles and aunts nearby. Dad kept his promise.

I learned my first Somali words from Mustafa. He also taught me how to break a street lamp (with a sling and a well-aimed stone), how to get my sister to give me her glass of milk (by spitting in her cup), and how to avoid homework without once getting a reprimand from the teacher (by calling in sick, and then copying from friends).

Mustafa spent his mornings roaming the city and his afternoons chewing *chat* and plotting some new intrigue. He often got away with his mischief, but from time to time he would be jailed—and then it would take all of my father's connections, and a good deal of expense, to get him released.

Mustafa loathed work. He didn't have to pay for his meals or lodging, and had some income from real estate—but nevertheless he delighted in swindling money from others. In the early days, the most frequent victim was his older brother, who owned a flourishing business. He had a huge retail store in the

Somali part of town that sold kitchen supplies: sugar, cooking oil, flour, pots and pans, readymade clothes, fragrances and the like. When Mustafa was in need of money, he would send me, note in hand, to his brother. I never knew what was written on the note, as it was scribbled in Arabic, but knew that my arrival signalled terrible news to Mustafa's brother. He would grumble the moment I walked in, but usually gave me some money in an envelope to deliver to Mustafa. Good news to Mustafa meant a quarter to me.

Sometimes his brother would refuse to send any money to Mustafa, which signalled sibling warfare. Mustafa had various options in his arsenal, but his favoured weapon was the mansion the two of them had inherited from their parents. A huge building with many rooms on its two floors, it was fenced in by stone walls and located in a lively part of downtown. Mustafa owned the whole ground floor, which he rented out to a renowned contraband smuggler, who I suspected was Mustafa's accomplice in his various schemes. The upper half of the house was the residence of Mustafa's brother and his family.

The day after he had been snubbed by his brother, Mustafa would dispatch a team of masons, carpenters and hauliers to his house before the break of dawn, with orders to disassemble each room, brick by brick, stone by stone, so that it could be moved and readily reassembled for an unnamed purchaser. But, before the demolition started, he would alert his brother to the sale, advising him to prop up his rooms and avoid expensive losses. His brother had never been able to buy Mustafa out, because no matter what price Mustafa set there was always someone, somewhere, who doubled his brother's bid. Building materials were not expensive in Jijiga, and nobody knew who would pay such an insane price for something so worthless, but in the end a settlement was always reached in which Mustafa got some money in return for promising not to sell the building for another few months.

A few years passed before this perpetual circus finally folded tent. Dad intervened: Mustafa was cajoled into selling his half of the property to his beloved brother, and was forced to concentrate his resources on original schemes.

Property tax is one of the most unpredictable expenses in the life of an Ethiopian landowner. No one knows for sure what the rate will be and when, if ever, someone will be dispatched to collect it. Some people live and die without ever hearing from the taxman, while others may get a surprise call decades after they register their land.

The tax collector in Jijiga was a rather eccentric man, about the same height as Mustafa but much older. He wore an eye patch and carried a huge leather bag and a cane with a retractable knife. As he walked from door to door, collecting taxes, he was escorted by a man in uniform who carried a rifle. He was said to be a wealthy man, with money buried in various places in his backyard. The money had been wrapped in antelope skin, sanctified by three sorcerers, two medicine men and a renowned curser—a treatment that would render completely blind anyone who tried to open the bag, except the taxman. This, however, did not deter some desperate souls from attempting to share in the loot. In fact, not a single month passed without someone perforating the dark soil in his backyard under the cover of darkness. In the morning light, it looked as if the gods had turned up his backyard with a diabolical ferocity.

Mustafa did not dig in the taxman's backyard. He merely tried to look like him and act like him. He bought himself an eye patch and clothes that might have come from the taxman's own wardrobe, and sprinkled some wet ash on his hair to close the age gap. He hired himself an escort, whom he dressed like the taxman's guard, and armed him with a borrowed rifle. He then dispatched two respected burglars to buy him old tax receipts, if they could, or retrieve them from their hiding places, if they could not. The landowners on the new taxman's list were, like most Ethiopians, illiterate. They would only look for the familiar insignias on the receipts, not the words that were written on them.

The project would have been successful, and Mustafa a rich man, had it not been for his untimely decision to swindle his hired escort. He paid the escort ten percent of the proceeds, but then immediately dispatched one of the two burglars to retrieve it. He then paid the successful burglar fifty percent of what he had collected, which would have been a good deal if he hadn't dispatched the second burglar to reclaim the first burglar's loot the very next day. The second burglar was also promised half of what he brought back, but, before he could even finish counting it, Mustafa took it from him, arguing that the second burglar had not taken part in the actual tax collection and that, anyway, he had already been paid for retrieving the tax receipts from the unwary public.

These little indiscretions earned Mustafa a two-year prison sentence.

Following his release, Mustafa became the very picture of piety—for a while. He read the Koran out loud at regular intervals throughout the day, loud enough to scare the songbirds off the trees; prayed five times a day on his colourful mat, head pointing east; and declined any food from our kitchen, preferring the Muslim restaurants in town. He even walked through the compound with his eyes fixed on the ground. This piety of his was far more annoying to Ms. Yetaferu, the other permanent guest, than his brush with the law had been. She carefully watched his every move and eavesdropped on his prayers, to make sure that he did not, in any way, contradict her own communion with God. Alas, she had forgotten that Mustafa prayed in Arabic, of which she could not understand a single word.

Ms. Yetaferu was, in many ways, a sad foil for Mustafa. She was somewhat deficient in her sense of humour, quite predictable in her manner, and she walked about with a nervous and suspicious look on her face, as though the world around her was conspiring to pull the ground out from under her feet. She was no relation to us, nor had anyone in town ever come to visit her, and yet she had been around for as long as I could remember. Mother gave her shelter because she and Ms. Yetaferu happened to be from the same home town.

Ms. Yetaferu was an Orthodox Christian, like us. She believed in the sanctity of the Orthodox Christian Church, and in its superiority over all the other churches that had followed in its footsteps. But most of all, she believed in the saints and their ability to mediate or intervene on behalf of parishioners who found themselves at odds with Christ. If one needed any kind of help, she was convinced, one could always appeal directly to the saint—for rains, say, or a good harvest—and the saint would deliver, unbeknownst to Christ. After all, there were far too many saints for Christ to keep track of.

Like us, she also worshipped the *Adbar*—the traditional sacred tree of the family. The huge tree rooted in our front yard was like no other tree in the compound: its roots needed frequent watering, and incense and *ood* needed to be burned under its huge trunk. She made sacrifices before the *Adbar* at

13

the beginning of each month, and knew to make only small requests of the *Adbar*, for the sake of expediency.

What annoyed Dad most was how she worshipped, with equal fervour, the spirits of her ancestors. The old woman burned incense and *ood* behind her door and invited the spirits to sneak in, camouflaged by the smoke. Her *Wukabi*, or personal spirits, required three days of uninterrupted blessing each month and endless festivities. So Dad tried to get rid of her by wedding her to a solo barroom entertainer and then chasing him out of town, with his new wife and his violin in tow. It didn't work. What Dad failed to understand was that the woman was married already, to her *Wukabi*.

Ms. Yetaferu never worked a day in her life—though, unlike Mustafa, it wasn't because she was lazy or loathed work. Everyone knew that she was the first to get out of bed in the morning; that she was the one who prepared the household's first of three coffee ceremonies each day, waking the neighbours and inviting them to join her; that she read each individual's daily fortune from the dregs in the mugs, before sending them off to work; and that she never went to bed before the hyenas had reclaimed the town, descending in droves from the mountains like an army of ants tracking sugar grains. The reason Ms. Yetaferu never worked at all was because there was not a single day in the year that was not sacred to her.

The Ethiopian calendar is divided into thirteen months, each thirty days long except the last, which is only five or six days (depending on whether it is a leap year). Every day of the month is assigned to a saint or two: day one is dedicated to St. Raguel and the *Adbar*, day two is St. Samuel's, day three is St. Libanos's, and so on. Of course, not all saints are created equal. Indeed, only a few of them are considered saintly enough to warrant an official holiday, preventing the farmer from tilling his land and the carpenter from felling a tree. No fisherman, for instance, can fish on the nineteenth day of any month, because it is St. Gabriel's day; nor on the twenty-third day, as he has to pay his respects to St. George; nor on any one of the other nine days throughout the year assigned to the saintliest of saints. Other individuals have their own favoured saints throughout the year, further reducing the number of days they are allowed to work.

Compounding Ms. Yetaferu's scheduling problem was the fact that some of the saints' days coincided with spirit days, forcing her to make a grave decision, choosing one over the other. She always placed her *Wukabi* ahead of any saint, though in some cases she was able to go to church in the morning and return home early enough to reconcile with her spirits. On such days she would close the door and windows of her room and use pieces of rag to plug any crevice that might let in light, to avoid detection by the saints while she communicated with her spirits.

All told, Ms. Yetaferu's holidays, each of which demanded prayers and sacrifices and prohibited doing any form of work, consisted of 263 saints' days, 52 Sundays, 9 other Christian holidays, 13 *Adbar* days, 36 *Wukabi* days (some of which coincided with saint's days) and 12 days to worship her ancestors' spirits. Altogether in an average year there were 368 consecutive days on which she was not able to work. Alas, the calendar was three days too short for her to complete her prayers.

THE LANGUAGE
OF THE ANGELS

————————

B EING BORN and raised in Jijiga, a multicultural
mixing bowl, I was insulated from Amharas'
mythical view of the world—until, at the age of
nine, I went to the eastern highlands. There, while visiting my
mother's cousins, I discovered how deeply rooted the prejudices were.

As a clergyman in Ethiopia's oldest Christian denomina-
tion, the Orthodox Christian Church, my uncle Yeneta followed age-old traditions with staunch vehemence. He always
wore a white outfit: a pair of white breeches, a loosely fitted
white shirt that fell below his knees, a white turban, and a *netela*
in which he invariably wrapped himself regardless of how hot
or cold it was.

Like so many priests before and after him, Yeneta rose
before dawn every morning to begin his communion with
God. The early morning prayer was carried out in the inner
room of the church. Every detail—the scented air, the music,
the decor—was made consistent with his holy prayers.
Entrance to this room was forbidden to all unordained souls,

except on special occasions when children were permitted to enter in order to receive a piece of bread and a sweet beverage, the "flesh and blood" of Jesus.

Except for Sundays, or when he presided over funeral masses, Yeneta would return home at around ten in the morning. On his way home, many believers would bend before him in a clear demonstration of their humble stature. The priest would give them his blessings and permit them to kiss the crucifix that he proudly dangled from his right hand. In his other hand he carried, like so many priests before him, a *chira*—long strands of bound horsehair mounted on a decorated wooden handle—which he periodically shook over each shoulder to deter flies from defiling his clean and holy person.

Yeneta's influence and position in the community were never more apparent than during the season of Lent, as he gave divine commands and passed judgment on his humble parishioners. At the age of nine, I was persuaded to attend one such event, an early morning service, in the company of two distant cousins and Yeneta's daughter-in-law. After the sermon, we were ushered into the confession room, which adjoined the burial tomb of a famous feudal lord who had lived nearby. The sparse, furnitureless room was dominated by a single portrait of Jesus, crucified. His dark complexion and Mediterranean features were more reminiscent of a youthful Yeneta than of the poor Jewish man they purported to represent. The wild plumes of exotic incense that rose from a pair of giant incense burners, the few chandeliers that held lit candles, and the small basin for baptism were the only items to relieve the eye of the walls' baleful stare.

The parishioners slowly filed into the room and assumed what I suspected were their usual positions around the perimeter—backs to the wall, shoulder touching shoulder, faces sober and inscrutable. I was pressed into a corner, from which I was able to observe what went on.

Yeneta's entrance was announced by two teen-aged deacons clad in colourful gowns who were dangling incense burners from their hands and reciting passages from the Holy Scriptures. Two more deacons, adults this time, slowly walked into the room followed by Yeneta. In a subdued tone, Yeneta uttered a few divine platitudes before making it known that confessions were to begin. A respectably dressed man by the door was the first to unburden himself of his guilt. He cleared his throat uncertainly, leaned towards Yeneta in a desperate attempt to maintain his privacy, and quietly announced: "I have bitten my tongue."

After generations of sins, the church and its parishioners had developed a unique dialect, forged out of common language, consisting of euphemisms that made the act of confession more endurable. To have bitten one's tongue meant to have lied, deceived or perjured; to have got around the ladle meant to have indulged in food forbidden during the Lent season—animal products, though not fish.

The next to confess was a woman who had "cried with one eye," or lusted. The priest swiftly pronounced judgment: she was to pray five times at the altar of Jesus. A few confessions later, a young man, obviously struggling with his shy and reserved nature, admitted he had "fallen off the bed." Yeneta commanded him to pray seven times and light two candles at the foot of the dark, stylized Christ that hung from the wall.

It occurred to me then that I too had sinned. Indeed, I had fallen off my bed just the other night, having been entangled in one of those perpetual nightmares in which I was being chased by a foe. I was desperately trying to outrun my assailant, but, as so often happens when one dreams, I was running on the spot, and the creature was quickly closing the gap. I made one final attempt at evasion, concentrated all of my energy upon a single escape, and darted out, only to knock myself out of my bed. I hadn't thought anything of this until I witnessed the young man's remorse. Moved by the gravity with which his confession was made, I cried out loudly before everyone, "I too have fallen off my bed."

The sobriety that hung like a pall over the room was immediately broken. I could hear muffled laughter lightening the air. Though his lips did not curve or betray the least emotion, Yeneta's eyes were dancing. One person pinched my ear, another lightly slapped my head, and yet a third, my mild-mannered cousin, leaned over and whispered in my ear not to open my mouth again unless it was suicide that I was after. Later I learned that to have fallen off the bed meant to have indulged in sex—a forbidden act during the fasting period.

YENETA COULD, and did, inspire fear. One day, I encountered Yeneta's eighty-year-old frame in the dimly lit sanctuary adjoining his bedroom, as he read from the holy book in a singsong rhythm. His long hair was bound inside a turban. His white beard fell to his chest.

Yeneta's Bible was perhaps the oldest one in all of Ethiopia. The cover was made of finely polished *qwara* wood, rubbed with bruised herbs and oils and wrapped in sheepskin. The pages themselves were made of sheepskin and beaten fine as bond paper, and were inscribed in an ancient liturgical language called Geez. The Bible was so heavy that it had taken two men to lay it on the table in Yeneta's sanctuary, from which it would never be removed.

"Yeneta," I asked, "what is the language of the angels?"

The venerable priest stopped his rhythmic reading of the Bible. His eyes flashed angrily, like wildfire. He rose to his full height, six feet three inches tall, and stared into my eyes for a full measure of eternity before shaking his head in disappointment and sitting down.

"Indeed," Yeneta said, "you make me wonder if you are Amhara or if you were found in the dump."

I found out that the Divine Author delivers in Amharic, and that the Devil speaks Oromo.

Not all amharas are created equal. In fact, there is no other ethnic group in the nation with such a pronouncedly prescriptive system of interaction. Aside from class distinctions, the two forbidden groups that a pure Amhara can never associate with, let alone marry, are the *Budas* and the *Lalibelas*.

A *Buda* is someone known to possess the evil eye. Traditionally, *Budas* were involved in the blacksmith and pottery trades, living and working in the isolated, rundown quarters of the city. Nowadays, *Budas* live and work among the highest ranks of Amhara society, and are only persecuted if it is established that they are definitely responsible for the sickness or death of someone in the community. *Budas* are held responsible for those sudden afflictions that come upon people in public places. If, for instance, one experiences a piercing pain while laughing in public and such a pain persists for days, it is the work of a *Buda*. If someone who is handsome comes home sick after attending a public event, it is the result of the evil eye. These illnesses can often be cured by chanting special sacred words, but sometimes an expert must be called. The expert begins by trying to determine which one of the known *Budas* attended the social event. Then the patient is brought before the guilty *Buda*, who is made to spit upon the victim, thus releasing the patient from the awful effects of the evil eye.

In those instances where the expert is unable to determine which *Buda* attended the social event, the forehead of the victim is stamped with a hot iron brand. The "signature" will show up on the face of the guilty *Buda*, thereby enabling the alert neighbours to spot him or her right away. A *Buda* with a noticeable facial scar would seldom venture out of doors.

Budas also have a mysterious way of transforming themselves into hyenas, or of joining a pack by riding on the back of a hyena. Hyenas are the most common, notorious predators in Ethiopia. They break into barns and compounds and steal donkeys, horses, goats and sheep. Hyenas, although cowardly and sheepish individually, are so fierce in a pack that no one would dare to confront them. *Buda* experts are engaged in the villages in order to determine whether or not any known *Budas* are travelling among the hyenas so they can be held responsible for the lost property.

The other group pure Amharas are forbidden to associate with are the *Lalibelas*. *Lalibelas* are people who, through a genetic inheritance that makes them prone to leprosy, are forced to beg out loud before sunrise at specific times of the year. A *Lalibela* may be a successful businessman or a renowned fortune-teller and financially well off, but because of a divine judgment must beg before dawn or become immediately afflicted with leprosy. If *Lalibelas* do not beg and howl before sunrise, their limbs fall off and their faces become deformed beyond recognition.

This practice was maintained for generations, until the military junta assumed power in 1974 and declared that howling before daybreak while begging—a practice that disrupted the pace of the revolution—was illegal and punishable by summary execution. Many *Lalibelas* suddenly discovered, to their astonishment and delight, that nothing happened if they ceased to beg.

MEMORIES OF
MEMERAE'S SHED

———————————

A S A CHILD OF the Amhara community, I was brought up according to time-honoured aristocratic moral codes. A child was expected to have unfaltering respect for his parents, elders and all authority figures, and to be strictly obedient without complaint. Children raised with decent values would never speak to their elders unless spoken to, would give way to an elder who was about to cross their path, would rise from their seats if an elder passed by, and would never put their hands in their pockets when answering an elder. Infraction of any of these unspoken rules would mark the child as undesirable. Such a child was considered unfit to be friends with the other children, and was marked for further disciplinary action by the school authorities. Persistent defiance and unruliness could even lead, in an extreme case, to disinheritance, since respect for elders was not only a measure of a child's character, but a reflection upon the family as well. A well-behaved and respectful child, on the other hand, was rewarded. Word of the child's good behaviour quickly spread to the parents and other notables in the community, serving as a priceless character reference.

The corollary of this moral code was the commonly held belief that a spanking now and again would help a child to grow up "straight," like a well-tended tree. If a child grew in a "crooked" manner, it was believed that no form of discipline could straighten him. It was the business of the entire community to see that each child grew like that well-tended tree. A child who swore in public, for example, would likely be spanked by a complete stranger, who would then thoroughly investigate that child's family tree with a view to taking the matter up with the irresponsible parents.

My MOTHER HAD peculiar beliefs about the ways in which the futures of her children were determined. She believed that a child had to enrol in school at the precise age of four years and four days to be successful as a student; that children needed to have their gums massaged with the ashes of *werka* wood in the early hours of the morning in order to grow a mouthful of well-structured teeth; and that a child needed to drink a glassful of a murky and bitter beverage made of *kosso* flowers every three months to purge and cleanse the bowels. I was registered in school at the precise age of four years and four days.

I spent my first two years at a private school, reading, writing, and solving riddles composed in Amharic, the language of kings. The school was quite modest. Three of the walls were made of dried twigs, and the fourth was the wall of our teacher's home. I remember that the walls were unstable, and we were constantly reminded not to lean on them. If the water delivery man tied his donkey too close to the wall, the animal would nibble at the dried leaves, pulling the building askew with each branch it tugged at.

The roof of our classroom was also made of dried twigs. We could see the sky through it. High above, the birds watched us from the heavens. Black kites flew overhead, to make sure that we did not carry brown paper bags. They knew that the butcher wrapped meat in brown paper. If they saw anyone walking outside with a brown parcel in hand, they snatched it away from him. We always covered our books and things in old newspaper. Thrushes, perched on the roof, sang for us. They also dropped on our heads. We always moved our stools out of the way when the birds were on the roof.

The floor of our little classroom was as God created it, dirt. It was sprayed with water twice daily to keep the dust devils from rising up in the middle of a session. But the ants were allowed to roam free. They travelled in a very long column from one end of the room to the other. The ants always watched us as they went up and down, to make sure that we were paying attention to the teacher. If a student happened to fall asleep in the middle of a class, an ant would depart from the parade, climb the leg of the student, and pinch him on the thigh before resuming its march.

Our teacher was called "Memerae" (My teacher) Beyene. Memerae did not have legs. Or, if he did, we never saw them, as he was always inside a sack. The sack was tied at his waist and covered everything below it. He dragged himself on the ground. Or better, he swung himself along. He would prop himself on two wooden supports, which he held in his hands, lift his body an inch above the ground and swing himself forward. Looking at him above the shoulders, as he came from a distance, it seemed as though he was riding a diminutive roller coaster.

Memerae Beyene was a monk. His faith and trust were placed in St. Michael. He himself travelled hundreds of kilometres from his hometown to serve the church of Jijiga. When he wasn't teaching, or sick and bedridden, he was to be found in the confines of the church, reading the Bible aloud, drowning out the courtship songs of the starlings, and caring for the rich dead, who are better housed than the living poor. Memerae was an angry man. No one saw him smile, ever. Many believed that he had no teeth. He was a hateful man. He hated everyone and everything, including the *Adbar*. He wished that someone would cut down all the sacred trees in town. He even hated the *Tsewa*.

The *Tsewa* is a group of twelve women who favour a common saint and make a pact to worship together on the saint's chosen day. Each month they make sacrifices together, sharing the miracles—afflictions cured, lost items recovered, all as a result of the saint's unmistakable interventions. The sacrifices consist of snacks and *tella*, a locally brewed beer. Each ceremony lasts one full afternoon, or until all of the *tella* has been consumed and the ladies are happily drunk. If one sees a respectable woman staggering in the street, it is a sure sign that she is coming from a *Tsewa*, and one must help her get home safely. *Tsewa* meetings rotate from one household to the next, so that each member incurs the expense only once per year.

Memerae liked saints, but thought that one should only make sacrifices in church. Nobody agreed with him. Many people suspected he was secretly a Catholic, and that he might even eat pork! Mam warned me never to accept food from

Memerae, but I didn't have to worry because Memerae never invited anyone to share a meal with him.

All we learned in school was Amharic. There were no mathematics, science or sports sessions. For as long as we remained in that dingy school, two long years, we poured our time into learning the intricacies of this ancient language whose alphabet contains 268 characters. Half of the front of the room was covered by a chart. Memerae would sit on a huge tortoise shell beside the chart, holding a long stick in his hand, and lead us through the rows. He would strike each letter with a learned confidence, and announce *"Ha-Hu-He-..."* and we would follow after. When we finished the chart, he would begin again.

After a few weeks, we learned the sequence by heart, and no longer needed to watch the chart. Instead, we watched the birds through the roof while repeating after him: *"Ha-Hu-He-..."* But Memerae did not like this. Whenever he caught a student looking elsewhere, he commanded him to stand up and name a letter picked from the chart at random. The student would invariably fail to give the correct answer, and Memerae would invariably pinch the boy's cheek very hard, making him cry.

We were pinched so often that we soon began to carry small bottles of baby oil with us and rub it on our cheeks, to make it harder for Memerae to get a hold on our skin. But Memerae did not like that either, and started using the ruler.

After a couple of months, I got so tired of the monotony that I would start to cry immediately after Mam woke me for school in the morning. I told her that all we learned was the alphabet, that I could already recite it from beginning to end without looking at the chart, and that I no longer needed to attend school. One day I rolled myself in the blanket and refused to answer her. She sat by my bedside and told me the story of how one grain at a time brings good fortune.

ONCE UPON A time there was a King in Shewa. He spent his days and nights listening to stories. Storytellers came from villages all over the countryside to tell tales to the King, but after a few years there were no stories left in the country that the King hadn't already heard. He sent messengers to neighbouring kingdoms looking for new storytellers. After a few more years, he had heard all the stories in the land. Finally, in desperation, he decided that what he needed was a storyteller who could make him cry out, "Enough! no more! I am done with stories." If such a person existed, the King swore to make him a prince and give him a great piece of land.

Many came, hoping to become princes and wealthy landowners, and the King always listened to their stories eagerly, without saying a word. One day a poor farmer came to tell the King a story that would make him cry out in protest. The King smiled at the poor farmer and said: "Did you know that many famous storytellers have come here, without telling me enough, and here you are, in your simple innocence, expecting to be made the owner of land, and awarded the title of prince? I know already that you are wasting my time, but nevertheless you may try."

The farmer seated himself on a rug, at the foot of the King, and began his story.

"Once there was a peasant in Axum who sowed wheat," he said. "When the crop ripened, he mowed it, threshed it and stored it in a granary. It was the best harvest he'd ever had. But there was a small hole in his granary, barely large enough to pass a straw through—and that is the irony in this tale. When all the grain was stored and the farmer went home, delighted, an ant came and entered through the hole. He picked up a single grain, which he carried away to his anthill to eat."

"Aha!" said the King, becoming more interested in the story, as it was one he had not heard before.

"The next day," the poor farmer continued, "another ant came through the same hole and found a grain, which he also took away."

"Very well! Continue!" said the King, showing more interest.

"And the day after that," the farmer continued, "another ant came and carried away another grain."

"Aha!"

"And the next day a different ant came, and he took one more grain."

"Yes, yes," interrupted the King, with some signs of impatience, "I understand all that. Let us proceed with the main thrust of the story."

The farmer made himself quite comfortable on the rug, and continued with his narrative: "The following day, a different ant came, and took one more grain. And the day after that, another ant came, and took another grain."

"Let us cut short the details and get on with the story," the King yelled, betraying his anger with the farmer.

"The day after that, another ant came and . . ." the farmer continued.

"Please! Please!" yelled the King.

"But Your Highness," said the farmer quietly, "there are so very many ants in this story." The farmer once again made himself comfortable on the rug, and continued where he had left off: "And the day following that, another ant came, and took another grain. And the day after that . . ."

"You should stop dallying," the King screamed. "After all," he noted with gravity, "the story is the thing."

"But this is the essence of the story," the farmer replied. "And the next day another ant came and took away another grain. And the day following that . . ."

"But," the King interposed, "all this is mere detail, let us get on with the plot."

"Certainly," the farmer said, and continued with his tale: "And the day after that another ant came, and took away another grain. And the day after that . . ."

"Stop!" the King shrieked. "I want no more of this!"

"Your Highness," the farmer offered, "the story must be told in the right sequence; the granary, after all, is still full, and must be emptied. That is in the next story. And the next day . . ."

"No! No! It must not be!" the King yelled.

"And the next day another ant came and . . ."

"Enough, enough, you may have the land and the title of prince!" the King screamed, rushing from the palace, fuming.

And so, the poor farmer became the owner of a large expanse of land, and a respected prince.

I wanted to be a prince, like the farmer, and so I stayed in school.

Approximately three months after we started school, the routine changed. Memerae brought a new chart, on which the alphabet was completely scrambled, and it became our turn to lead him through the maze. He would pick a student from his list, and make him go over the chart out loud. Another would follow, and another, until we had all been over the chart. Whenever we were close to memorizing the latest chart, a new one would appear.

Once Memerae was completely satisfied that we could identify each of the characters, he taught us why certain of the letters repeated themselves. There were sixty-three such characters. For instance, there were six characters representing *Ha*, two for *Se*, four for . . .

Because it was rude to associate a king with something so intimate as a kiss, the *ki* in king would be different than the *ki* in kiss. As the sun was a symbol of power and eternity, the *su* in sun would be different from the *su* in sugar, which was a perishable item. And, as power was something for the gods and kings, the *po* in power . . . We spent the rest of the year learning to identify celestial and imperial features, and to distinguish their spelling from that of everyday things. No individual would be accorded a learned status who lacked the ability to recognize such subtle differences.

Before the first year was out I had come to like the school better, not so much for what it offered as for the entertainment that I discovered around it. The school was right across the street from the church, and I could slip into the church compound to watch the monks and deacons performing their heavenly duties. As parishioners came to the church at odd hours in order to make emergency requests, or offer sacrifices, I would hide behind the huge columns and listen as they pleaded with St. Michael.

Once I heard an old woman tell St. Michael that she had just killed her neighbour's cat, wrapping it in an old rag before dropping it into a dried-up well. She explained that the cat had been stealing beef from her kitchen, poaching the strips that she had hung to dry from the line. She had done all she could to keep the cat at bay, closing the doors and windows of her kitchen, but the animal always managed to find a way in. She asked for forgiveness, placing a box of candles at the door. I thought that the lady was quite mean, killing that cat, so as soon as she was out of sight I found the box of candles and threw them away. I knew that if St. Michael didn't find those candles, he would soon come after her.

Another time, I overheard two schoolgirls ask the good saint to help them pass their exam. They were much older than me and quite pretty. They promised to bring the saint incense and *ood*, if and when he kept his end of the bargain. That night, when Mam reminded me to study, I told her that I needn't bother any more; all I needed was a few sticks of *ood* and a bag of incense for St. Michael. She told me that my books were much closer to me.

My other pastime was haunting the cemetery behind the church. It was a large graveyard populated by a strange array of tombstones and some scattered shrubs. Most people gave the cemetery a wide berth, avoiding it altogether at high noon and after sunset, when the ghosts of the dead were known to rise. These ghosts would tease passersby, tossing a handful of dirt in their eyes or causing some other mischief.

After having lunch I would hide behind one of the shrubs at the edge of the cemetery and watch the courageous people who dared to dart through the graveyard. There were only ever one or two of them during these ominous hours, and they scanned their surroundings nervously, carefully weighing a change in wind and quickening their pace at the slightest unexpected noise. It occurred to me that I could be of some help if I tossed a stone their way, without showing myself.

The first stone, as it hit the ground, always had a hypnotic effect. The individuals would freeze in their tracks, scrutinizing their surroundings with the greatest care. Having seen no living soul in the area, and knowing that the wind had not changed its direction, they would resume their journey, picking up the pace even more, believing, perhaps, that their ears were playing tricks on them. As soon as they turned their backs, I would toss another stone. This time, they would not look up for proof, but would run as fast as their legs could carry them, fleeing from that cursed place. The women sometimes dropped what they were carrying, but I never once touched what was left behind.

WHEN I WAS growing up, our favourite game was to dare someone either to do something courageous in the cemetery at night, or else to chase a wild hyena. Once, when I was seven or eight, my friends and I dared a fat boy, who had just moved into the neighbourhood, to drive a nail into one of the graves. Four of us, including his younger brother, watched as he proved his manhood.

It was a beautiful night. A quarter moon hung low in the sky, and the desert heat gave way under a gentle breeze. After dinner, as our parents congregated in the compounds, we snuck out of our rooms to meet at the rendezvous before heading to the cemetery. Once we arrived at the graveyard, the four of us watched and waited, while encouraging the fat boy to get a move on. When he was fifteen metres from us, he chose a grave. He searched for signs of a ghost and, finding none, sat himself down on the hard soil and began hammering the nail into the ground, stopping only to scan his surroundings from time to time. Satisfied that the huge nail was driven deep, he decided to run. But when he attempted to stand, a ghost grabbed him by the shirttail. We watched as he stumbled and fell. Just before fainting, he let out a savage cry.

The rest of us ran home as fast as we could, sneaking back into our rooms without being detected. This boy would have spent his night in the graveyard in the grasp of that ghost had it not been for his younger brother, who told his mother about the incident.

That night was quite memorable. His mother was hysterical—crying and pulling out her hair. The neighbours emerged from their compounds and crowded the streets. The hyenas wisely avoided their usual route, in order to escape blame for the crisis. Mam betrayed an anger that I had never before seen as she unceremoniously pulled me out of bed and ordered me to lead the way to the fallen fat boy. Outside, the rest of the boys stood cowering under the burning gazes of their mothers.

The search team consisted of eight women, five men, four children, three dogs and a drunken bat. The men carried lanterns and clubs, and the women their senses. We did not have much difficulty in establishing the general area where the boy had disappeared, but the continuous calling of his name got no response. His mother became more and more desperate by the minute. My own mother was beginning to frighten me, promising me that if anything happened to the boy she would leave me here, to let the ghosts decide my fate. I began to cry.

Fortunately for me, one of the men finally spotted the boy. He still lay on the ground where he had fallen, his eyes rolling out of their sockets, afraid that the moment he called out the ghost would strangle him. As the crowd descended on him, the lanterns cast eerie shadows over his terrified face. His mother crashed through the bushes and fell on her dear boy, shedding tears of jubilation. When she tried to lift him, she discovered that the tail of his shirt was nailed to the ground.

That night, my mother beat me for the first time in my young life. For reasons I did not understand, she was crying as she whipped me, shedding more tears with each successive lash. I cried out, not only because of the pain she inflicted, but because of her condition. Mam was, to me, a symbol of sanctity and serenity. Seeing her in this distraught state pained me. I knew then that I had done something terrible and unforgivable. That day, I decided to change for the better. I decided that I would become more like my older sister Meselu and make my bed in the morning, come straight home from school, and no longer kill birds with my sling.

But before the week was out I had my own challenge to answer: I had to prove how close I could get to a pack of wild hyenas without blinking my eyes. I had chased hyenas numerous times, and didn't think the challenge was too big. That night, I snuck out of my room as usual and met my friends at our customary rendezvous. The final destination, this time, was a bridge at the outskirts of town. The bridge spanned a wide valley that was bone dry year-round, except for a brief period during the rainy season when it overflowed its embankments and caused major damage to the neighbouring areas. At the time, the valley was dry.

The only building near the valley was the police station. The residential areas were much farther away. There was a tiny door at the remote end of the compound that was seldom used and always unlocked, as no one would willingly walk into a police station. The last street lamp cast its glow a few feet from this door. From here, the bridge was a distant wilderness.

At sunset the hyenas would congregate in this valley, under the bridge, refining strategies for the night, deciding which neighbourhood to attack and voting on who should mate the female in heat. They would settle all their personal differences before invading the town. Sometimes they'd bring their kill back to this place, and share the feast in peace. Over the years I had learned their routine, and so knew when to attack them and when to keep my distance. I knew, for instance, that it would be suicidal to confront a pair of hyenas having a private moment, or to approach a pack as it sat down to dinner. That night, hiding in one of the small pockets of the bridge, I regarded them carefully as they approached. They seemed to be at ease.

My friends took their places some distance away. The hyenas soon began crossing the road in ones and twos. I waited until the last one had made its appearance before jumping out of my hiding place. I yelled a few brave words and tossed stones at the nearest one. This was when the confused hyena was supposed to run, so that I could chase after it until it passed from sight.

But the hyena didn't run away. I yelled more words, and hurled more stones, but it stood its ground defiantly, staring at me with demonic determination. Something told me I should just call it a night. I took a few tentative steps backwards, my eyes on the enemy, but the hyena made up for the difference by taking a few measured paces of its own. I called over my shoulder for my friends, but there was no response. When I looked back and saw the last of them breaking into the police compound, I decided, for better or worse, to run.

Knowing that those wretched animals, although graceless, could outrun the wind, I ran as fast as the gods permitted me, crashing through the thorny bramble and jumping over an open ditch with the reckless abandon of a feverish devil. I could hear the hyena as it trotted behind me, scattering gravel under its claws, and was painfully aware of its desire to clamp its steely jaws down on me, but I hoped to reach the glaring street lamp first so that the gods might see me and dispatch a policeman to intervene. I was a couple of steps from the doorway of the compound when I heard their laughter. There were now half a dozen hyenas within arm's reach. As there seemed to be no time left for divine intervention, I jumped the last metre, crashing through the entrance with the savage determination of a blind goalkeeper.

Once I was safely behind the stone walls, I knew that I would live. I opened the door a crack to taunt the hyenas from my newly acquired position of safety, but they continued to run past me, multiplying in number. I discovered then, with a great blow to my pride, that they had not been chasing me after all. They had spotted a street dog farther up the road, and were closing in for the kill.

BEFORE THE FIRST year of school was finished, I was able to read, albeit with the tentativeness of a Sunday-morning drunkard, and to write, with the appropriate *k* for King and *h* for Haile Selassie. It would take the better half of the second year for me to fine-tune these skills. Before we were considered educated, however, we had to spend a few months on poetry.

In Ethiopia, poetry is second only to the achievements of kings. Poets are sought after and treated with great reverence by the ruling class. In ancient times, poets were invited to read at the king's palace and light up the festivities at a feudal lord's manor by composing odes that both celebrated triumphs over adversaries and advised the lord of the condition of his serfs.

The most popular form of poetry, known as the *kinae*, offers one message to the untrained ear and another to cultured listeners. The key to the *kinae* lies in the contradictory nature of the Amharic language. When assembled in sentences, these contradictory words interact, forming rather potent cocktails. Generations of oppression, without freedom of speech, gave birth to this tangling of meanings and intentions. If a man had been mistreated by a feudal lord or local chieftain, he would compose a *kinae* to read at a social event, a poem that was sweet and heart-rending to the untrained ear, but quite biting to the lord—one of the intended audience.

The peasants, by and large, were illiterate and unable to put together a recondite *kinae*, so the poets did it for them. A poet might compose a *kinae* to inform the lord that the taxes he had levied on his subjects were excessive, about the brutality of his son, who raped and plundered the locals, or as a plea for forgiveness on behalf of the man he had recently thrown into his private jail. The feudal lord was often trained in the interpretation of the *kinae*, but if he doubted his own judgment, there were always one or two monks beside him to shed light on the subject. Poets were usually exempt from the repercussions of their *kinae*, as lords were generally reluctant to be seen as monstrous persecutors of humble poets. Besides, the poet could always plead his ignorance, claiming that his intentions were misread, and offer apologies.

Memerae was at his best when reading us poetry. He would sit on his tortoise shell and read out loud two or three lines from a *kinae*, asking the class to give him the "bronze" or obvious meaning, as well as the "gold" or hidden meaning. He would allow us a few moments to reflect on the words, repeating the *kinae* twice or more as we struggled to unravel the words. Each *kinae* is like a small universe concocted of infinitely small magnets, each with a negative and positive force. We would dissect it with our little brains, and then present our view of how that particular universe functioned. Memerae was never angry at us for giving wrong interpretations; he simply emphasized where it was we should look for clues.

I remember a *kinae* that Mam told me as a bedtime riddle:

መሽ በሩን ዝጉት ከቀረ ልማይ፤
ተከፍቶ ማደሩን ሕይወደውም ሆይ።

The bronze meaning is: We have waited long enough for Mr. Limadae to come home. It is now late in the evening. Please latch the door; I don't feel at ease having to go to bed with the door still unlocked.

The gold meaning is: Now that you have decided to deny me what I had come to expect as my due, there is no point in keeping up this relationship. I am not a person who can easily forgive and forget.

We were never intended to compose a poem, as that requires years of disciplined training. Few ever aspired to write poetry, and when a student of poetry finally succeeded, he marked the end of his training by composing not only a *kinae*, but also something called a stranded poem. One can draw a jagged line through a stranded poem, from top to bottom, breaking it into two independent pieces. Each of these halves rhymes and has its own meaning; put together, the two pieces form a body that gives a third and entirely different meaning.

There was no celebration when our two years of school with Memerae came to a close. He simply told us that we were ready to begin our formal education, and sent us to public school.

ALULA'S MORALITY

O NE HAD TO be at least seven years old in order to enrol in public school. At the beginning of each academic year, the school director, Mr. Taddesse, would determine the ages of the newcomers and their eligibility to enrol. He stood in front of the flagstaff near the main gate, with the self-assured air of a bold lizard. Mothers stood outside the gates in a jagged line with the young ones, newly dressed in starched outfits. Their heads hung to their hands as the school guard let their children in, one at a time, to hear the verdict.

Mr. Taddesse wasn't one to bother with birth certificates; he knew how easily they could be rewritten with a good handshake. Instead, he decided the eligibility of each child by asking us to touch our left ear with the fingers of our right hand, hand crossing over the crown of our head—without tilting. I was unable to touch my ear, but Mr. Taddesse let me register because he knew my parents.

The public school was a pleasant change from Memerae's shed. The classrooms were in actual buildings: the concrete block walls were whitewashed and clean; the windows had glass panes, and we were allowed to open them; the floor was newly tiled and the roof was a corrugated metal sheet, without holes for the eagles to watch us through. We didn't even need to bring our own stools, as the school already had tables and chairs. We had more than one teacher, and all of them had real legs. Everything in that school seemed to be well thought out, from the duration of each period to the punishments inflicted on the unruly.

My early days in public school were characterized by terror and torture at the hands of the very people who were supposed to be our nurturers. They seemed to believe that they had to exorcise all of our childhood demons with the whip. And so in each classroom there came to be a single object on which all of our vague childhood fears were focused—the "persuader." The persuader was a whip fashioned out of a bull's penis. After it had been soaked in oil for weeks, rendering it supple and strong, it had been mounted on a wooden handle. The whip made pain take on individual colours; for each wrong we committed, the whip inflicted a separate hue.

Only a philosopher can give the wrong answer and be lauded for his intelligence. We were rewarded with the persuader. Persistently incorrect answers earned you one good lash, skipping homework merited two lashes, a fist fight would get you three lashes, and a paper ball mischievously propelled towards the teacher would get you five lashes.

Not all wildness was punishable by the whip. If a boy pulled the hair of a girl sitting in front of him, the teacher would have him kneel before the class, hands stretched at his sides, for the rest of the period. If a boy slid a looking glass underneath a girl with the intention of peering under her skirt, the boy would be made to crawl across a gravel field on bare knees, back erect, brick balanced precariously on the crown of his head.

The school director was called upon whenever the lashings failed to show results. Our director, Mr. Taddesse, was imaginative in his punishments. He once threw a student bodily out the school window. He was also known to crack children's heads with a chalk duster that he threw with the ferocity of a maddened devil. Sometimes the punishments were meted out to suit his own personal needs. If, for example, he had work to be done in his garden or barn, for the rest of the semester the student would be sent to his home at the end of each school day. When his wife went to market she was invariably accompanied by one or two sulking schoolchildren who were made to carry her bags like coolies. In our minds the school director was the very personification and logical extension of the persuader, the bull's-penis whip.

My attendance at public school turned out to be more a measure of my tolerance for physical punishment than of my academic excellence. The thrill of being in a real school had not yet worn off when I began feeling sick each morning at the thought of going to class. In the first three years, not a single month passed by without my shaking hands with the persuader. The purpose of this punishment was completely lost on me—if it was meant to be a corrective measure—because with each lash I received, I plotted vengeance.

It has been said that only a self-educated man truly worships his teacher. I loathed mine. The culmination of my frustration occurred during my fourth year in school, at the age of nine. The focal point was my teacher in the course called "Morality." Mr. Alula was, by far, the oldest teacher that I had ever had—he was about sixty. He was five feet eight inches tall, heavy-set, and his head was completely bald except for the scant white hair that salted the periphery of his scalp. He came from the northern highlands, and therefore had both the accent and the manners of an outsider. He was also the only man in town to own a slave, from the Wollamo ethnic group, whom he had brought along from his home town.

Mr. Alula taught us that it was immoral to answer an elder while looking him in the eye; to neglect lending a hand to your teacher's wife as she came from the market with a handful of bags; and to swear in the name of our father when the father of all, King Haile Selassie, was still on the throne. He also made sure that we led our lives by the moral standards that he set for us. The class usually began when Mr. Alula introduced a student who had broken one of the many sacred moral precepts he had so painstakingly drilled into us. Sometimes the lesson revolved around a rule that he had neglected to teach us. Knowledge of such a rule, he assured us, would have been bred into any child from a decent family.

"Ahmed," he would call, commanding that student to stand up: "I saw you throwing a ball yesterday over the head of an elder. I should not be surprised if you are struck down by lightning any day now."

"Aster," he would say, turning to a girl in the front row, "I also saw you yesterday: you were running in the street. What a shame to such a decent family as yours. A lady never runs. A lady walks humbly with her eyes on the ground."

"Nega," he would continue, after pausing for a few seconds, "I do not know if you are human, or a walking chimpanzee. Don't fool yourself into thinking I did not see you during recess today. I watched as you made a loop out of your belt, slid your feet into the loop, and mounted the utility pole using your belt as a bracket. I can't say anything to you, because you are completely hopeless, but I will speak to your father on the way home."

On such days, I would rush home before him to release our dogs from their secluded shelter. The dogs were huge, semi-wild, and as aggressive as famished caracals. They seldom barked, but everyone in the neighbourhood knew that they were merciless to trespassers.

I would wait for Mr. Alula outside the compound and, when I saw him turn the corner, I'd step inside. I'd whistle for my dogs to come and stand by my side, then open the gate of the compound at the first knock, and step back so that Mr. Alula could take note of my company.

"Is your father home yet?" he'd ask.

"No."

"Your mother must be home," he'd say. "Call her for me."

"She's not home either."

Suspicious of my story, he would say: "I will go in and check for myself. Put a leash on those dogs for me."

"I can't," I'd respond.

"And why not?"

"Because . . . because they don't obey me."

"But," he would contradict, "I can see them standing by your side. Is this one of your mischiefs, or has the Devil got into you?"

I would keep quiet as Mr. Alula stood his ground. Unsure of what to do next, he would shift his eyes from the dogs to me, and back to the dogs. Unwilling to be outwitted by a nine-year-old boy, he would gather his courage and take a tentative step forward. The dogs would glance at me for guidance and, noticing that I wasn't smiling, they'd assume it was war and dart out at the trespasser. Mr. Alula would pull his leg back just in time, his whole body trembling from the near-death experience. I'd continue to stand my ground, defiantly. Mr. Alula would wave his index finger at me, and the finger would shake so badly it threatened to come loose from his hand. Trembling, he'd warn me that I would get my due.

Mr. Alula usually managed to reach my parents eventually. Mam was never happy to see him, but she was always polite. She would hear his complaint in detail and watch as his hands vividly mimed the scene, showing her just how I had done this thing or that. Mam would thank him for his angelic supervision, but as soon as he was out of earshot, she would wish him immediate death. Mam's opinion was that Mr. Alula was a spiteful man who hated children, not only because he had none of his own, but also because he had been hammered on the head by a melancholic devil.

Dad was always glad to see Mr. Alula. He would invite the teacher in and open a full bottle of fine *arake* for the occasion, which the two of them would drink as they talked through the night. Dad had a very high regard for morality, and believed that Mr. Alula was the most moral person in town. After all, Mr. Alula was from the northern highlands, the seat of all great kings, the place that holds all the virtues of the old kingdom intact—and Dad, well, he was just a second-generation settler in the Islamized east, with an incomplete knowledge of the ethical conduct of pure Amharas. And what's more, Mr. Alula owned a slave—further evidence of his high moral standing.

Mr. Alula maintained a strong moral view on all things from everyday affairs to how the kingdom was run. No matter what issue Dad brought up, Alula had the solution, one that even his enemies could not dispute. For instance, when Dad mentioned the recent uprising of a Somali tribe close to Jijiga, Mr. Alula argued that the King's soldiers should not be sent. He reasoned that the army's business was only to defend the frontiers of a nation from invading enemies; that the rebellious Somali tribesmen, although unruly, were citizens of the nation; and that if the army were once allowed to indulge in internecine strife, there would be no end to the dilemma. He convincingly argued that it was immoral for the King's musketeers to raise arms against this troublesome tribe.

The moral solution to this perpetual problem, continued Mr. Alula, gulping down his *arake* and wiping his mouth on the sleeve of his jacket, was to dispatch another Somali tribe against them. The two tribes must already be ripe for a fight, perhaps because of an argument over grazing land, a dry water hole or the direction of the wind. A couple of truckloads of *chat* and half a dozen camels sent to the tribal chiefs would do the trick. The friendly tribe would raid the hostile tribe, burn their settlement to the ground, and bring them to their knees. To the casual observer this might seem immoral, but that would be because he was only a casual observer.

A couple of years would pass, and the defeated tribespeople would rebuild their home. They would resume paying taxes and allow safe passage throughout their territory to the King's musketeers. The most moral thing for the kingdom to do, then, would be to forgive back payment of the taxes, provide some camels and goats to the tribal chiefs as a form of indemnity, and offer the kinsmen a few boxes of rifles to better protect themselves next time. Indeed, Alula argued, not many rainy seasons would pass before the friendly tribespeople rebelled, making it necessary to dispatch their old enemy to bring them into line; thus making the initial immoral act completely moral.

Mr. Alula felt strongly about animals, especially dogs. He had three dogs himself, and like all the other dogs in the community they were kept for protection, chained behind his house, where no outsider could see them; better yet, where the dogs could see no one except familiar household members. This kept their animal instincts and fighting spirits high. He had a contract with the local butcher so that each morning the head and heart of a bull were delivered, fresh, to the dogs. He made certain that each dog received the correct proportion of meat, brains and heart, and that there was not a single morsel of bull's lung in their meal. (Everyone knows that bull's lung completely robs dogs of their vitality—the lung is for cats.) And he supplemented his dogs' diet, every now and then, with wild bee maggots, to hone their savage intuitions.

Mr. Alula's passion for dogs was so high, in fact, that it extended beyond his own charge. He strongly believed that if your neighbour neglected his Christian duty to look after his dogs—if he didn't chain them during the day, feed them, and water them—then it was up to you to do the right thing, and kill the dogs.

In Mr. Alula's words: dogs running wild are a menace to a neighbourhood; they dig through the fences and grates of your compound, making your property vulnerable to hyenas; they hound your chickens and sheep; they steal the food from your dog's mouth; and, as though that wasn't enough, they spread rabies. His solution was to give them pieces of meat laced with potent poison.

It might appear, on the surface, as if you are punishing the dogs. In actual fact, it is your neighbour who pays for his negligence. Without the protection provided by his dogs, his property is vulnerable not only to burglars and sorcerers who would sneak in under the cover of night and plant some ominous fetish in the compound, but to hyenas as well. Dogs seldom provide an impenetrable defence against determined hyenas, but they alert their owner so that he can make a timely intervention before the barn is raided.

According to Mr. Alula's thinking, the loss of his dogs makes your neighbour realize their material worth, so that when he gets replacements, he will make sure that they are properly chained, fed and watered. The immorality of killing the dogs is, therefore, temporary and fleeting. The fact that the new dogs are treated well makes the whole act completely moral.

Alula's Rules of Morality had some surprises in store for Dad. For instance, Dad, like many members of the community, had always maintained that the hyenas that invaded the town after dark should be mercilessly killed. They not only posed a great threat to property, but made it immensely difficult for anyone, without proper protection, to venture outdoors in the evening. The streets of my childhood were deserted after nine o'clock, with no street dog, beggar or lizard in sight. It looked as though the entire town was under siege.

Mr. Alula proceeded to shed light on the morality of wandering hyenas. He explained not only why it was moral to permit the hyenas to reclaim the town at night, but why we should encourage them to do so by throwing discarded bones into the streets after the compounds were locked. He persuasively argued that without hyenas, the city would be forced to hire street sweepers to remove the carcasses of goats run down by speeding trucks, or the remains of street dogs hacked by angry butchers, or the vultures killed in battle over decaying meat. Without timely intervention by the hyenas, the city might even have a homelessness problem.

Sleeping outdoors in Jijiga was the ultimate suicide. It was a vanishing act. The hyenas would cut you up into pieces quicker than the gods could put you together. They would devour you, your shoes, bracelets, linen and anything else you had touched. Beggars knew this; they might go hungry, but they always had shelter. They would pull together their slim resources with ten or more of their colleagues and rent a room with a strong door and eighteen latches. Mr. Alula did not enjoy the spectacle of people being eaten by hyenas; but he was a moral man, and had to make tough decisions. He was willing to sacrifice a few individuals so that the rest would have homes. Homelessness, concluded Mr. Alula, is a vivid indication of a shortage of hyenas.

I NEVER LIKED Mr. Alula, a fact he was well aware of. I got into serious trouble with him once, when I ran out of ink during a Morality class and so was no longer taking notes. I was simply sitting and watching as he wrote diagonally, from one end of the blackboard to the other, talking to the wall. His head mesmerized me; the shiny scalp with the slight salting of white hair at the periphery was quite enthralling. As I watched, the back of his head mysteriously changed its appearance and I could see the face of someone with a grey beard and tiny eyes, which were crossed in an unnatural way. The mouth of this stranger was slanted, more vertical than humanly possible. It was staring at me with a demented look, winking at me and crying at the same time. I quickly realized that it was the Devil, teasing and testing me. A shock ran down my spine and the hair on the back of my neck stood up. I was both afraid and courageous, calm and perturbed.

I fished a piece of rubber band from my pocket, made a V out of my left thumb and index finger, and fastened the band around it. With my free hand, I tore a piece of paper from my notebook, rolled it, and bit it with my teeth to make it strong. Tucking the paper wad into the end of the band, I aimed my weapon at the eye of the Devil, pulling the rubber as far as it could go without breaking before releasing. I hit my target.

The Devil lost his eye, but it was Mr. Alula who screamed, dropping the chalk to the floor and rubbing the back of his bald head with both hands. His first impression was that he had been bitten by a mutant mosquito, but, noticing the wad of paper at his feet, he quickly realized that it had been no act of God. Looking around him at the little devils in the room, he demanded to know who the culprit was. Instead of answering, the students were laughing, cherishing the moment, having never before seen such a contorted face on the almighty Alula. Unable to contain his anger, the teacher let out a torrent of abuse and ordered us all to kneel down. Walking from row to row and looking each student in the eye, he ordered a few suspects to stand and face the chalkboard. I was among them.

Mr. Alula ordered us, the selected few, to empty our pockets on his table, and he proceeded to go through the items with keen interest, looking for some clue. Unsatisfied with what he saw, he ordered us to turn our pockets inside out. That was when I knew I was in trouble. The rubber band dropped to the floor and Mr. Alula regarded me with the tortured look of someone who had just broken a healing bone.

"Nega," he mumbled, "it is you again, is it?" It was a question to which he did not expect an answer.

With a defeated look in his eye, Mr. Alula surveyed the class, which had withdrawn into distressed silence. He allowed everyone else to return to their seats, then turned to me. He stared for a long moment, weighing forms of punishment, deciding which among them would be suitable for the atrocious crime I had just committed.

"Stand facing the class," he muttered, reaching for the persuader. He flexed the whip, rolling and unrolling it.

"Bend over and hold the end of the table," he commanded, recovering from his initial shock, and becoming once again the familiar Alula.

With the ferociousness of an aging lion fighting some feckless upstart, Mr. Alula raised the persuader high above his head and dropped it on my rear end. It felt as though someone had made a long incision in my flesh before sprinkling chilli pepper in the wound: the sensation was more scalding than boiling water, more bristling than dry ice on one's soul. Mr. Alula whipped me for five generations, pausing only to stretch his arms now and again or to wipe the sweat that gathered on his brow with the sleeve of his jacket. There was a gasp of collective torture from the class, and a few students shed tears. Mr. Alula liked tears, so I refused them, though inside I wept tears that rolled from my heart like flames. I felt I might burn down from the inside out, turning into an ashen heap. I knew right then that this was going to be a battle that would not end in my defeat.

When he was exhausted from having exerted himself so wildly, Mr. Alula dismissed me, the persuader still dangling from his plump fingers. I headed for my seat, limping, gathered my books and things, and left the classroom quietly. At the gate of the compound, the watchman inquired why I was leaving school before class had been dismissed, and he demanded a note from the teacher. I looked at him for a long while, the contempt and anger that was building in me showing plainly on my face. The contents of my stomach were churning, and threatening to spill out all over his starched uniform. But I refused to open my mouth. Instead, I hurled my books at his smug face and walked out of the school compound with a resigned spirit.

Once outside, there was no stopping the tears that coursed down my cheeks as though they had been waiting a thousand years to break free of the tortures of schooling. I sobbed, not because of the pain—the persuader had numbed all the nerve endings, and so I felt none—but because I knew that I had, just then, ceased to be a carefree schoolboy and become a man: a vengeful man who had just picked a fight with the entire world.

Mam demanded to know why I was home so early, but I didn't stop to answer her. Instead, I headed for my bedroom, sank my face in the pillow, and refused to acknowledge her presence. The primitive instinct that all mothers share told her that this was not your usual run-to-mamma incident, but it took quite a bit of persuasion and petting on her part before I opened my mouth.

On seeing the wild tangle of lash marks cut into my behind, the bruises that marred my nine-year-old skin, Mam jumped from the bed, her hands covering her mouth to stifle a scream. She thought she knew who the culprit was, but wanted to hear it from me. I merely told her what she already knew.

Confirmed in her belief that Mr. Alula was indeed the Devil's messenger, Mam vowed that he would never set foot in our home again. She promised me that she would not let this incident pass, that she would first seek justice from the school director, and then from the *Adbar*. Then she tended to my wounds by soaking dried leaves and roots in water, adding some divine oil to the mixture, applying this poultice to my skin, and covering my back with a clean wet towel. After instructing me to lie still, she left the house.

Mr. Taddesse, the school director, came to see me at the end of the day. He joined our family for dinner, and spent most of the evening drinking *arake* and speaking in subdued tones with Dad. Before leaving, the director came to my room, woke me, assured me that I would be all right, and said that I should just stay in bed until I felt better. I spent the next four days at home, recovering.

Even after my wounds were healed and I could walk again, I still harboured a great deal of resentment against Mr. Alula, and felt that I could not go on living unless I exacted some form of justice. But my boundless rage did not make me reckless. I carefully studied the situation. My good friend Wondwossen and I spent many hours dangling from a tree across the street from Mr. Alula's residence, deciding on what needed to be done.

Mr. Alula and his wife lived in a compound with two other families. The compound was not fenced in by a stone wall, like our residence, but by a wooden one. In the middle of the lot there was a water well with a creaking windlass, and a big kitchen shared jointly by the three families, which belched out torrents of smoke throughout the day. The only barn in the compound was owned by Mr. Alula, and housed his four prize cows. The barn was fenced in by wooden planks and reinforced by thorny twigs. It had a strong door, but no roof.

Like many families in the community, Mr. Alula hired a

shepherd boy to take care of his cows. The boy would make his rounds early in the morning, gathering sheep, goats, cows and bulls, which he would turn out of town to graze. Shortly after sunset, the boy brought them back, walking them along the main route and separating out a few at each juncture to find their own way home, which normally they did.

Watching this clockwork routine, I was struck by an idea. I climbed down the tree, feeling a rush of excitement, and urged Wondwossen to hurry after. I told him about my plan, and he thought it was the best thing, next to a blazing firecracker taped to the tail of a wicked cat. We decided to meet the next day, with our water pistols loaded and ready.

Iт WAS SATURDAY afternoon. Wondwossen and I kept Mr. Alula's residence under intense scrutiny, watching for the cows to come home. We waited, hidden in the bush, full of excitement at what we were about to accomplish.

As the afternoon wound down, passersby became a rarity. Life reverted to the compounds: chairs and drinks were brought out and neighbours joined in, sharing the feast and gossip alike. Children ran and played under the watchful eyes of their parents.

The cows kept their schedule. The shepherd boy separated Alula's four from the countless others, which he drove ahead. The routine was so well practised that no one waited for the cattle at the gate. The cows sauntered the thirty metres with ease, queueing at the gate of the compound to enter one at a time.

That night Wondwossen and I changed the routine a little. The moment the shepherd boy passed out of sight we left our hiding places and walked slowly towards the unsuspecting cows. I approached the one at the head, and after rubbing her neck to gain her trust, lifted her tail and injected the special fluid from my water pistol into her back end. The cow seemed disoriented. She stood in her tracks as though the earth's gravity had finally taken hold of her, then with a mad fury she leaped high above my head and landed on the ground with a savage thump. She ran wildly past the compound, her hind legs kicking at the sky, as though she were trying to buck an invisible rider. Wondwossen administered the solution to the other cows, and they soon joined in.

Mr. Alula's neighbourhood was transformed into a wild Roman circus. The cows ran back and forth, kicking at invisible enemies with their hind legs. Their eyes were protruding so wickedly that they threatened to pop out of their sockets any second. Their mouths were foaming as though they had gorged themselves on a box of detergent, and they were moaning loudly, pleading with their God to intervene. Wondwossen and I were too shocked to run away. The spectacle was too much; it was not what we had expected. We wished we had thought of some other plan, but it was too late.

Disturbed by the commotion, a girl wandered out of the compound. I could see where she stood, frozen in her tracks, overwhelmed by the scene around her. Her jaw dropped and her eyes blinked wildly, as if she were trying to slow down the reel running fast in her brain. But no effort could change the bizarre spectacle unfolding before her. She turned and fled, wishing to alert an adult to the strange and frightening occurrence. But before she could reach the safety of the compound, one of the cows rammed her savagely, tossing her body into an open ditch as it headed for the gate. Once inside the compound, the cow charged towards a woman who sat washing laundry in a large metal basin on the ground. As it passed her, the cow stepped on the edge of the vessel, overturning it. Caught in the sudden lake of suds and soaked clothes, the animal slowly and ungracefully toppled over, where it remained for a while before finding its legs.

Two other cows struggled to enter the compound. Unable to decide which would go first, both thrust their heads inside, pushing and shoving. The door was knocked from the rickety wooden frame, and part of the fence came crashing down. Once inside, the two cows continued their mad dance, sending everyone indoors. Mr. Alula was seated in a rocking chair, sharing a bottle of spirits with his neighbour. He pulled his chair out of the way before making a valiant attempt at calming the animals. Indeed, one of them appeared to heed his soothing words: as she stood facing the kitchen, she let loose a wild torrent of urine. Then, remembering the steps to her dance, she threw her hind legs high, catching Mr. Alula in the balls and sending him flying. He came to a rolling stop in the black soil, soaked with laundry water.

One of the neighbours, a young soldier, quickly intervened. He drove the cows back with a bat, pulling Mr. Alula to safety. He then called for Mr. Alula's slave, who was in the backyard, and together they managed to herd the cattle into the shed. Mr. Alula was taken indoors, as the rest of the household gathered to assess the damage and discover what events had precipitated this mayhem. The soldier found us where we stood transfixed and asked us what we knew about the cause of the disaster, which was, of course, nothing. He shook his head with sorrow, speculating that the cows had eaten some poisonous weed, or had been touched by a paid curser.

People from the other compounds gathered in the streets, trying to learn what they could about the incident. Wondwossen and I walked away unnoticed, with mixed feelings of happiness and distress. We were satisfied that no one would ever know we had injected the cows with a chilli pepper solution. And, as no one was seriously injured, we felt the mission had gone divinely.

Early the next day, Mr. Alula came to see Dad wearing a bandage over his head. He was convinced that Wondwossen and I had given his cows something to drive them mad, and wanted to know what it was. The cows refused to be milked the night of the incident, and the morning after as well. Mr. Alula had asked the shepherd boy if any of his other customers had experienced similar problems. He had been assured that they had not. Whatever had happened to Mr. Alula's cattle must have taken place after they turned the corner.

Dad asked me, a resigned look on his face, if I had anything to do with it. He promised he would not punish me, as the cows were still alive. He explained that knowing what the cows had eaten would help them find the right herb to restore their vigour. I strongly objected to any implication that Wondwossen or I might have poisoned the animals. I recited the story that Wondwossen and I had agreed upon: we had been out hunting birds with a sling as they came home from the countryside and we had just been passing by Mr. Alula's residence when we noticed the dancing cows. Mr. Alula was not convinced.

Mam intervened on my behalf: "Don't torture my boy any more; you've already done enough harm to him," she snapped, taking me by the hand and leading me to the kitchen. Mr. Alula left our home a dejected man, still convinced that Wondwossen and I were the culprits, but not knowing what we had done.

After seeing the visitor out, Dad came into the kitchen to ask me one last time if I had done what he suspected I was quite capable of doing, but I held my ground. He turned to Mam and suggested that perhaps it was time for me to see the medicine man. Mam acknowledged that she had been thinking about it for quite some time.

A few days later, Mam came into my room with a glass of milk, to tell me that we were going to see a medicine man the next day. She assured me that nothing bad would happen, that I wouldn't even be injected with a needle. Mam promised to take me to an Arab shop afterwards to buy me sweets, so long as I didn't tell anyone.

THE MEDICINE MAN lived in the Muslim part of town. The man was ominously big, with a very long beard and a moustache that covered his mouth. He wore a black patch over his left eye and a white turban perched on his head. His house had two rooms, the front one much larger than the back. The doors to both rooms faced the street, and were aligned. The medicine man sat in the back room facing the door. One could easily throw a stone from the street and knock the turban from the learned man's head.

When Mam and I walked in, there were eight men in the front room, seated along the perimeter of the wall, chewing *chat*. The room was enveloped in a haze: a wild mixture of burning incense, *ood*, and centuries-old sweat. It was stiflingly hot and uncomfortably quiet. A light, transparent curtain hung over the doorway to the inner chamber. The stillness of the air was accentuated by the dead immobility of that gossamer curtain. A housemaid sat on a stool in the middle of the front room, brewing coffee over a portable burner fuelled by a stack of charcoal.

"Can I help you?" she inquired.

"We are here to see the medicine man," replied Mam, who looked noticeably ill at ease.

Without further ado, the maid stood up and walked into the back room to inform the holy man. He must have given his consent to see us because the maid waved us through. Together, we were taking a couple of tentative steps forward when a crow flew into the filmy curtain, screeching frightfully, and clipped me on the shoulder in its mad struggle to escape into the open air.

"Don't take one step farther," the medicine man commanded. "You are being followed by an evil spirit."

Mam pulled me close to her bosom. I could feel her body trembling, and thought for a moment that she had forgotten how to speak. We stood still.

"Go back and bring me two bottles of highland *arake*, a roll of Akuda *chat* and twenty birr in cash, wrapped in a green banana leaf," the medicine man ordered.

Mam bowed her head in submission, and we left the room in silence.

The next day, Mam and I returned with the order in hand. The medicine man received us with a slight nod of his head, showing us to our seats while mumbling messages to the spirits around him. He sat on a mattress that was laid on a raised platform. There was a huge incense burner before him, into which he threw lumps of incense from time to time. His savage crow

was perched on the only other piece of furniture in the room—
an inverted bamboo basket, to which it was strapped.

After what felt like an eternity, the medicine man ceased his
mumbling and turned his attention to us. He opened one of the
two bottles we had brought him and sniffed at the *arake*, determining its purity. Satisfied, he poured a small quantity of the
alcohol into a colourful glass, and tossed it at the foot of the
door. He untied the roll of *chat*, which Mam had carefully
placed on the mattress. He checked it for freshness before
determining if it was to the liking of the spirits. Satisfied once
more, he turned his attention to our final offering, the one that
came wrapped in a green banana leaf. He nodded to Mam, to
pronounce his trust, and with that gesture told us he did not
need to check the contents. The banana leaf, still folded, was
shoved under his pillow, unopened.

The medicine man directed us to draw closer the rags we
sat on so that we could face him, with only the incense burner
between us. One of the divine gifts of the medicine man was to
know in advance why each person sought him out. But he
always asked, regardless. People knew that he was already
familiar with their problems, and so were quite frank.

Mam broke the silence. "My son has been running into all
sorts of problems lately," she began, with a slightly nervous
edge to her voice, though she seemed to be composed.

"What sort of problems are we talking about here?" asked
the medicine man, who radiated a knowing confidence.

"He seems to have a problem with his teachers. Not a
single month passes by without him getting whipped or dismissed from class for bad behaviour," she confessed, a tortured
look on her face. "I pleaded with the *Adbar* to intervene, but
the *Adbar* must be tired of my continuous pleas, because no

good has come of it. I hope you can do something for him."

The medicine man still wore his most learned look as he nodded his head and expressed agreement with Mam's unimpeachable conclusion that he was the only one in town who could solve such an intricate problem.

"When exactly did the problem begin?" he inquired.

"Ever since he enrolled in public school," Mam answered. "Maybe it is because the building is erected on someone's grave, but he hasn't been the same since the first day I brought him there."

"Come closer, young man," the medicine man commanded, instructing me to kneel down before him, assuring me that he intended only to read my aura and not to harm me. He opened my left eye wide with his fingers, and asked me to roll the eyeball first to one side, and then the other, before moving on to the next eye. Then he took my palm in his hands and read my life as it was written in the criss-crossed lines of my pink skin. After he was done, he instructed me to grab a generous amount of incense from the container at his feet and throw it in the huge burner.

The smoke rose high and heavy from the burner, becoming so dense that I could hardly see my mother, who sat no more than a metre from me. Uncertain which way to turn, the smoke hung in the midst of the still air, choking me. Various animals emerged from the thick plumes. I saw an elephant standing on its trunk, a horse with six legs and a dog with a crocodile's body. They all ascended higher and higher until the last of them withered into nothing.

"Put some more incense on the burner," he commanded, as he watched my entire life unfold, past and future, in those dark plumes. Then the medicine man muttered some sacred words in a language that only he could understand—to aid him in unravelling the mystery of my affliction. He sat before the smoke, turning his head from side to side, so that not a single detail would escape him as he poked the unburned incense into the centre of the fire with a piece of *chat* stick. Then, as though struck on the head by an invisible hand, he made a quick start, dropping the *chat* stick on the ground, and turning his one eye on Mam.

"Your son has been invaded by evil spirits," he announced. "I can see two of them inside him now."

Mam sighed, feeling both distress and relief. This confirmation put her mind at rest, but she felt regret, knowing she could have brought me to the holy man much earlier and eased her life, as well as mine, much sooner.

"I suspected as much all along," she finally admitted. "I thought he ran into them when opening an empty room at school. I've always told him to stand sideways after opening the door to an empty room, to let the spirits out without startling them," she elaborated, "but he never listens."

Indeed, Mam had taught me about the invisible world that was always with us. She had told me about the spirit world we cannot see, which, nonetheless, is as real as the one we live in. Like us, the spirits go about their daily business, visiting each other, solving riddles and sometimes even fighting one another. We are influenced in many ways by the spirits we encounter. When a tree is about to fall on your head, for example, it is a good spirit that alerts you, without your knowledge, to step aside, thus saving your life. And when you see an unattended fruit basket, it is a bad spirit that urges you to steal a banana. Yes, there are good and bad spirits, but there are no good or bad people.

The spirits that we pass through, or those that pass through us, need reasons to stay with us for good. Normally, our relations are fleeting. That is why we don't steal bananas at every hour, or escape accidents every time. One of the reasons spirits remain lodged in a person is because they are disoriented. That is why Mam always told me not to walk into an empty room right after opening the door. One should always give spirits a chance to compose themselves.

"Have you done anything about this problem?" asked the medicine man, suspecting that Mam might have.

"Well, his teachers have been at him for years. One of them almost skinned him alive, recently. His father whips him and I . . . I knock his head once in a while," Mam said, unburdening her grief.

"Beating him will not solve the problem," announced the medicine man, beaming with learned confidence.

I almost jumped out of my seat with delight. I had always sensed that whipping me was not a good idea, and here was a man, a very learned man, proving me right. I felt bad for being suspicious of him. All along, I had considered this medicine man, with his wild beard and unbecoming eye patch, more like a retired devil than a wise and holy man. Now I was quite ashamed of myself.

"Beating him," elaborated the holy man, "only harms his body; it can't rid him of the evil spirits. What you must do is smoke them out."

I was puzzled. How could one smoke something out of someone?

The medicine man reached for some pouches under his mattress, and handed Mam various types of herbs and substances I had never laid eyes on before.

"This should cure him without any trouble. But if for some reason the evil spirits resist the treatment, there is a second option." He interrupted himself for a moment, to receive a cup of coffee that his maid brought to him, sipping it twice before putting it down.

"As I was saying, if the evil spirits refuse to budge, you should tie his hands and legs behind him and . . ."

I stood up, ready to flee. I realized I had been wrong in assuming that this man was learned and holy. He was indeed the Devil, and I was not going to let him or anyone else tie me or . . .

"Sit down, young man," he pleaded.

But I was not to be convinced. I stood waiting for him to take back his words. Mam beckoned for me to come to her, whispering in my ear that she did not have to do everything he said and that I should not be overly concerned. I believed Mam and decided to sit. Not wanting to be too near the Devil, however, I pulled my piece of rag closer to Mam's.

"Does your boy understand Somali?" the medicine man asked.

"I am afraid he understands some," Mam replied.

The holy man turned to me and inquired, "*Afan Oromo ni-bekta?*"

"You could sell him in Oromo," Mam assured him, smiling at me.

Satisfied, Mam and the medicine man started communicating in Oromo. The man did most of the talking while Mam listened intently. Once in a while she asked him a question and he elaborated a point in detail, using both of his hands as well as his one eye. Before we left, he gave Mam a package wrapped in a brown banana leaf, which he pulled from a corner of the room without having to stand up.

Mam and I walked home in silence. She was lost in thought and didn't seem to be aware of my presence. Once in a while I would ask her a question, which she would answer with a smile, nod or monosyllable. Before we got home, she stopped at an Arab store to buy me cookies, as promised. She pulled a handkerchief from her bosom, untied the knot and gave the Arab a few coins. Mam does not like us to eat in the street, for fear of the evil eye, so she took me to a small bar owned by her friend, where she bought me a bottle of Fanta and told me to finish eating my cookies. Mam told the bar owner where we had been and what the medicine man had said. When she reached the part they had discussed in Oromo, she neglected to translate it.

The weekdays passed without anything happening. I thought that Mam had forgotten about the medicine and I decided not to do anything that would remind her of it. On Saturday I was awakened from my sleep early. I always sleep in on the weekends; it is only the women of the house who awake with the birds. I complained to Mam that it was too early for me to get out of bed, but she told me we had visitors in the living room who wanted to see me.

The visitors were two young soldiers. Dad had helped one of them, a neighbourhood boy, get recruited into the army. He often came to see us with one friend or another, and Mam often made them stay for lunch or dinner, reminding him to celebrate the coming holiday with us before he left. Mam often said the young soldier was like a son to her. I also liked him. Once in a while, he gave me a ride in his Jeep. The Jeep actually belonged to the officer who was usually sitting quietly beside him. I guessed the officer could not drive and so got the young soldier to drive him to work.

In the living room, all of the furniture had been pushed towards the walls, creating an unusually open space, in the centre of which was a big incense burner. Mam told me to take my shirt off, but I became wary and stood there, undecided. The two soldiers grabbed me by the hands, and removed the shirt from my back. I was too scared to think and did not know what was going to happen. I began to review the reel in my head, backwards, spinning it faster and faster, trying to find out what I had done in the recent past to warrant a military invasion.

Mam tried to calm me down, explaining to me that she was just going to smoke the evil spirits out of me, and that she was not going to hurt me. I was seated on a stool by the burner. Mam brought out a blanket and placed it over my shoulders, while the two men held me down. She sprinkled the herbs and powders on the blazing charcoal, waited for a few moments, until the smoke was very dense, and then gave the soldiers the cue to throw the blanket over both the burner and my head.

Enclosed in a dome, surrounded by flame and smoke, I felt that I was in hell. I couldn't breathe. I couldn't see. The heat was so overwhelming that I thought I would melt like a candle if I stayed enclosed a moment longer. I tried to get up, but was held in a steel grip. I tried to push the fire away, but an invisible hand pushed it back. I became dizzy and was about to collapse into the flame when angels held me up. Encouraged, I pulled my waning strength together and attempted to stand, but the devils pushed me back into the flame. Finally, I became the fire.

Generations passed before the flame lost its vigour, churning out dark and stifling fumes. I walked through the oppressive haze for fifty-five years and a day, before coming to a bright light at the end of the tunnel. When I stepped from the tunnel, I had arrived in a land of clouds, with no earth, trees or buildings in sight. I could see people walking briskly on the clouds: they stepped from higher clouds to lower clouds without missing a beat. When I looked down, I noticed that there were others walking upside down on these same clouds, as though they were a bizarre reflection of the people above, as in a still pond of water. I realized that there was no gravity here, nor any sort of earthly laws. It was an entirely different realm.

When I recovered from the shock of being in this new world, I started to notice details that I had overlooked in my initial shocked state. The people I saw around me were quite different from the ones I was used to: they had long and strong legs, as they did a lot of walking, but their arms were tiny, mere stubs that dangled from their shoulders. I realized that they didn't do any physical work and so had no need for strong arms. I didn't see any ears. It was eerily quiet in this realm, and so I supposed they had no need for ears. Once in a thousand years there was a loud announcement that came from the clouds, shattering the serene atmosphere. Everyone would stop and listen to the heavenly message, lifting their stub arms high so that a small ear would open in their armpits like a blooming flower. So they did have ears, after all. But why, I wondered, would they sprout from such an unnatural place? I soon realized why. It was unbearably cold here. An ear on one's head would not last a single second. It was -10,000°C.

Looking still more closely, I noticed that they did not have eyes, or a mouth. They had antennae, like butterflies, to direct their travels through this realm. They were not in need of eyes, as everything was blinding white. They only needed the antennae so as to avoid running into one another, and so they could find their way on these multi-layered clouds. Mouths had no purpose either. They did not eat, because they were spirits. And they never spoke. If, once in a while, they wished to pass a message to another, they simply bent over—to communicate with their only orifice.

It was an alien world, but here I was the alien. The fear in me subsided only when I realized that no one paid any attention to me. I was curious as to where these spirits were coming from, and headed to. What was hidden in those castles of clouds? I tried to find out, but when I attempted to take a step I discovered that I had frozen to my tracks. I had stood too long in one spot, and my boots were glued to the immobile cloud. Now I understood why they spent their lives walking.

While desperately struggling to free myself, I noticed that the aliens had stopped to watch me. Their antennae were pointed at me like the horns of a herd of wild goats, ready for a fight. A chill ran down my spine. I could not run because I was glued to the spot; I could not speak because my mouth was frozen shut. I was frantic. The strange creatures came closer and closer, finally feeling me with their ridged antennae. They ran these coarse instruments all over my body, in order to determine my shape and find out if I was one of them. Realizing that I was an intruder, they decided to strangle me. A hundred mutant hands held my arms; others held my feet. When one of them put his hand around my neck, instinct took over. Startled, I jumped up. When I opened my eyes, I found Mam sitting next to me, taking my pulse.

"You've slept the whole day," she whispered. "Raise your head and eat something. You haven't eaten yet, you know."

I was relieved to see Mam, but still confused. I asked

myself: what am I doing in bed with my pants on? and what time is it? When I looked through the window, I saw that it was pitch dark outside. My head was throbbing and my stomach was churning, as though it could not decide whether it wanted to stay with me or not.

"I'm not hungry," I replied, gathering my waning strength.

"At least have a glass of milk," she implored.

I shook my head to say no, because I knew that I could not hold it down.

"Drink it. Let it come out if it must," she said, reading my mind. She lifted my head and trickled the warm fluid into my mouth. It relaxed my jaws, but my stomach did not welcome it. Mam cajoled me to finish drinking, and I did. My head had hardly touched the pillow when the milk came out in a white gush, punctuated with dark ink.

"Let it come out. It will do you good," Mam said to encourage me, as she held my chest.

The entire contents of my stomach spilled onto the floor, and my stomach itself struggled to follow. I coughed, and tears rolled down my cheeks. When I blew my nose, a tar-dark fluid emerged. Mam held a piece of rag to my nose, and urged me to clear it out, which I did.

Terribly exhausted, I lay back on the bed. I wished Mam would leave me alone, so that I could sleep, but she still hovered over me. She asked me if I wanted this thing or that, but I had no energy to reply. I felt so drained I could hardly keep my eyelids open.

Mam soon woke me again, to give me some herb juices that would settle my stomach. She sat on the edge of the bed, pleading with the Virgin Mary and the *Adbar* to help me recover.

Encouraged by the medicine staying down, she came back with my favourite dish, dried beef stew, and another glass of milk. I ate and drank half of each, and felt better. Before she left to sleep, Mam brought the framed portrait of the Virgin Mary, holding baby Jesus in her arms, and laid it beside my pillow. She reminded Jesus' mother to look after me while my own mother went away to rest for a little while.

The next day I was well enough to walk around, but Mam urged me not to leave the compound. Wondwossen came and stayed with me for the whole afternoon. We unfolded discarded tin cans, hammered them flat, and cut them into various shapes from which we assembled toy airplanes and cars. We took our slings and hunted the owls and bateleurs that were invading the pigeon's nest in our backyard. Before Wondwossen left, Mam served us snacks and glasses of milk.

On Monday I went back to school. The school had changed a great deal, or maybe I had changed. Weeks passed and I did not see the persuader. Even if I failed to do my homework, I was not whipped. Instead, I would be sent out to collect rubbish from the compound, or sent to kneel down outside, with arms outstretched, a stone held in each hand. I didn't mind either punishment. Mr. Alula had also changed. He didn't talk to me much any more, and when I asked him questions he gave me the right answers.

One day he was teaching us the significance of a flag to a nation. He spent half an hour explaining to us why the Ethiopian flag was so important that it was flown the world over, why our national anthem was so significant that even the Americans played it when the King visited, and why it was our privilege to rise early and hang the flag on its post.

Each school day began the with students lining up in front

of the flagstaff, singing the national anthem while the flag was slowly raised. At the end of each school day, we lined up again to watch as the flag was lowered, before being neatly folded and placed in the director's office. Every government office in town had a flag post at the entrance; the flag was flown during work and put safely away at the end of the working day. When flags were raised or lowered in government buildings, the national anthem was played by a trumpeter; everyone on the street would stand still, dropping whatever they were doing, until the flag was in its place. Neglecting to pay your respects by standing still would mean being stopped immediately and reproved for your conduct. Only Somalis were known to be disrespectful of this tradition, and I thought that the moral of this day's lesson was for the Somali students in the classroom.

Mr. Alula ended his lecture by emphasizing that a flag was symbolic of the identity of a nation; that when it was flown on its mast it signified the independence of the nation; and that there were many African countries that did not have the freedom to fly a flag, as they had been colonized.

I had never thought of that before. Soon, an idea presented itself to me, and I raised my hand to ask a question. Mr. Alula peered at me over his glasses. Clearly, he detested my rude interruption, but he nevertheless allowed me to speak.

"Does that mean that when we lower the flag at the end of the day, we no longer have freedom?" I inquired.

Mr. Alula's hand remained suspended in air, his fleshy frame turned to hastily sculptured clay, and his glasses slid down his nose until they were propped up by his upper lip. When he finally recovered his composure, Mr. Alula gave me the answer: "Your mind thinks like the Devil's. Get out of my class."

I didn't mind being outside. It was the end of the rainy season. The air was breezy and refreshing; the sun was mild, having abandoned its scorching heat under the incessant rains; and the fields were covered with dark green grass. This wild grass appears out of nowhere every rainy season, growing to a height of about two feet before disappearing again into the dust. In the open country, the Somali women harvest the stem of this grass by carefully peeling off each layer of blade that holds it to the ground. They dry and dye the stems different colours and sell them at market. Other women use the colourful stalks to weave baskets of every shape and size, some to carry things, others to hang from the wall in decoration.

The grass on campus was never harvested. The school director wouldn't permit it. It was never trimmed either, but grew wild, providing a good hiding place for a kid who wanted to avoid class. I soon discovered an even better use for it. I admired the strength of the grass—it couldn't be torn out with one's bare hands. I figured that if I grabbed some stems in one hand, and another bunch from a foot or so away, and tied the tips together before hiding the contraption from sight, it would make a very good trap. I could then sit a safe distance away, and watch people stumble and fall as their feet got stuck in the trap.

The boys who came crashing down always got up fast, full of rage and looking for a fight. When the girls fell down, they would laugh or cry. A girl who had fallen once was easy to identify. She walked slowly, raising each leg to her chest, as though she were marching in tune to some alien army beat.

I was busy working on the grass, dashing from one end to another, when I heard someone calling my name. It was the school director, Mr. Taddesse.

"What are you doing out of class?" he demanded, holding one of his arms around his chest and massaging his goatee with the other.

"I was thrown out," I replied.

"Who is it this time?" he asked.

I told him who it was and why.

Mr. Taddesse chuckled and added: "You asked the wrong question. How would you like to come to my office and have a cup of tea with me?"

Mr. Taddesse put his arm around my shoulder as we walked together.

"Mr. Alula has not forgotten what happened to his cows," he remarked, looking down at me and smiling.

I did not say anything, because I had nothing to do with the cows.

"How did you like that medicine your mother gave you?" he inquired, still smiling.

I told him that I did not like it.

"Maybe it worked," he added.

"I guess so," I said, "because Mr. Alula did not whip me today."

Mr. Taddesse's office was one of two big rooms that faced the main gate of the compound. The other room was for the rest of the staff. There was a short corridor separating the two rooms, decorated with huge photographs of the King, the deceased Queen, and the princes. Mr. Taddesse's office was decorated with animal parts—the horns of mountain nyala, walia ibex and oryx covered all the walls, except for the space behind his chair. The faces of the animals were long lost; only a piece of the forehead between the horns remained. There was a hairy hide hung on the wall behind the director's chair. The animal must be too cold without its fur, I said to myself. I remember looking at the walls and thinking that perhaps Mr. Taddesse could see only war in creatures around him.

The director let me in first, suggesting that I take one of the two chairs across from his desk. He went to get us some tea. I adjusted the chair so that I could sit facing Mr. Taddesse. Before long he returned with a tray on which there were two glasses of tea, a bowlful of sugar and a teaspoon. He placed one of the teacups at my end of the table and took the other one himself. Mr. Taddesse then went on to sweeten his tea. He added two spoonfuls of sugar to his cup, stirred it, then passed the sugar bowl to me. I took the spoon out of the bowl and dumped the sugar in my tea until the fluid overflowed the glass. I always put an inch of sugar in my tea when Mam was not around.

Mr. Taddesse was smiling at me as I was attending to my tea. His hands rested on the arms of his chair, his right hand massaging his goatee. He sipped the tea twice before breaking the silence.

"Someone punctured the tire of my car while it was parked in my driveway," he remarked. "You wouldn't happen to know who might have done it?"

"No," I replied, bending over to sip my tea without lifting it from the table.

"I am sure it was not you," he added.

I assured him it was not me. I liked Mr. Taddesse's car, and would not do it any harm. Actually, it was a truck, a very tiny Land Rover, with a cargo area much smaller than the hood. It was an old truck, and Mr. Taddesse only used it on weekends. The truck never started on its own, so every weekend he looked for someone to push-start it for him.

We, the neighbourhood kids, learned the routine. We'd gather outside his compound before he even looked for someone to lend him a hand. It wasn't because we liked Mr. Taddesse, but because he gave us a ride around the block. When Mr. Taddesse was late for his drive, we'd knock at his door, to remind him that we were there to push-start his car.

Dad did not have a car of his own. Once in a while, he would be driven somewhere in the government Land Rover. But he never allowed me to join him on a trip. When I wanted to ride in a car, I would walk five kilometres out of town to the checkpoint where trucks going to and coming from Ogaden were searched for contraband by the finance officers. Only a few trucks went through the checkpoint on any given day, so I would wait for hours, watching for a trail of dirt to rise on the gravel road, a vivid indication of a speeding truck. I often succeeded in getting a ride back to town, but once in a while, the Somalis would refuse to take me with them. If they lost their contraband to the finance officers, and were unable to make a deal, they would become furious, abusive and hateful towards all Amharas.

"You would not damage my car even if I whipped you?" asked Mr. Taddesse.

"No," I replied, draining the last of the tea down my throat and waiting for the sweet syrup to flow. When I looked up, I noticed that Mr. Taddesse was waiting for further assurances. "I would burn down your barn," I told him, to make him feel better.

Mr. Taddesse shot off his seat, fuming and promising me many bad things. I didn't understand why he was so angry; his barn was old, and its straw roof hung down over the fence, becoming a nuisance to passersby.

"If you even think of getting close to that barn, I will shoot you," Mr. Taddesse barked, his nose drawn close to my own.

I knew that the director owned a gun, a very big gun. Once every few weekends, he would go out of town, hunting, and return with a gazelle or oryx in the back of his truck. The whole neighbourhood would gather in his compound to glimpse the kill. The animals that Mr. Taddesse shot were always caught while performing some odd act: some were killed grinning, some were sticking out their tongues at the director, others were staring at him rudely. The oryx he killed were much bigger than me, so I knew he could easily kill me.

"You know that you have a very serious problem?" the director noted.

"Yes," I acknowledged, "it is Mr. Alula." Then an idea presented itself to me: "Why don't you shoot Mr. Alula?" I asked.

Mr. Taddesse sat back in his chair, relaxed. Massaging his goatee with his fingers, he replied: "Because he did not burn down my barn." I thought it was because Mr. Alula was far too big for him to fit into the back of his truck.

I stuck my finger into my glass and cleared the few remaining grains of sugar from the bottom. Mam did not allow me to do that. She thought it was savage. But Mr. Taddesse did not mind.

When I finally finished my tea, I looked up at the director, grinning. He smiled at me and handed me a piece of paper to wipe my fingers with.

"Is your father back in town yet?" he asked.

"Yes, he came back two days ago."

"Tell him that I will come to see him tonight, after dinner," he commanded, walking me to the door.

The family was out in the open air when Mr. Taddesse arrived, chatting and drinking *arake* with the neighbours. Mam got him a chair and he joined the group. Shortly after I retired to bed, Mam came to have a word with me. She sat at the foot of my bed while she talked.

"You told Mr. Taddesse today that you would burn down his barn," she said, without any sign of anger.

"Yes, but I am not going to do that any more, because he will shoot me," I replied. I did not tell her that I was working on a different scheme, one that would let me avenge myself without getting shot, in case he decided to beat me up.

"You know," Mam struggled, "life is not a boxing ring. One has to learn to accept defeat every once in a while without putting up a fight. No one is strong enough to live on their own. Everyone, including the rich and famous, needs to be part of a community. You are far too young to understand this now, but someday you will grow up and remember my words."

Mam went on to tell me a story about why it is important for everyone to be part of a community.

ONCE UPON A time, a leopard and a fox decided to hunt together. They went to a village called Kuni, where they found some animals grazing. The fox, being smarter, quickly tripped and captured a cow. The leopard captured a goat. The fox and the leopard drove their catch home and put them in their separate barns.

The leopard wasn't happy that the fox had the larger animal, so that night, while the fox was in bed, the leopard snuck into the fox's barn to steal the cow. But he found that the cow had given birth to a beautiful calf and decided to steal the calf instead.

Early the next morning the leopard woke the fox to show him the miracle. "Look how lucky I am, Mr. Fox," the leopard said. "My goat gave birth to a calf."

"Impossible!" replied Mr. Fox. "Only cows give birth to calves. Goats can only give birth to kids. The calf must be mine."

"But you can see for yourself that the calf is with the goat," argued Mr. Leopard.

"Yes," Mr. Fox replied, "but it could also be with an elephant. Nevertheless, only cows give birth to calves."

The fox and the leopard argued this way for many, many hours. Finally, they decided to look for a judge. The first one they found was Mrs. Gazelle.

"Mrs. Gazelle, please be a judge for us," Mr. Fox requested.

Mrs. Gazelle looked at Mr. Fox with suspicion: "Yes, what is it?" she inquired.

Mr. Fox told his story and Mr. Leopard told his.

Mrs. Gazelle weighed her decision very carefully. She was more afraid of Mr. Leopard than of Mr. Fox. Mrs. Gazelle stood a safe distance away from Mr. Fox as she gave her decision.

"Years ago," she began, "cows gave birth to calves, camels to camels, lions to kits, and goats to kids. But the times have changed. Nothing stays the same. Now, goats are permitted to have calves, as God is my witness!"

Mr. Fox didn't agree with the judgment, so the three of them went looking for another judge. After finding Mr. Hyena, Mr. Fox and Mr. Leopard told their stories. Mr. Hyena was also afraid of Mr. Leopard and put on his most learned look as he gave his decision.

"As everybody knows, no ordinary goat can have calves. But goats owned by a leopard can, as God is my witness!"

Still, Mr. Fox was unsatisfied with the judgment. The four of them, Mr. Fox, Mr. Leopard, Mrs. Gazelle and Mr. Hyena, went looking for another judge. They found Miss Klipspringer. Miss Klipspringer heard the story of Mr. Fox and Mr. Leopard with an anxious look. She also was afraid of Mr. Leopard, and decided that the calf belonged to him.

"Well, Mr. Fox." said Mr. Leopard, "it seems that there are no more judges in this land, so the calf is mine."

"No," replied Mr. Fox. "There is Mr. Tota."

Tota was a very small monkey with a very long tail. He had a human face, and was very intelligent. Tota was not afraid of Mr. Leopard, because he could jump higher and faster.

Mr. Fox, Mr. Leopard, Mrs. Gazelle, Mr. Hyena and Miss Klipspringer went to see Mr. Tota. When Mr. Tota saw the five of them coming, he climbed a tall tree and began nibbling a leaf.

"Please be our judge," Mr. Fox said. He then told his story, and Mr. Leopard told his. Mr. Tota listened to them both with a far-off look in his eyes. When they had finished, Tota slowly turned to the tree trunk and started massaging it. The animals stared at Mr. Tota with puzzlement.

Mr. Leopard broke the silence: "So what do you think, Mr. Tota?"

"Wait a moment, can't you see that I am busy?" Mr. Tota replied with an irritated look on his face.

"What is it you are doing?" Mr. Leopard asked.

"I am milking the tree," Mr. Tota replied. "I have eaten my lunch and now I must drink some milk."

"What a stupid animal," Mr. Leopard said. "No milk can come from a tree. Everybody knows that."

"If a calf can come from a goat, then certainly milk can come from a tree," Mr. Tota replied.

Mr. Leopard was embarrassed. His face blushed. He broke into a nervous smile and said: "Yes! Yes! I can see the milk coming!"

The other animals knew that no milk could come from a tree. They also discovered that Mr. Leopard could be defeated if they were brave.

"God knows that only a cow can have a calf!" they shouted together.

Mr. Leopard looked at them all with shame. He could defeat them each, one by one, but could not defeat them all together. Also, he could not live alone in the jungle.

"I am sorry, Mr. Fox, the calf is yours," Mr. Leopard conceded, his eyes staring at the ground.

And that is why, Mam concluded, even brave and strong creatures need to do what the community says, because no one is strong enough to live by himself.

ON FRIDAY, when I got home from school, I could see that Mam had bought a goat as big as a dwarf bull. If it was a holiday and we were expecting a lot of visitors, she might purchase a sturdy bull to share with two or three neighbours, but we had never bought such a mammoth goat before.

"How come you bought such an ugly goat?" I asked Mam.

"Well, you know," she demurred, "it's a special occasion."

"So, why didn't you buy a bull instead?"

"A bull wouldn't do."

"Why not?" I asked.

"You'll know soon enough," was her cryptic answer.

I gave the goat a dish of water and went out to play. Soon, I had completely forgotten about it.

When I got out of bed the next morning, the two soldiers were back in our living room, smiling at me and each offering me a hand to shake. But I knew better and darted under the huge living-room table and out the front door, evading my two enemies and running for my life. They caught up with me before I could leave the compound. As I cried, they comforted me, telling me that they were here to celebrate a feast.

"Can't you tell by the size of the goat?" one of them wondered out loud.

I calmed down, believing that perhaps one of the saints' days demanded a mammoth goat feast.

Usually Dad slaughtered the goat and I gave him a hand. He would hold the goat upside down, with his foot on the animal's head, while I steadied its four legs. Dad would say a few words of prayer, then slit the animal's throat. The goat would then be hung upside down from its hind legs, while Dad opened its belly, dumping the contents into the dog's bucket. I would help him skin it, then rush inside with various parts before the eagles got word that we were celebrating.

That day Dad stood by and watched as the soldiers did the slaughtering. When I asked him why, he told me that this occasion required a special kind of skinning. Indeed, the soldiers did not open up the belly of the animal. Instead, they carefully peeled the skin from the goat as though they were undressing someone. I thought that God would be happy to see how the soldiers did not in the least mar his careful creation.

The skin of the animal formed a huge pouch. The leg

openings were carefully laced up, and the refuse—the blood, urine and feces—was poured into the sac. It was a strange fetish I was witnessing, but I did not ask many questions. As I was standing at ease, waiting for the goat to be taken apart, the soldiers jumped on me, held me to the ground and took off all of my clothes. They tied my hands and feet together behind my back and plunged me into the goat's skin.

I was too shocked to put up much of a fight. Once inside the mire, I tried to keep myself from suffocating by poking my head out for air. But the soldiers pushed me down, adding water to the unsightly mix until I was completely drowned. While gasping for air and swallowing instead that greenish-red liquid, I tried to enlist the only aid I knew: I called out for my Mam, but she remained indoors, crying.

Millennia passed and I was still in the goat's skin. The kingdom on Earth rotted away and vanished. The three pillars supporting the Earth, anchoring it to the universe, gave in and the planet plunged into a different universe. It was a goat's universe and goats ruled all creatures, on air, land and sea. The goat king, with a golden crown on his head and a thousand medals on his chest, was ferried about on a golden carriage pulled by six hyenas. All of the government officials were goats, and they often complained about the ungoatly behaviour of the sheep, the cow and the donkey. They were particularly dismayed by the lack of manners shown by dogs, who always lifted one leg to relieve their bladder; and they were simply incensed at the laziness of cats, who sat on windowsills grooming themselves, waiting for someone to take care of them.

The goats tried to reform the world and succeeded in many ways. They tamed humans and made pets of them, putting collars and chains round their necks before taking them out for walks; they trained frogs in meteorology, so that they could tell when it was *not* raining; they taught mice many languages, so that they could spy on their neighbours; and they trained horses to walk on their front legs, so that they could support the sky with their hind legs.

The goats commanded earth and sky. Birds no longer flew, having forgotten how. The goats had stolen that knowledge from them, so that the sky was filled with goats, hovering over their property on earth. Aristocratic goats roamed the city streets, wearing monocles chained to the vests of their threepiece suits. These goats always massaged their goatees as they addressed the commoners—the sheep, the cows and the donkeys.

When the aristocratic goats grew too large for their world, they decided to wage war on the world of lions and leopards. Their judgment became more and more clouded as they consumed oceans of *arake*. Then war broke out between the two worlds, but all the goats had for a weapon was the persuader— the bull's penis. The lions and leopards descended on these pitiful animals, destroying their properties and killing them mercilessly. Hundreds of goat years passed in war. The goat civilization crumbled. The only pillar supporting their world gave way and their planet was plunged into oblivion.

The goats' planet fell through thousands of universes, which were clumped together like bubbles of soap, before the planet lost its momentum and came to rest in one of them— our universe. I awoke with the sad knowledge that I had come back to a place where goats were ruled by humans.

BOOK TWO: CLOUDS

FEKADU'S WORLD

AVING FINISHED my elementary schooling, I
entered Grade 7 at the high school. My generation was fortunate. The high school in Jijiga
had just been built and was ready to welcome us as soon as we
left the old public school. In the past, students had had to
leave town for much larger cities in order to further their education. The modern school system in Ethiopia was still in its
infancy: there were just a handful of high schools to serve the
millions of aspiring students. Only the financially privileged
and the socially established could afford to send a child hundreds of kilometres away for what was commonly considered
a luxury.

The excitement of being among the most learned youths in
town was intoxicating. The fact that we were going to be
taught in classrooms unlike anything the town had ever seen
before was so significant that we were often stopped in the
street by students attending the old school who wanted to hear
about the miracles.

The first day we came to class the high school director

called a meeting in front of his new office. He told us to remember always that our beloved school had been built with financial aid from the Government of Sweden, and that we should do our part for the generations to come by keeping the building and the furniture as they were now. We loved the Government of Sweden. We did not know, however, if Sweden was in the same universe.

The only drawback to high school was the shortage of teachers. The teachers from the old public school were too ignorant to teach high school. We were to be taught by university graduates, who had been blessed with a degree. But that first year, and for many more to come, students had to miss one subject or another because of the lack of staff. Even after a teacher had agreed to come and we had celebrated the occasion by placing welcome signs on the wall, he might quickly leave us in the middle of the term, half-taught. We were always short of teachers, mostly in physics, mathematics and chemistry. There were too few graduates from the only university in the country, and teaching is seldom the first choice of those who possess a degree.

The chemistry laboratory was the wonder of the town. In this room were strange things that the city of Jijiga had never before known. The walls were lined with beautifully crafted cupboards that had glass windows, complete with handles bearing the inscription of the lion. The cupboards were filled with all kinds of glasses and bottled liquids. One huge table sat at the front and many others were laid carefully around the room. The tables were unlike any others in Jijiga: they were made of a smooth and shiny Formica, which everyone thought came from the fourth universe. There were even high, three-legged stools cushioned like the King's throne itself.

We were led into the chemistry lab one day by the school director, who explained the use of various fixtures. We were not allowed to touch anything, because there were things in the room from which the atom bomb could be made. After the visit, the room was locked up, awaiting the appointment of a chemistry teacher.

There was a watchman in the school whose job it was to make sure that no one stole anything. He walked around the compound, chasing students from buildings; we had no business being near the building during recess. But we always managed to sneak behind the chemistry lab and peer through the big windows, cheerfully anticipating the day we would be allowed to build the atom bomb.

A few months passed and, as the items on the shelves started dwindling, it became alarmingly clear that someone was robbing us. Before the school year was out, all the bottles, beakers and tubes—even the stools—had disappeared. Only the tables remained, and that was because they were anchored to the concrete floor. Strangely, the building itself hadn't been damaged. The door wasn't broken and the windows were intact. Everyone, including the pigeons on the roof, was depressed by the events and wondered how this could happen under the watchman's careful eye. Indeed, the watchman never left the compound before everyone was gone, every building was locked and the main gate was chained and padlocked.

Only later was it discovered that the watchman was distressed at the idleness of the chemistry lab. Appalled that so many good things had been locked away, never having been used, he wisely elected to redistribute the items so that someone could make use of them. As long as nothing left the country, he reasoned, the equipment served its original and rightful purpose—benefiting the people of Jijiga.

And so the markets were stocked with graduated cylinders, U-tubes, retorts, wide-mouthed bottles of various sizes, burettes, pipette tubes, evaporation dishes and incandescent burners. The big bottles were the best-sellers—many people could put them to good use. The graduated cylinders followed, as people realized that they could now be sure of the exact amount of *arake* they consumed. Afterwards, people began wondering what they could do with the rest of the merchandise.

It is easy to imagine a nomad stopping by the stand, picking up a U-tube with rubber cork fittings and brass tubes sticking out of its ends and scratching his head, wondering what possible use he can put it to. Unable to figure out a purpose for the object, he reluctantly returns it to the table. Meanwhile a respectable lady snatches up a pipette tube and examines the oddly shaped device with the utmost interest. The tube, with its central bulging belly and tiny bulb ends, captivates her. Unlike the nomad, she quickly figures out a use for the strange tube. She decides that she will burn *ood* in its belly, so that the aroma will be retained longer, and buys three.

The tea rooms of Jijiga received most of the bounty. The stools with high legs and comfortable cushions drew a lot of customers. The tea rooms dramatized the uniqueness of their establishments by serving tea filtered by laboratory funnels and delivered to the customer in half-full beakers. The sugar was presented in an evaporation dish and the milk was offered in a test tube.

Aside from the loss of our beloved lab, the high school was a delight for us. Here, there was no persuader. The teachers, being young and graduates of university, were too civilized for that. If a student persistently made trouble for the teacher, the teacher resolved the problem democratically. He would dismiss the class, keeping only the troublesome student behind. The teacher would lock the door and windows of the classroom, move the first two rows of tables back to create an open space at the front, and invite the bully to a fist fight. The two would then knock each other down, tear each other's shirt to shreds, and pull out tufts of each other's hair, until one of them admitted defeat, or until the bell rang, announcing the end of the session. The rest of us would gather at the windows at the back of the building and cheer them on, so that they wouldn't lose momentum. When the differences were settled, the door of the classroom opened and the pair would walk out together, wiping the blood from their noses and nursing their wounds.

Not all teachers believed in settling differences by slugging it out. Some believed in dialogue. If, for instance, an idle student remarked on the bare scalp of a teacher by calling him "bald," while disguising his voice, the teacher would not demand to know who the culprit was. Instead, he would continue writing on the blackboard with his back to the students, and provide a subtle retort: "Fuck your mother."

HIGH SCHOOL WAS for me, as for many of my peers, a window onto the larger world, a world that had long been kept from our view by aging imperial drapes and our families' careful planning of the vista. But when the veil of secrecy was unceremoniously thrown aside by students from the countryside—children of peasant families who had been given the rare opportunity of being educated past the elementary level—what we saw didn't look right. Indeed, those of us who grew up in Ethiopia's towns and cities had never guessed at the existence of such a complex land tenure system. It systematically excluded the vast majority of peasants from land ownership, forcing them to eke out a living by working the lands of the chosen few.

There were four such students in my classroom alone, all boys. The girls were kept at home, to provide help, until they turned thirteen and were old enough to marry. The boys stood out in the small crowd because of their strange accent and their age. All four were much older than we were.

One of the boys became a good friend of mine. His name was Fekadu Lemessa. He'd come from western Ethiopia, following his younger sister, who was married to a private in the infantry in Jijiga. When I first saw him, Fekadu was so poorly dressed that he did not even have footwear. Students made fun of his bare feet and odd accent, though not to his face. The boys knew that if they became embroiled in a fist fight with Fekadu, he could easily knock them out with one quick punch.

Fekadu never actually knocked anyone out. One needs to associate oneself with a group before making an enemy, and Fekadu kept to himself. Even during recess, when students formed groups and set out to play ball or chatted away, he could be seen pacing up and down at the remote end of the compound, all by himself. Wondwossen and I thought the boy felt inhibited because of his modest background and found it difficult to integrate with the student body. We made more than one attempt to include him in our small group, but he invariably declined. A semester passed before the boy became trusting enough not to cross to the other side of the road when he saw someone he recognized coming his way. Yet another semester would go by before he betrayed a smile.

His transformation achieved its highest rung, luring all sorts of curious glances, when he stopped to answer a greeting and shake hands. "Mighty glad you could help," he'd say, at the slightest gesture of goodwill. Fekadu was from the Oromo tribe, but his Amharic was so archaic that he could have easily passed for an archbishop if he had wanted to. In the classroom, on those rare occasions when he stood up to speak, the students looked questioningly at each other, wondering whether or not to say "Amen" at the conclusion of his presentation.

"What does your father do for a living?" I asked when I'd got to know him better.

"He is a serf," he replied.

I asked him what a serf was.

"A serf is a sharecropper," he told me.

When I asked him what a sharecropper was, he paused to take a good look at me. Reading the ignorance on my face, he proceeded to explain: "A sharecropper is someone who works the plot of a feudal lord for a share of the harvest."

I was puzzled. Why would anyone hire himself out as a labourer when he could easily apply to get a piece of the government's land? In Jijiga, if you spoke refined Amharic and promised to make good use of the fields, your land request was easily granted. Surely, Fekadu's father spoke polished Amharic.

"How come your father did not apply for a piece of the government land?" I asked my friend.

What I learned shattered my world. Menelik II, King of Kings of Ethiopia, was not the saint Mam had portrayed him as, but a merciless tyrant. I now knew he was at the heart of the tenancy problems. Fekadu told me that when the Emperor brought Western Ethiopia under his control in the late nineteenth century, he confiscated all the land and divided it into three parts: one-third each was then given to the Church, the State, and worthy local people—the latter being the traditional leaders of the region. The Church's share was further divided among its hierarchy. The State's share was also broken up and granted to various warlords who had helped to subdue the region and were now overseeing its administration. Since there was no paid army in those days, the warlords paid their officers and men in kind: they broke down parts of their own land share and gave them to their soldiers to work.

The recipients of the State's share of land were required to participate in the kingdom's efforts to strengthen its might. In time of war they would provide mules, rations and other items necessary for the war effort. In some cases, they even equipped their tenants and led them into battle. The Emperor further rewarded these model citizens by exempting them from paying taxes, and permitting them a generous leeway in interpretation of the law.

For conquered people, like Fekadu's father, the loss of two-thirds of their land meant earning a much harsher living as tenants. The new landlords had little affection for these people, as they were their former enemy. For the privilege of working the land, the tenants paid in kind: as much as half of their produce went into the landlord's coffers. They were also required to provide a tithe of their produce to the central government and another to the local governor. Though they were not owned by their landlords per se, and could theoretically pack up and leave, the position of these tenants was for all intents and purposes indistinguishable from that of slaves.

Despite these brutal circumstances, the tenant had one consolation: he was socially better off (although economically less so) than someone who earned his living as a skilled worker with no land to till. For only an outcast worked as a blacksmith, weaver, trader, skindresser or potter. Indeed, the peasant was too proud to be seen in public with one of these handymen, even when they were from the same ethnic group. During hard times, if the tenant was forced to hire himself out as one such labourer, he would travel many villages away from his home, where no one knew his name.

In the northern and central highlands, home of the old Christian kingdom, agricultural land remained hereditary and inalienable. Each male descendant of a founder was entitled to the use of the land granted his ancestor. Thus the land was the communal property of all the descendants. When a boy was married he would be allocated a small parcel of the land to work on, and when someone died or ceased to farm, his lot would be divided among the others. No one was allowed to sell or mortgage his share of the land, or to transfer it to someone outside of the family. In this ancient culture, tenants were extremely rare.

There were no feudal lords or tenants in Jijiga or the surrounding regions. It was a land of settlers and nomads who pretty much stayed out of each other's way, unless it was to trade, collect taxes, or wage war. The nomads roamed the vast countryside, settling their tribal differences peacefully through the clan chief, as they had for hundreds of years. But even the Somalis were not perfect. Once every few rainy seasons, they found it absolutely necessary to shed some blood among themselves, and settle a few outstanding issues. Right about then, the kingdom would make its discreet appearance on the horizon, a few boxes of rifles in hand, encouraging them to resolve their differences without outside intervention.

The Amharas and other highland settlers were governed

by the written laws, the Civil and Criminal Codes of Ethiopia. There were policemen in starched uniforms, shadowy lawyers whose identity no one guessed at, and judges taking bribes. People tended to settle their differences through elders, sorcerers and witches, though, since courts were expensive and the government's mediation was considered a last resort. One had to bribe the clerks, ushers, interpreters, the man holding the washroom key, and the presiding judge in order to succeed in a court of law. It was a bidding war, where the litigant doubled and tripled his opponent's offer until the opponent had completely exhausted the money stashed in his backyard, sold the jewels his wife had inherited from her ancestors, and even mortgaged their centuries-old bed.

The judge in Jijiga was a very respected man, a pillar of the community. Sought after for wedding ceremonies, the settling of family disputes, and to recommend the right herbal medicine for unique afflictions, the judge attended all social occasions, and never missed observing a Sabbath. The Church regarded him as angelic. Four priests, six monks and nine deacons had already vouched for his saintliness, recommending that he be given the status of sainthood when he retired from this mundane world. The Archbishop in Addis Ababa, however, remained unconvinced. He demanded further evidence in the form of visible works—in the footsteps of St. Tekle Haimanot, whose noble deeds were written all over the northern highlands—before he would even consider granting such a monumental request, placing himself firmly between the judge and the mighty gates of Heaven.

Many parishioners of the Church of St. Michael in Jijiga believed that if the judge could raise enough money to build a bigger and better church, to be named after the venerable

St. Gabriel, the Archbishop would be shamed into naming him a saint immediately after his death. Building such a church would cost forty thousand birr. So it was not, after all, the Archbishop who stood between the judge and the pearly gates, but forty thousand birr.

The people of Jijiga knew that the judge took bribes, but they also understood that his many expenses could not possibly be met by a modest government salary. The judge had seven growing daughters, a mansion with thirteen bedrooms, three housemaids, two guards in blue uniform, a Land Rover that required frequent waxing, and a wife who worshipped far too many saints—she was a member of nine *Tsewas*. The judge also needed to raise forty thousand birr for the Other World.

Though the judge took bribes, he never permitted the money and favours he received to get in the way of his judgment. It was, after all, an open court. The bribe's only consequence took the form of a hulking man who stood at the door to the courtroom, blocking evidence and restraining witnesses.

The courtrooms of Jijiga were open to the public, so the populace could witness democracy at work. Once, I was dumbstruck when the presiding judge ruled that a middle-aged man who had thirty-two stab wounds in his chest, as well as a gashing bullet wound to the crotch and a severed head that had been discovered four days later in a far-off village, had committed suicide. I remember thinking that the learned judge had made a terrible mistake, but quickly realized that he could not have reached any other verdict, as all of the evidence and witnesses were missing from the court.

As a young boy who'd grown up inspired by this democratic atmosphere, it was a shock to learn about the existence of such a monster as the "Feudal Lord" who kept a world of peasants on his leash, deciding what crops they would grow and what their share of the harvest would be. I asked many questions, but above all, I wondered why ownership of land, which in my boyish imagination was no different from any other personal possession, should require a complex tenure system, and armies of musketeers for enforcement.

THE DEVIL-TAMERS

My INTEREST in the political life of Ethiopia grew steadily in the 1960s. During school recess, Wondwossen and I listened while Fekadu told us in his ancient drawl about the difficulties of life in the countryside. I'd come to know a great deal about serfdom, but the one subject I could not entirely fathom was a feudal lord running his own prison cell.

At home, Mam and I talked about the things I'd learned from Fekadu. She always heard me out with unfaltering interest, even while attending to her kitchen chores, and never contradicted the story. Not that it was new to her, but hearing it from me must have given her a new perspective. She would sigh and conclude each session by reminding me that Ethiopia was a large, diverse and complex country.

One day, Mam asked me to bring Fekadu home for lunch. She took an immediate liking to the boy, giving him Dad's old clothes and shoes. Fekadu never failed to say "mighty glad," bowing until he almost touched the ground when receiving each gift. Mam did not feel comfortable with his expression of gratitude and asked him to be a little more at ease. But that was like asking a bird not to sing, a hyena not to laugh.

Though Dad's clothes were a little too big for Fekadu, the shoes must have been too tight, because he cut a small window for his little toe. I was always distracted by his wiggling little toe—it looked like a tiny mouse trying to emerge from a cave it had outgrown.

Fekadu soon got a part-time job doing laundry for some of the schoolteachers, and running errands for housewives, so Wondwossen and I seldom saw him after school. We hung around with boys from other groups, talking about the same subject: the feudal lord and his modern-day slaves. As word trickled in from young people in much bigger cities, it seemed to us that the entire student body in the nation was, somehow, entranced by the same issue.

We believed that serfdom must have been introduced without the knowledge of Emperor Haile Selassie. After all, we had shaken hands with the King, receiving a crisp one-birr bill, when he visited the school. He did not seem like the kind of person who would stand by and watch a feudal lord herd a world of serfs to his private jail. Hadn't His Highness outlawed the slave trade while still a young man, impressing the world outside, and earning the nation a seat in the venerable League of Nations? How could the same king, at the summit of his power, stand by and watch while millions were held under a thinly disguised form of slavery?

Haile Selassie was a hero not only here at home but all over the wide expanse of sunny Africa. Hadn't he, for instance, intervened in the Sudanese civil war, when our northern neighbours were cutting one another's throats in the most savage way? And hadn't he successfully mediated peace among them, shaming his kinsman Christ, who had failed to achieve just that? And didn't he go on to found the Organization of African Unity, breaking the ground for a towering building in Addis Ababa where leaders of African nations would gather each year and whisper in corridors about how to quash uprisings and unleash the most effective coup?

Certainly if the Emperor had been aware of the full extent of the rural problem, of the atrocious ways in which a few landowners were governing the vast countryside, he would have done something about it. One couldn't expect a single person, even if he was the King of Kings of Ethiopia, to know everything that went on in his vast domain. Someone had to alert His Highness, and we, the most learned youth of Jijiga, along with many other students, believed it to be our patriotic duty to do just that.

But how could one get such a sensitive message across to the Emperor, past all those Royal Guards, fortune-tellers and Devil-tamers? Should we send petitions through the Post Office? But what if the feudal lords got hold of the package and came after us?

Finally, we concluded that the best way of getting the message across was by cutting out the postman and the Devil-tamer. We would make public demonstrations along the major streets of Jijiga, past every government building, waving placards and chanting: "Land to the Tiller!" Jijiga had never seen any form of demonstration before. We were thrilled to be the first to bring yet one more novelty to this dusty city.

Five students, including myself, volunteered to organize the rally. We prepared the placards with the "Land to the Tiller!" motto clearly written in big black ink letters on a white background. On the appointed day we sent coded messages to each classroom so that the students would be ready. The piece of paper bearing the coded note was passed from hand to hand, desk to desk, before the classroom doors opened and smiling faces emerged. They came out in ones and twos, to the complete bewilderment of the teacher, who was not aware of the revolution brewing under his nose until the buildings had been completely vacated.

In all, two hundred students gathered on the football field, cheering and radiating confidence under the light breeze of a spring morning. We were about to change the world for the better. The teachers, the school director and the rest of the staff congregated near the school flag, wondering what was happening and who was responsible for the uprising. We ignored them. Today we were the leaders, the teachers of a new lesson.

We quickly formed a ragtag line and proceeded towards the unknown. Some overzealous students suggested that we break a few windows in the School Administration Building to mark the occasion, but they were drowned with criticism. No window-breaking. No insults. The only words to be repeated, loud and clear, were those written on the placards. The only action to be taken was to march peacefully to the government offices, to the main market, downtown and then back to school. Then we would take the rest of the day off.

As we proceeded to the City Hall, our procession attracted a great deal of attention—more, in fact, than we could ever have imagined. The populace of Jijiga was too stunned to breathe. All eyes were on us. Even the street dogs, which had seen all manner of bizarre acts in their reckless lives and were inured to anything that did not affect them personally, stopped their bickering and watched our small demonstration. The dogs stared at each of us with puzzlement, tilting their heads first one way and then the other. Their attention was drawn to what we held over our heads. The dogs read the placards, twice. Then they became engaged in a heated argument about what "Land to the Tiller!" meant and how it would affect their territories, the lines of which were painstakingly redrawn every few seconds.

A camel laden with firewood piled sky-high, stood stock-still in the middle of a crossroads watching us. A young soldier, driving an army colonel in full uniform, honked at the camel. The camel pissed on his Jeep. The Somali nomad pulled the beast by the rope tied to its upper lip, savagely tearing the lip in two. The lip bled. The camel's mouth exuded white froth, but the beast held its ground. The camel wanted to know what was going on, pleading with passersby, in his guttural voice, to read the placards for him. Camels don't read Amharic, as they are uncivilized. A sheep nibbling a banana peel decided to help. It read the placards with one quick glance. Looking up at the curious camel, the sheep pronounced: "B-a-a-a-a-d!"

The City Hall compound was guarded by an armed police-man who was housed in a tiny wooden sentry box. His head appeared at two-second intervals, bobbing outwards before retreating back into the box. He was startled awake from his catnap by our noise. He fumbled with his gun, and his flyers. For a brief moment he was not sure if he was still napping, turning a new page in his dream. But our deafening noise could have awoken even the dead. The guard raised his rifle threat-eningly, but unsure of whether to point the barrel at us or not, he swept the gun before us, drawing a line in the air that we understood not to pass.

The guard kept us in check for a long moment, until someone made a flurry of telephone calls. We were finally allowed to proceed. But no one came out of the grey, mysterious buildings to greet us. We could make out faces glued to the windows of the rooms upstairs, and on the ground floors there were some curious figures in the doorways. As we approached each building, the faces disappeared from view. But that didn't deter us. We marched up and down the driveways twice, shouting our mottoes, until we were convinced that there was not a single soul in the building who could later blame us for keeping him in the dark.

Our next destination was the Municipality Building, but we were intercepted halfway by policemen wielding heavy clubs. We hadn't expected to be disrupted by the police. We hadn't broken any windows or street lights or even insulted the Governor's maid. Certainly, there was some misunderstanding. If we could only get a bit closer to them, if they could only read what we had written on the placards, we would see comprehension spread across the face of each officer, who would say: "Our mistake! Pardon us! Allow us to escort you through the southern quarters of town, as no one can tell what those temperamental Somalis are capable of!"

We took a few measured steps forward, when all the wrath and anger that had long been held under a tight lid in the murky fortress at the end of town showed itself. We received a rude and violent awakening. Now we knew why the police had been recruited from a hostile tribe more than 1,500 kilometres away and kept isolated, speaking Amharic among themselves in a strange accent. The proof was now on the street, snapping tender bones, spraying virgin blood.

With the ferocity of a black lion whose territory had been violated, whose females and young were held in siege by unrelenting hyenas, the police attacked, chasing us up and down the open field, crushing our bones with their boots. The first to fall were those the beast identified as the patriarchs—those holding the placards. But very soon everyone had felt their hard wooden clubs.

I doubled up on the first impact, as the club hit my skinny thigh, and rolled on the gravel road, screaming. I watched, helplessly, as scores of others fell around me with bloody faces and broken arms. Some were punched in the stomach so hard that they rolled towards the open ditch like soccer balls that had got out of hand.

I struggled to stand, but my wounded leg had completely given out on me. Fearing that the Devil-tamers would soon return to finish me off, I dragged myself across a thorny field and headed for a compound on the near side of the road. It was a residence, fenced with tightly spaced barbed wire. I pulled myself through the wire, shredding my clothes and skin into a thousand long, narrow pieces in the process.

Still fearing for my life, I limped through the first open gate I saw, which brought me into a very narrow alley. In front of me was the open gate of another compound, and I made for that, pushing aside the bewildered housemaid who was empty-ing some trash into a garbage container. The maid cried. The dogs barked. I tripped on the protruding root of a tree inside the compound and collapsed on the ground.

When I raised my head, I saw a burly man in uniform wielding a heavy black club. Unceremoniously, and without asking any questions, the man grabbed me by the lapel of my jacket and started dragging me towards the front yard.

"Stop," commanded a female voice.

A startlingly beautiful woman in her mid-twenties came into the garden. The woman regarded me carefully, her face changing colour as she sensed my agony. "Who has done this to you?" she inquired, with mounting concern. When I told her who it was and why, a fleeting smile passed over her sweet face. "So that's what it is?" she responded, waving the guard away and leading me into the garden, her arm around my shoulder. She had heard the commotion outside, but thought that a Somali nomad had dismantled his helmet-shaped hut, bound the contraption to the back of his camel, and then tangled his cargo in a power line, getting himself into trouble with the irate neighbours.

The young lady was aghast that the children of decent families, such as her own, should be subjected to barbaric treatment for doing what children had always done: silly things. Her long, unkempt hair and transparent dress seemed to amplify her beauty, as she asked me questions and dressed my wounds. She took me to a faucet on a lone standing pipe in the garden and washed my hair. "The cold water will calm your nerves," she said, still smiling.

I was transfixed by those large and sweet eyes, eyes that had not been reddened and dried by the eternal dusty winds of Jijiga. She must have been very rich to live in one of the villas that had recently sprouted in the midst of the city. The building was exotic; even the fence of the compound was unique, being only two feet high, and topped with ornamental iron bars. This couldn't possibly protect her from the evil outside, I thought. Then I remembered the brute in uniform who had dashed to the backyard the minute he heard the dogs barking, in order to confront the trespasser.

"I want to send someone over to your place so your mother knows that you are fine," she said, flashing her white teeth. "You know I can't let you go out now. Those animals will pounce on you before you turn the first corner."

I ached to go and find out what had happened to my friends. I could see through the dark bars of the fence that the world had resumed its usual rhythm. Hawkers were shouting out loud. Donkeys carrying jerricans full of water criss-crossed the road, farting. And a street goat, the most reliable of all informants, showed itself to me. The goat jumped onto the fence, poked its head through the iron bars, and looking straight in my eyes nodded its head twice, telling me that the world outside was back to its normal chaos and that I need not stay locked away any more.

"I am going," I announced.

"No you don't. Can you go past him?" the lady challenged, pointing at the compound guard who was still hovering over me. "Don't be silly. Wait until your mother gets here."

The young lady dispatched one of her maids to fetch Mam.

It did not take long for Mam to dash in, panting. Mam seemed to have forgotten her manners. She did not greet the lady of the house, or acknowledge any of the people standing around me. She slumped on the concrete stair beside me, and started unravelling one of the bandages on my arm to examine my wound. Her hand was shaking. Satisfied that it was nothing but a ragged ugly line, Mam went on to examine my legs and my back. All this time, she did not say a word to anyone, com-pletely drowned in her fears and concerns. Finally, glad that I was still in one piece, that I had once more proven to the world that I had nine lives, Mam let out a deep sigh. She covered her eyes with the end of her *netela* and silently wailed. These were cries of jubilation.

The lady of the house sat quietly by Mam's side. Putting her arm around Mam's shoulder, she comforted her. Mam turned her head away from the lady as she dried her eyes and blew her nose into a handkerchief that she had pulled out of her bosom.

"How can I ever thank you?" Mam mumbled, looking at the mistress of the estate with pleading eyes.

"It was nothing," the young lady replied, still smiling. "It felt like having my own brother around. Nega looks, in many ways, like my own young rebel. The last time I saw him was almost a year ago. I am from Nazareth, you know," she added.

The woman invited both Mam and myself in. The two of them sat in the living room, chatting. I was taken to the dining room and served like a visiting dignitary by a young maid in uniform. Once in a while the mistress of the house beckoned the maid, advising her what sort of tidbits to include in my menu. I ate my fill, and was about to fall asleep in my chair when Mam announced that it was time for us to leave. We thanked my benefactor, the maids and the guard. Mam invited the young lady to come over with her husband for the coming holiday; the woman gladly accepted the invitation. I wished that Mam hadn't included the woman's husband.

On the way home, Mam broke the bad news to me. She told me that, as a result of our irresponsible adventures, over a hundred students had been roughed up by the police; that seven students, two low-flying angels, and a devil in a wheel-chair had been injured so badly that they had to be hospitalized. The only fatality of the day was an aging stork who, like many of us, neglected to make a timely retreat. The street dogs were looking into the funeral arrangements. It was, indeed, a day of indiscriminate mayhem.

All this because we suggested land reform? It was hard to grasp. There had to be a mistake, a breakdown in the chain of command.

The time of reckoning was the following morning. When the school gate opened, dignitaries were gathered in the compound anxiously waiting to offer apologies and promise a thorough investigation of the terrible error. That was what I appreciated most about the monarchy. When the kingdom was challenged by an opponent, and felt justified in flexing its brute muscle, it dispatched 10,000 soldiers, 110 tanks and 28 cannons to subjugate 200 nomads with old, cranky rifles. And now, when it felt that it had done wrong, and was ready to offer apologies and make rectifications, the kingdom dispatched the Governor of Jijiga, the Chief of Police, two generals from the Mechanized Brigade and a whole array of lower brass. Even the school director was dressed in a three-piece suit, with matching necktie.

We were told to assemble in front of the Chemistry Lab. The dignitaries led the way, climbing the three low steps of the porch in the most refined manner, assembling at the centre of the platform in the proper hierarchy. The military police stood facing us on the ground below, their backs to the wall, Uzi machine guns tightly held at their chests. The students arranged themselves in small clumps, which seemed reluctant to merge. The influential group could easily be identified, as the beautiful girls were with us.

One of the generals gave orders for us to come closer for better communication. "Can somebody tell us what all the noise was about?" the same general continued. I was aching to spill my guts, to recount the atrocities committed by the police, which the high brass had obviously heard about but could not appreciate, as none of them had been dragged over the thorny fields or beaten like dumb cattle. I wanted to demand direct communication with the Emperor so that we could settle the "Land to the

Tiller" issue once and for all. But I lost my nerve. I had never been a good speaker, and today my emotions got in the way.

The general repeated the question. There was an eerie restlessness among the students. Dresses shuffled. Heads turned one way or the other, whispering. But no one volunteered to answer. Finally the general made the decision for us. Pointing at my friend Wondwossen, who was standing next to me and who was, even at that age, about six feet tall, thus standing out in the small crowd, the general commanded: "You, with the baseball hat, tell me what you were doing in the streets yesterday."

"We were . . ." Wondwossen began to reply when the general curtly cut him short.

"Never say *we*. Say I. The only living soul in this great nation who can say *we* is Emperor Haile Selassie I, King of Kings of Ethiopia, Conqueror of the Lion of Judah. Never forget that!"

"But I am speaking for all of us," Wondwossen reasoned.

"Aha! So, you are the leader of the uprising!"

"No, I am not the leader. I happen to share the same belief as the others and march under the same motto."

"Then explain what your motto is."

"We were . . ."

"There you go again! I told you never to say *we*!"

At this point the other general saw the light. "What is your name?" he demanded, looking down at Wondwossen with undisguised contempt.

"Wondwossen."

"Who is your father?"

Wondwossen repeated his father's name twice, but the general could not place him. If a student had reached high school in Jijiga, he must have come from a decent family. All decent families in town knew each other. Someone whispered something into the general's ears.

"Well! Well! Well!" the general beamed, his decorated chest heaving, "your father is a good friend of mine. I didn't know that he had such a grown-up boy. I will let him know what a fine boy he is raising."

This didn't sound quite right to us, but all of a sudden every student wanted to speak his mind. The small gathering turned into chaos. Someone threw a stone at the dignitaries, and the military police fired shots into the air. We dispersed. School was closed for another day. Now it was clear that the struggle awaiting us would be long and treacherous.

Before the school year was out we held another demonstration. We were better prepared than the last time, but the outcome was no less disastrous. Most of us were rounded up and detained. But we didn't spend the night in jail. Before sunset, our families came to the detention centre, escorted by the police chief. The chief made a speech in which he blamed our families for our unruliness. He expressed a wish that we would not meet again under similar circumstances, but if we did he would not be responsible for the things that might befall us, and our parents shouldn't hold him responsible, as he had given them a timely warning.

During the next year and many years to follow, like many of my peers, I was thrown into jail twice or more per year for advocating "Land to the Tiller!"

The first time I spent a night in jail, I was only fourteen. It was a sobering experience. The jail was a rundown building with no windows in its cells. The concrete floor was broken into so many fragments that it took me a while to realize that it was not poorly laid gravel. The room was full of human faces. Every inmate had cut out a tiny strip of floor on which he slept or sat, never leaving his place unless he absolutely had to. Because of lack of space, fist fights were common.

Half the jail inmates were old-timers—thieves, burglars, murder suspects. They preyed on the newcomers, demanding money, cigarettes and valuables. Money could buy you safety and also a space to sleep on. Sleeping had its own routine. Everybody lay on his side, breathing on the back of his neighbour—for there was no space to sleep on one's back. There were no mattresses, blankets, bedsheets or pillows. Many used their shoes to prop up their heads. Every few hours the whole human tide received its cue from the man at the end of the line, and turned over. Those who spent more than a few nights in jail could do this drill while deeply asleep, I was told.

In the small hours of the morning the jail room was raucously opened and a man in a deep state of inebriation was thrown in. The man stumbled, knocked over the urine bucket behind the door and spilled its contents on us. The poor fellow, who was already half asleep when he stumbled in, would be asleep for the next few days, for the old-timers beat him mercilessly. They finished with him only after thoroughly searching his pockets, taking his silver necklace and his shoes. We spent the balance of that night on our feet.

As the years passed and the student demonstrations proved to be unrelenting, the police refined their response. Detention became longer. Torture routine. The persuader of the old school was replaced in jail by "The Snake," a two-tongued whip fashioned by Satan himself in his own spare time. The whip cut through your skin and soul, burning so deeply into your flesh that you could smell it roasting for three days after.

In the classroom, the teacher would call upon the largest of the students to restrain the trembling limbs of each boy who was whipped; in prison, the large silent boy was replaced by a variety of torture techniques. There was the "helicopter," where the prisoner's hands and legs were tied behind his back and a pole was hoisted through the rope, raising his body far above the floor. There was the "spread-eagle," where the prisoner was stretched out like a piece of drying hide, his arms and legs tied to the far columns of the building. And the "pilgrim," which involved suspending the prisoner by his hands, a canteen of water laced to his penis and balls.

Torture was systematic. Indeed, it was a natural extension of childhood. By night children might fear the howls of the hyena, its distant cries charging the thin desert air with terror. But by day the hyena hides in the belly of the cactus and if one slits the belly open, the hyena wanders out—disoriented by the light, dazed and cowardly. In the morning we children would batter the daylight-dumb beast with stones and knock it with sticks, slowly destroying it. I don't know why we did it, only that we did, and that it had always been that way.

And so by turns we feared and struck the government. Systematic imprisonment and torture only refined the movement. We snuck under the cover of the desert darkness and painted slogans on the whitewashed buildings of downtown stores, spread handwritten pamphlets in the market stalls and the major streets, and always managed to appear in person during outdoor festivals holding the same old placards, "Land to the Tiller!"

Years passed, but no change was effected. The movement

became a divisive issue between the students and their families, who saw the uprising as little more than an attempt to destabilize the establishment. Fathers and sons would sit across from one another at the dining table in sullen silence. The Church had pronounced that when a son rose against his father it marked the end of the world: the proof was in the Bible. It had been foreseen many generations before by a young man in the barren mountains of the Jewish homelands. Civilizations had perished, great cities and monuments had been razed to the ground when the young rebelled against the old and decided to reshape the world consistent with their radical visions.

We had the vision, but lacked the followers. The Somali nomads, who as a conquered people would elsewhere identify themselves with the student movement, turned a deaf ear. The land tenure system in Ogaden, as in many other pastoral regions, remained largely intact. The Amharas disliked the arid lowlands, as they feared that they might contract malaria there, and so they let these nomadic people administer their parched lands themselves. For the Somalis of Ogaden, land was common property. The various clans met from time to time to discuss how best to make use of grazing land or deal with a drying-up water hole; and, when there were insurmountable differences, they settled them the usual way, with guns.

The student movement had become a predictable nuisance, to be dealt with by the persuasive boots of the police; by their mute, hard clubs. All the signs said that the monarchy would easily survive this uprising and last well into its third millennium. Then something happened in the northern highlands, where land tenancy had never been a problem, that ultimately changed the course of history.

THE EXORCISTS

THE MAIN RAINS failed. Seeds died before breaking out of the ground. Drought threatened millions of lives. But this was not the arid lowlands of the coastal regions around the Red Sea and Ogaden—it was the northern, temperate highlands of the Tigre and Wello provinces. The year was 1972.

The loss of one or two harvests shouldn't, normally, trigger a famine. These areas would have weathered the bad times had it not been for three significant factors. First, the rains in the preceding two seasons had been so erratic that the harvests had been minimal. Second, the government had failed to heed forewarnings and stock up on grain supplies. After all, Ethiopia had been subjected to similar conditions far too often for the government not to see the inevitable outcome. The 1965–66 famine, which had wiped out almost a third of the population of some of the same areas affected by the recent drought, was still in living memory. Third, Ethiopia's farming practices were antiquated.

ETHIOPIA IS potentially a rich country: it possesses extensive tracts of fertile land with dependable rainfall, and mineral resources that include gold and platinum. Ethiopia could feed herself, and still export a great deal of agricultural produce. In other words, the 1973 famine was not an entirely natural disaster. Failure of the main rains had withered the affected areas, it is true, but the devastating consequences of the famine were largely man-made.

The road to misery was paved when the government turned a blind eye to the systematic destruction of the nation's forests. Only a century ago, 40 percent of the country was covered by trees, most of which were hundreds of years old; by 1973, only one-tenth of that remained. The destruction of the forests was swift. I had witnessed, in a mere decade, a densely forested highland region being transformed into a desolate landscape.

Slaying the forests triggered a chain reaction. The soil, once shielded from the torrential tropical rain by the dense vegetation, was carried away. Each year 1.6 billion tons of fertile soil was lost to erosion, much of it settling in lakes and creeks, reducing the country's supply of fresh water. Some of this soil ended up in neighbouring countries.

With the soil gone, not only the farmland was lost but the rains also failed to replenish the groundwater. In many regions where there were once countless brooks and streams, water is now mined from a deep-lying aquifer. The depth of these wells increases from year to year, and in time the inevitable happens: the underground water reservoir is depleted, resulting in mass migrations of the people who depend on it.

Ethiopia has the largest number of domesticated animals in

Africa, eighth in the world. About 27 million cattle, 42 million sheep, 17 million goats and millions of camels roam the countryside, taking up 61 percent of the land. This is a mixed blessing for the country. The herds are responsible for a great deal of environmental damage, as overgrazing accelerates soil erosion.

The pastoral regions can support only 21 percent of the cattle population, 25 percent of the sheep and 75 percent of the goat herd. A responsible government would harness the economic potential of these regions, while curbing the detrimental environmental effects, by building slaughterhouses and meat-packaging plants in these regions, encouraging the nomads to evaluate their wealth with a method other than a head count. The ravages of the relentless droughts are too well known to the nomads for them to turn down a sensible offer.

The explosion of the human population is one factor that is seldom addressed. In 1960, when I was a tot, the population of Ethiopia was 20 million. By the time the 1972 drought swept the country, the population had almost doubled. In 1996, the population stood at 58 million. The United Nations reckons that, if the present trend is maintained, by the year 2050 Ethiopia will be the ninth most populated country in the world, with a population exceeding 200 million. Food production is unlikely to keep pace with the population growth.

The archaic land tenure system also played a role in fostering the famine. The peasant had no incentive to enhance his production, since his share of the produce was limited to what the feudal lord deemed sufficient for his sustenance. Even during abundant harvests, the peasant seldom noticed an increase in his meagre granary.

The peasant used a centuries-old, labour-intensive method of farming that required three or four runs over his plot before the seedbed was ready. The finely pulverized soil also aggravated the wind erosion problem. The seeds used by the farmer might have been resistant to the adverse elements, as a result of natural selection, but the yield was meagre. The various research centres in the country managed to produce varieties of seeds that both resisted the adverse elements and gave higher yields, but they did not make it to the peasant's plot.

Agriculture being the driving engine of Ethiopia's economy, the attention it received from Haile Selassie's regime was at best pitiful. Barely 2 percent of the national budget was allocated to this economic sector.

The latest famine might have come into view in 1973, but it had been in the making for many, many years.

As soon as the main rains failed in 1972, the Ministry of Agriculture responded by conducting a survey, the results of which were submitted to the Council of Ministers. After careful deliberations, the policy-makers made two critical decisions: first of all to do nothing, in order to avoid embarrassment to the Emperor, who was portrayed to the world outside not just as the oldest ruler in sunny Africa, but also as a caring and considerate father figure; and secondly, to actively suppress any news of the drought or any talk of famine. So began a series of cover-ups that would ultimately lead to the demise of the monarchy.

The human price of the royal indifference and unaccountability was 200,000 dead by the time the famine was harnessed. This is not surprising considering that the peasants lived hand-to-mouth, saving nothing for the next season. But there was much that could have been done. The drought was localized.

There was surplus harvest in other regions of the country, which to the astonishment of the Devil himself was being sent out of the country. At the time, the government had the financial resources to purchase the surplus grain and distribute it among the needy. Ethiopia received more than half of the U.S. foreign aid to black Africa. Between 1952 and 1974, U.S. military aid to the regime was over $270 million, and economic aid was over $350 million, but the money was being saved for a rainy day and the rains didn't come.

In 1973, news of the famine had started to leak. Three professors from Haile Selassie I University (now Addis Ababa University) went to Wello province to assess the situation; they returned with pictures of the dead and dying. An exhibition of these pictures was mounted on campus. Students reacted by fasting, demanding that the university send the money it had saved to the starving provinces. They waged a public awareness crusade, displaying the gruesome pictures to the awe-stricken community, and organizing a campaign to collect food and clothing for the victims of the drought. The students demanded that the regime declare a state of emergency. They initiated a number of demonstrations, including a trip to Wello province that would include the drought-stricken in the mass rally. The monarchy considered this to be the ultimate form of sedition. The police were dispatched to restore order, bullets were fired, and a few young people lost their lives. Soon after, the three professors were dismissed from their posts.

It would be mid-1973 before the government finally acknowledged the existence of famine, and made it clear that it needed, and wanted, help. The World Food Program, UNICEF, the Food and Agricultural Organization (FAO), the United Nations Development Program (UNDP) and the U.S. Agency for International Development (USAID) were all consulted. The government's position, however, was that if the cost of aid was making news of the famine public, then it would do without the aid. The international agencies pondered this logic, debating whether to save lives or to save face for the Emperor. The decision was to do nothing.

The cycle of cover-ups and indifference finally broke down late in 1973 when an English journalist named Jonathan Dimbleby filmed the crisis. The footage shocked the outside world out of its apathy, and donations from Oxfam, the British Save the Children Fund and others began to trickle in. A total of 14,800 tonnes of grain were distributed among the needy in 1973, barely a kilo a month per person. Even when the floodgates of the food supply finally flew wide open, the needy saw only a trifle, because a good deal of the stuff was diverted, by ever-alert government officials, to local markets. In Jijiga, one could buy bags of imported flour, powdered milk and tins of cooking oil at reasonable prices. The local traders couldn't compete with the prices or quality of produce offered by the government-official-turned-merchant. The sacks and various containers of donated food had "Not For Sale" printed boldly on them—but that was a note the aid donors had scribbled to themselves, to remind them not to sell it to us.

The end of 1973 was a very busy time for government officials. When they were not busy siphoning off donated food to local markets, they were scurrying to hide the famine-stricken from view, sometimes locking them up in camps, as was the case with the town of Kobbo, where 290 prisoners died of starvation before the authorities decided, a fortnight later, to look into the situation.

On the bright side, 1973 saw the lethargy in the palace

lifted. In November of that year, the Emperor finally decided to visit the affected areas. People still held His Highness in high regard. In Wello, the dying combed their hair, straightened their clothes and lined the streets to welcome the entourage. The stones that lined the roadsides were painted white, and green grass was flown in, to serve as a carpet for the King and render the scene less stark. It could not hide the surrounding misery.

The King was truly appalled by what he saw. He was moved enough to disregard his personal security and walk among the crowd to comfort the dying. But he did not promise to alleviate their pain and suffering. His Highness reminded the victims that such acts were beyond human capacity, that they should seek guidance from the Kingdom above. Purchasing the necessary grain would have cost a few million dollars. The Emperor would have liked to help, but he was not a wealthy man. After all, all he had was $1.6 billion, and it was tied up in Swiss banks.

The year 1973 was not a good one for the monarchy. The oil embargo imposed by OPEC had resulted in economic crises the world over: Ethiopia was no exception. The Arab oil-producing countries raised the price of oil by about nine cents a gallon. After careful consideration, the regime decided to raise the price of a gallon of gasoline by twenty-five U.S. cents. The immediate effects of this hike were felt by public transport, primarily taxis. The government wasn't completely insensitive to the needs of the poor: it decided that taxi fares would remain unchanged.

In Ethiopia, taxis are not a luxury. They are the only reliable and affordable transportation for the urban poor. With a typical fare of ten cents a trip, most couldn't ask for a better deal. The taxi drivers had a very slim profit margin, and couldn't absorb the price hike in gasoline without going bankrupt. In February 1974 they decided to strike, shutting down the public transportation system completely. This had a domino effect, igniting a riot that had been in the making since a series of educational reforms was proposed two years before.

The controversial Education Reform Bill, which was proposed in 1972, savaged the modern education system while it was still in its infancy. Education beyond the primary level would no longer be free; there would be no new schools offering a secondary education, severely restricting the number of young people who would study past the primary level; and university education, still an embryo, would be born but wouldn't be allowed to grow beyond infancy. In answer to a decades-long demand on the part of the teachers for better pay and working conditions, the government offered an all-round solution: their pay would be reduced and their working hours and the number of students per class would be increased. The teachers weren't amused: 17,500 of them joined the taxi drivers already on strike.

The regime was unperturbed by all the looming crises. As long as the armed forces were behind the throne, why should one lose sleep over such minor details? The military was the best-trained and -equipped fighting machine in Africa; it had long since demonstrated its coercive power by ruthlessly suppressing countless instances of internecine strife.

But 1974 was an ominous year for the monarchy. A mutiny of non-commissioned officers and enlisted men broke out in the province of Sidamo. A broken water pump triggered the revolt. For months, the enlisted men had complained to their officers about a lack of proper drinking water, requesting that their damaged pump be repaired. No solution was offered. Out of desperation they decided to draw their water from the officers' well, an act that the officers found disrespectful. The enlisted men responded by arresting their officers, refusing to set them free until either the Prime Minister or the Minister of Defence came to inspect their wretched living conditions. The King did not think it appropriate to send a minister on such a trivial mission, dispatching instead a much-decorated general—Lieutenant-General Deresse Dubale. This officer found himself taken prisoner as well, and forced to live alongside the enlisted men, eating the same food and drinking the same water. In a week the general fell ill.

The army uprising was the straw that broke the back of the aristocratic camel. Following the Sidamo mutiny, a second one broke out in Asmara, Eritrea, followed by a third at the headquarters of the Fourth Division in the capital, and another one a few miles away at the Debre Zeit Air Force Installation. The working classes and government employees joined the revolt, students intensified their protests, and the nation was soon riddled with strife. The Emperor made many hasty concessions, but far from having a calming effect, this indicated to many that the monarchy was quickly losing its grip on power.

By the middle of 1974 the question was not whether the monarchy would last the year, but what would replace it. Not only was there no opposition political party—there was no party at all. The only organization sufficiently organized to assume power was the army, and indeed the army did take over. On September 12, 1974, the Emperor was deposed, parliament was suspended, and the door to the unknown was thrown wide open.

The military junta was no more immune to the direction of

events than the man in the street, but it declared itself open to ideas. Postal stations were opened for suggestions, and all sorts of dialogues were encouraged for the purpose of determining what needed to be done. Radical young Ethiopians flocked from self-imposed exile abroad to make their mark on history. Political prisoners were freed from the penitentiaries to play a role in the dawning of the new era.

Barely six months after assuming power, and only weeks after announcing a vague form of "Ethiopian Socialism," the junta nationalized all banks and thirteen insurance companies, with no financial compensation for the owners; a month later seventy-two industrial and commercial companies were added to this list. Another month passed before the most sweeping and far-reaching measure of all was taken: all rural land became the property of the state, the peasant being granted only a "possessory" right to the land that he tilled, to a maximum of ten hectares. On July 26, 1975, all urban land and houses not physically occupied by the owners were nationalized. In all, 409,000 houses and apartments became the property of the state.

If the rural land policy had led to the demise of the feudal lords, the urban land policy effectively wiped out the nascent middle class. No one had anticipated such a drastic move; many were too shocked to raise a voice. My own parents had not lost much property due to these measures, but like my peers I was caught off guard and did not know what to think.

Soon after these events, the junta set in motion policies designed to help it administer the country more effectively. Towns were divided up into administrative zones known as *kebele* to look after the expropriated property and to keep a closer eye on subversive elements. Towards the same end, peasants were urged to form associations, one for each 200 to 250 families.

The junta took over power without bloodshed, and promised the nation that events would run their course without need for the gun. On November 23, 1974, however, fifty-seven officials of the fallen monarchy, two members of the junta, and twelve other military personnel were put to death without any form of trial or any admission that events had got out of hand. The Emperor was still under detention. There were still ongoing negotiations between the junta and His Highness on the spoils of the previous half-century. The Emperor refused to share his tidy pickings, piled up in Swiss banks, with the new upstarts, maintaining that the money saved was for his own brood. Sending the archbishop or priests from the Emperor's favourite church did no good. It became painfully clear to the junta that it couldn't, after all, hope to buy that new outfit. Home renovations had to wait. All those glossy catalogues with alluring pictures of machine guns, missile-launchers, armoured personnel carriers and majestic tanks had to be put back on the shelf until new sponsors were found. The junta decided, with a heavy heart, that the supreme ruler had to go. Late in August 1975, one of the Emperor's prison guards was instructed to snuff the life out of the old monarch. The guard achieved this by using the Emperor's own humble pillow.

THE EMPEROR'S DEATH came as a complete surprise to us. Like most people, I was shocked and dismayed, and wondered why anyone would want to kill the one man in the nation admired and respected, despite his recent shortcomings, by all ethnic groups. He was an old man—in his eighties—and frail.

Sparing his life would put not only a human face to the junta, but also a humane one.

The junta did not openly admit doing away with the monarch, as it did in many other cases. The truth would become public through word of mouth. But the vulgarity of the news broadcast was no less revolting: the Emperor was familiarly referred to in the equivalent of the French word *tu* instead of the appropriate, respectful *vous*. The public reaction must have been overwhelming because in subsequent broadcasts the proper corrections were made.

SOON AFTER THE November 1974 mayhem, there were wholesale massacres in the provinces. Peasants turned their machetes against their former bosses. For them, the revolution was a movement against Amhara chauvinism. High government officials were done away with in towns and cities with no rhyme or reason, by the officers now in charge of public administration. The judicial system and the courts were indefinitely moth-balled.

The main difference between war and peace used to be that in war the fathers buried their sons, while in peace the sons buried their fathers. The revolution redefined war and peace. I buried my father as I watched the Grim Reaper over my shoulder, making the roll call.

EARLY TO FALL

D AD WASN'T a feudal lord. He wasn't even of feudal origins. His father, Mr. Altaye, had been lured from his humble hinterland homestead by the high-flown promises of a newly conquered East, but succumbed to illness long before his young family had put down roots. Dad never said how his mother fared after the sudden death of his father, how she adjusted to her new surroundings. His family affairs were seldom discussed at our dinner table.

Dad moved to Jijiga when he came of an age to strike out on his own. Times were hard for someone with small beginnings and unbounded ambition. Dad was frowned upon by conquered Somalis, who resented his hegemonic background, and looked down on by men of his own ethnic group who'd already made names for themselves.

The one welcome break Dad received in his young life was being offered a clerical job in the newly set-up Governor's Office of Jijiga. Amharic was God's own choice for the medium of government and Dad, who read and wrote

Amharic impeccably, was picked—no questions asked—to fill one of the humdrum positions in City Hall.

Dad became a clerk at the tender age of twenty-one, and a clerk he would have remained for the rest of his life—in the absence of powerful connections—had he not taken a chance and volunteered for assignments farther south. As his career crept up the bureaucratic ladder, he was relocated from one small town to another slightly bigger one. Eventually, he had covered a great deal of the conquered region.

We lived in many towns in Ogaden where there were hardly any Amhara settlers—except for a few administrators, police and army personnel. These towns were quite far from Jijiga, some as far as a thousand kilometres. A highway, laid with gravel and rarely maintained, connected these remote places with the rest of the country. As there were no buses or other modes of civilian transport to serve these areas, the occasional traveller had to buy a seat in one of the few trucks that headed south. But it would be days before the traveller reached his destination, as he would have to catch a number of connecting trucks. Only Somalis can roam these regions at will: all others need to be escorted by the army.

The army convoy left town once every few months. All prospective travellers registered at the army headquarters well ahead of time to book a seat in one of the trucks. The ride was free, with preference given to government employees; those dispatched to enforce the wishes of the King; and prostitutes, who unselfishly rendered their services to the patriots at the front. A single convoy consisted of a hundred or more trucks, dozens of Jeeps armed with high-calibre machine guns, twenty or more cannons towed by the trucks, and thousands of soldiers armed and ready for combat.

I REMEMBER ONE such convoy. The day before the trip, army trucks are dispatched to collect our belongings. Beds, chairs, chattels and anything without a life of its own is loaded up, and covered with canvas to protect it from the infernal dust of Ogaden, before the trucks head back to the depot. Early the next day we gather with the other passengers at one of many pickup locations, escorted by relations, kissing, crying and wishing us Godspeed. Around midday, the convoy crawls out of town.

Ogaden is like no other region in the country. It is a vast, arid and for the most part flat expanse of land. There is no set-tled agriculture here, and only a very few buildings have the kind of foundations that promise longevity. No forests either. The sun's mirage over the horizon, resembling a periphery of ocean, is occasionally punctuated by acacia trees scattered over the landscape. These trees, as indigenous to the region as camels and Somalis, are hostile. They are dwarf trees, flat at the top, but giving little in the form of shade from the unforgiving sun. Their meagre leaves are protected by inch-long thorns, and only camels, goats and a few other animals dare eat them.

A few kilometres out of town the road shows little sign of use. Weeds sprout between the pressed-gravel tracks, animal skeletons litter the dusty trail, and birds build their nests in the middle of the highway. The convoy makes frequent stops to clear the road, permitting the kids to commune with nature. Mothers can be seen dragging children out and cajoling them to relieve themselves. Mam turns to me and asks: "Are you sure you don't want to take a leak? We are not stopping again for another hour, so it is either now or in your pants."

The convoy starts moving again. The same scenery. Fero-cious sun. Acacia trees with thorny leaves. A lone nomad dragging a camel loaded with two sacks of charcoal, which he takes to town. Once in a while, a group of Somalis is seen leading a caravan of camels: the soldiers cock their guns; the machine guns on the Jeeps are trained at the nomads; we are instructed to lower our heads. The Somalis, however, show nothing more than curiosity.

Occasionally, wild animals can be seen roaming around. A giraffe nibbling the thorny leaves of an acacia cocks its head above the flat top of the tree. It stares with anxiety at the metallic millipede speeding along the trail. Not believing its eyes, it turns sideways, to focus first through one eye then through the other. Realizing that its senses do not betray it, the giraffe shoots off with angelic speed. A meerkat comes out of its burrow in the ground, shaken awake by the rumbling engines. Unsure of what to do, the meerkat moves back and forth. Then, standing high on its hind legs, the meerkat lets out a wild shriek, following which its brothers and sisters emerge. They stare at the speeding convoy with baffled looks, watch the trailing dust with growing alarm. Shaking their heads in disgust, they plunge back into their burrows in perfect unison.

The soldiers shoot gazelles and any other animals with split hoofs that the Bible permits them to eat. They slit the throat of the animal and hang it upside down from the back of one of the trucks. They also kill hyenas, because they are God's enemies, but they never touch lions. The King loves lions. He has live lions in the palace and paintings or sculptures of lions on everything from the national flag to the bolts on his gate. No public building is complete without the statue of a lion. When an English contractor building a major bridge on the Awash river neglected to place a sculpture of a lion on all of its columns, payment was withheld until the corrections were made. So the soldiers do not shoot lions.

Birds commit suicide. They fly in the way of the speeding trucks, miscalculating the vehicles' speed, then collide with the windscreen and get smashed by the tires. Snakes crawl under the vehicles, thinking that they can negotiate a route, and get plastered to the gravel. A wide range of birds, from pygmy falcons to marabou storks, follow the convoy from high in the sky. They dive down, after the dust settles, to clean up the highway.

We reach our destination two or more days after we leave. Sometimes the local Somalis give us a reception, lining the streets and yelling something at us while extending a finger. Some even throw stones at us. The soldiers are never happy with the reception, but they are not allowed to kill the Somalis. They are permitted to fire a bullet in the air and then shoot at their legs. To save time, they shoot at their legs first and then fire in the air.

Once in town, we are housed in army barracks. We are always warned, before going out to market, of the harm that may come our way because the Somalis are not yet convinced that we are there to civilize them: to anchor them down to their sun-baked land; to appoint a chief from among them who speaks Amharic, and who would address them in Amharic while another Somali translates, until it is no longer necessary to have a translator, because all of them will be civilized and speak Amharic. Until that time comes, we are told to treat them with suspicion.

I never liked life in these places because there were so many things that children could not do. We could not play far from our home, for fear that the Somalis might snatch us and feed

us to hyenas. We could not take candy from these strangers—
if they somehow felt rich and handed us some—because it
might be laced with poison. And we were to keep a respectable
distance from their wells because, as everyone knows, there is a
devil at the bottom that would swallow us alive.

THE EMPIRE WAS expanding quickly, but God couldn't keep
up on His promise to multiply the number of Amharas and
populate the new frontiers. Christian Oromos were being
drafted at an ever-increasing pace, and it fell on a few scattered
Amharas, like Dad, to quickly Amharize the Oromos so they,
in turn, could Amharize their kinsmen—the Somalis of
Ogaden. Dad spent many more years in Ogaden, away from
home and family, hopping from one town to the next, fulfilling
the wishes of the Almighty in Heaven and the Emperor in
Addis Ababa. The rewards weren't generous. It was two long
decades before he attained a respectable position.

The revolution found Dad in the seat of the Governor of
Kabri Dahar, five hundred kilometres from Jijiga. The town
was smaller in size than Jijiga, but no less significant: it was a
major military base. The young revolutionaries weren't sure
how he got there in the first place, but with a name like Mezlekia
(which means "one that carries through"), and from an era
already past its days of glory, few doubted his reactionary
background. The revolution was already whizzing by, throttle
open wide, and it was unthinkable to slow its pace to look
into the background of the likes of Dad. The revolutionaries
decided on the spot that he would have to go the progressive
way. No trials were held, no questions were asked.

Dad's death would have remained a mystery, like those of

countless others who seemed to vanish without a trace, had it not been for an army officer who was brave enough to bring the news to us. We learned from him that Dad, along with a few army officers with suspicious backgrounds, met his end on the firing grounds of the military base in Kabri Dahar. His remains were buried in one of the mass graves that mushroomed with the revolution.

A thief and a murderer sent to the gallows for his crimes was held in greater esteem by the junta and the public at large than a man done to death for political reasons. The murderer's relations were entitled to his retirement benefits; his bank savings and investments were left intact. Friends and acquaintances of the condemned gave the bereft all the support they needed in their difficult time; candles were lit and bags of incense sacrificed by priests who spent countless hours praying for the departed's immortal soul in an all-out effort to save him from eternal damnation. But a reactionary was an immediate outcast. No one could afford to be associated with him. A political death sentence passed on him was also passed on to his family, albeit slowly and painfully. With the breadwinner gone and the community's support withdrawn, the condemned man's family found itself in desperate circumstances.

Our plight did not end with loss of the breadwinner. That was only the beginning. As we were shunned by friends and relations, placed in the bad books of local officials, and denied credit by the neighbourhood merchants, we began simmering under the skin. It seemed a foregone conclusion to many that we were destined for the Grim Reaper.

But my siblings and I were not ready to join those already under the dry sod. Not yet. I took a part-time job at a tailor's shop in the Muslim part of town, the only job I could find.

Mam tried her hand at many crafts before deciding to brew *arake*. I would walk from door to door, selling the bottled liquor to retailers, mostly local prostitutes. It was *not* an immediate success. In the beginning, retailers looked at me with pity in their eyes as my family's condition dawned on them, sampled the merchandise with slight suspicion before sorrowfully shaking their heads as if to say: "I wish I could be of more help, but I have to make a living, too," and returning the bottle to me. But Mam was from the highlands, a region renowned for its high-grade commercial *arake*, and in the end managed to distill a clear bottle of the spirit that didn't exude a forbidding odour. Those who offered to buy rarely had the money in hand. I would give them bottles on credit, checking back from day to day to see if they'd managed to dispose of it. They always managed to sell it eventually and I, in turn, got my money. No one ever failed to pay up.

Soon, Mam began taking trips into the highlands to sell tins of butter and smuggled bottles of perfume, returning to the markets of Jijiga with the much-desired highland *arake*.

Between Mother's entrepreneurial endeavours and my after-school job at the tailor shop, we always managed to have something on the table, seldom needing to dig into the bank in the backyard. Times might have been hard, but as Mam often reminded us, it turned the family into a pack of cornered lions—fierce, resourceful, and stronger than ever.

EARLY TO RISE

WITH THE military junta ruling the roost, socialism became a buzzword, more fashionable than bell-bottom trousers and dog-ear-collar shirts. Communist literature, which no one had seen before, flooded the streets. To accelerate the cause, the postal system became more efficient in the weeks after the revolution than it had been in its fifty-year history. After a request for books on "Scientific Socialism," a couple of weeks would pass, at most, before half of a library would arrive from China, and the other half from Moscow. And it was all free!

School work became secondary as we poured our time and energy into studying "Progressive Thought." In classrooms, students began demanding justifications for the subjects being taught. "How do polynomial equations help the downtrodden masses break free of their age-old shackles?" a student would challenge his bewildered teacher. "What is the relevance of the Three Laws of Gravity to the revolution sweeping the nation?" another student would challenge. It was already well known that the students were more versed in Progressive

Thinking than their teachers, and wished to prove that at every juncture. The teachers were simply out of their depth.

The two political parties that evolved during the creeping *coup d'état* started making inroads. No one had even heard of these parties before the outbreak of the revolution. The Ethiopian People's Revolutionary Party (EPRP) made its existence known only in August of 1975, while I was in high school, and the All-Ethiopian Socialist Movement Party (Meison) wasn't known until 1976. Both were formed by a community of exiles who returned to Ethiopia just in time to jump on the revolutionary bandwagon. The military junta allowed both parties, in the early days, to make their views known. Open debates were held on the issues and on the direction the revolution was taking. Those of us not yet primed with Communist outlooks were nudged into keeping the pace.

The EPRP—with its eye on the throne—maintained that political power should immediately be handed over to a civilian body. The Meison argued that the military junta should stay in power until the citizenry was well acquainted with the new ideology, further debates had been carried out, and a viable political party had emerged that would embody the conscious will of the people, and not just their emotions. The EPRP advanced the notion of an unlimited "people's democracy," whereas the Meison favoured a "controlled democracy," led by a political party that would emerge later.

The military junta, like the man in the street, gravely pondered the debate. It quickly realized it needed to alter its policy from the original, vague form of "Ethiopian Socialism" it had embodied, to the Soviet style of "Scientific Socialism." It also became apparent that the junta had to co-opt or destroy the civilian left if it intended to stay in power. The junta did both:

after establishing an ideological school (Yekatit 66) and an advisory political body (the Politburo), the junta outlawed the EPRP, and co-opted the Meison—who were urged to aid the junta in developing their own brand of political party.

The Communist ideology and the EPRP's policies gained a foothold when students from various parts of the country got together for a few months under the National Campaign for Development through Co-operation. The campaign was launched shortly before the junta nationalized all rural land. The intent was to fight illiteracy; prepare the peasants for the imminent land reforms; and, after the reform, help them organize grassroots organizations. Sixty thousand students, from Grade 11 to senior university fellows, were dispatched to the countryside to mobilize the peasantry. The students were to live and work with the peasantry, while the government helped with the grocery bills.

I was a Grade 11 student stationed at Jijiga at the time. Since the number of qualifying students from town was low, fewer than sixty, a good number of young men and women were assigned to join us from different corners of the country. There were no peasants to organize in Jijiga, and the Somali nomads were not keen on learning to read and write in Amharic—they preferred to fight Amharas. So we spent the days in group study sessions dissecting Marxist thought, taking each proposition apart, piece by piece, before putting it back together.

Initially, I was confused by much of the Communist outlook. I was, for instance, unable to understand how the Communist state could be a democracy when it was clearly stated, in black and white, that it was governed by the "dictatorship of the proletariat." But, I was quickly reminded by my campaign partners, capitalism was also a form of dictatorship, only it was led by the bourgeois class. Even though there are multiple parties in a capitalist society, and people elect their leaders by secret ballot, the system is designed to serve the needs and interests of the ruling class, the bourgeoisie. Communism cuts through all the red tape of secret ballots and the multiple party hogwash by electing itself.

When I pointed out the contradictions in Lenin's philosophy on the "self-determination of Nations" in a multinational society, I was drowned in criticism. Lenin grants that all nationalities, under a socialist multinational country, have a right to self-determination (including secession). But, he emphasizes, it is the obligation of the Social Democrats in such nations to fight against separation. As the Social Democrats were in the upper echelon of the regime, I wondered if this was not giving someone a piece of bread with one hand only to take it away with the other. But, I was reminded once more, under socialism all national questions are democratically addressed. And, since the aim of socialism is to create a stateless society where all nationalities can live and work on an equal footing, there is no justification for secession.

I decided not to ask any more questions.

The EPRP's point of view was discussed behind closed doors. It was receiving wider acceptance, not because of its well-thought-out and co-ordinated themes, but because many harboured strong prejudices against the junta. The army men had always been looked down on by the civilians, because of their modest academic and family backgrounds, and the intelligentsia felt insulted at having to take orders from these men of war. The other factor propelling the youth towards the party was their desire to conform. University students in every campaign appeared to identify themselves with the policies of the EPRP—the party still in the making. If such learned people chose the EPRP over the alternative, who were we, simple high-school kids, to argue otherwise? In later years, after the EPRP had made its violent appearance upon the stage, there would be a more sinister reason to abstain from challenging the party's outlook. These intellectual gangsters would prove to be a far more horrific threat to dissenters than the enemy in uniform—the junta.

The campaign produced results that were directly contrary to the regime's policy. The students, in many parts of the country, rallied the peasants against state officials, the police and administrators—most of whom were landowners. As a result, a number of students were put to death. With its resounding motto of "Ethiopia First!," the military junta's initial policy was a shade apart from other forms of African socialism, being more nationalistic than universal. The students, however, had already been exposed to the teachings of Marx, Lenin and Mao, and were attempting to use these imported ideas as principles of organization and education. The students' efforts to jump the junta's gun and urge the peasants to form collectives was in direct opposition to the will of the regime. Their attempt to oust former landowners from their midst created chaos, catching the junta unawares. By the end of 1975, the regime decided to recall the students to the cities.

The campaign in Jijiga was the first to fall apart, as a result of some minor political differences with the officers in charge, compounded by a lack of direction and purpose to the mission. Barely four months after setting up camp, everyone boarded the bus for home. No form of reprimand was initiated by the regime. The political waters were still once more, and the junta hoped that the incident would be forgotten, without causing further ripples.

SCHOOL WAS STILL out, and I spent the following months feverishly reading Marx, Lenin and Mao. I amassed more knowledge in those few months than I might have in years of study at some respectable institute in Moscow. I still had a few misgivings about the viability of communism and its various canons, but I kept these doubts to myself. Indeed, Marxist philosophy is filled with noble ideas—a classless society in which no one is economically exploited by another, a society where "Everyone works according to his ability and is provided for according to his needs," a society where there is no form of discrimination or favouritism, a society where . . . It was quite a neat package, but I suspected that it had been delivered to the wrong universe. I was willing, however, to take part in this grand experiment.

By late 1975, underground study groups were flourishing. One couldn't walk past a youth in the streets of Jijiga without getting an invitation to a group discussion. Wondwossen was in my study group, along with two other boys of my age, and a younger girl. We gathered each afternoon, behind closed doors. The week was divided in two: three or four days were spent on individual readings, and the rest of the week was spent in group discussion. For the discussion sessions, we prepared presentations that would each last a couple of hours, followed by questions and answers, and intense debate. Occasionally, members of another study group were invited to join us, so that we kept abreast of the tidal wave of Communist thought.

Shortly after the EPRP made its debut in August of 1975, the party's official publication began to spread like wildfire—underground, of course. The paper, *Democracia*, was handwritten, signifying its humble beginnings. From the outset, *Democracia* unleashed a torrent of abuse against, and a condemnation of, the junta and its civilian allies. Any measure the regime undertook, including land reform, was considered short-sighted and a failure. No form of compromise with the rulers of our nation would be considered, unless it resulted in the complete and immediate surrender of power to a civilian party—namely, the EPRP.

My colleagues and I, like most young people at the time, spent many evenings making duplicates of *Democracia* by hand. We scattered them in back alleys and market stalls, dodging the men in uniform who patrolled the streets—just like we had in the old days, as we painted slogans on the walls. Unlike the old days, this infraction carried a death penalty. But the law was something to be observed only when you had nothing better to do.

We were acting out of personal conviction. I was not a member of the EPRP, nor were any of my close friends. An invitation to join the party seemed imminent, though no one knew how or when it would come. The EPRP remained invisible, with no head office, and no delegates to contact. Only the overwhelming work done in its name testified to its existence.

GROWING PASSIONS

I T WAS A BLUSTERY day in Jijiga. The wind devils were
everywhere. Birds no longer dared to fly among the
gusts of wind that lifted rooftops into the sky, so that
one could see corrugated metal sheets and discarded tin cans
hovering overhead. A grid pattern was laid over the sky and
supported, every thirty metres, by whirlwind columns. People
ran indoors. Those remaining in the streets covered their faces
with pieces of cloth. A ten-year-old boy dashed past me on an
aging Peugeot bicycle. He stopped three metres from me, in
the middle of the street, regarding me carefully.

"Aren't you Kebede Tasse?" he inquired.

"No, I am Nega Mezlekia," I replied.

"In that case, this is for you," he said, handing me a folded
piece of paper.

I found the whole episode a bit theatrical, indeed, off-the-
wall. But I was also curious. Before I could ask him who the
paper was from and what it was regarding, the boy disappeared
into a dust cloud.

I could not wait until I got home to learn the contents of

the mysterious paper, so I hid myself in the meagre shelter of an abandoned truck and tore the paper open. I suspected that it might be from a secret admirer, as it was not uncommon for teenagers to send one another love letters through intermediaries—boys to girls, more often than not.

The message read: "Someone will be waiting for you at the northeast corner of the Ogaden Hotel at 5 P.M. on Wednesday. The subject will be wearing a white handkerchief on the left wrist. Tell the subject: 'X' wants to know the time ('X' being your initials). The subject only knows your initials. The password is: My watch is stolen. Destroy this note right away. Never tell anyone, not even your mother, about it."

My heart skipped a beat. It is certainly going to be a momentous event, I said to myself. It all seemed like something out of a James Bond movie. There was an exotic quality to the experience, a certain originality. I'd had girls slip a promising note into my school bag before, but this was unlike anything I'd ever seen or heard of.

On the appointed day, I was in fine fettle. I put on the widest bell-bottom pants that I owned, which often tripped me as I walked; combed out my Afro hair at least twice a minute, so it looked like a well-trimmed hedge; and rehearsed my lines so well that I could pass for a junior version of James Bond.

The time came. And, indeed, there was a girl waiting for me, but she was much too plain-looking, and my spirits fell. I used to pass this girl in the streets of Jijiga without looking twice. I felt that I had been cheated of something—I don't know what. But, I made an effort to be civil, and went through the secret code, which by now had lost its thrill. After passing the hurdle, she asked me if I knew what it was all about. I pleaded ignorance.

"You are being recruited to form a cell with me," she noted, with an exaggerated air of authority.

Each cell is a link in one of the clandestine chains that hang from the EPRP like the tentacles of an octopus. A cell consists of four or five people who receive their orders through one individual, who is in contact with a higher cell. Each member of the junior cell would soon be required to set up another cell, thus expanding the base of the party exponentially. No one says no to such an invitation. The EPRP was an invisible and invincible "friend" whose displeasure was more fatal than a thousand bolts of lightning.

Cell members met in complete secrecy. They never greeted each other in public, and never told anyone, including their closest friends, who the other cell members were. The secrecy was meant to limit damage to the party. If one person was arrested and tortured by the regime, they could name only a few individuals: the members of their cell group, and their one contact to a lower cell. In effect, only a single piece of the octopus's many tentacles would be amputated, leaving the body intact to pursue its normal life.

And so began my other life—unbeknownst to my childhood friend Wondwossen, and the rest of my buddies. The main duties of the cell were to ensure the broadening of the party's social base by bringing as many others under its umbrella as possible; to disseminate the party's line by spreading copies of the *Democracia* wide and far; and to point out anti-EPRP elements, so that the party could send its urban guerrilla units to do away with them.

As early as 1976, the EPRP had embarked on a nationwide campaign to eliminate their most obvious, as well as their perceived, enemies. The party spread terror throughout the land, as the bullet-ridden bodies of young men and women became a common sight on the streets. What it had lost in the form of open debate, it tried to win back at the end of a barrel. "Power! Power! Power!" became the three resounding mottoes of the party.

The fodder for the EPRP's guns consisted mostly of members of the other civilian party, the Meison, who were now in league with the junta. But it also included *kebele* officials, political instructors from the newly established ideological school (Yekatit 66), and various revolutionaries whose points of view were not to the liking of the EPRP. A few innocent individuals were labelled as pro-Meison, and met with violent deaths, because of personal grudges. Not only was there no appeal, but there was no way to ever know who had pointed the finger.

For a while it seemed that these terrorist actions were working. Power seemed a mere breath away. Then, the tables turned. The EPRP had underestimated their opponents' capacity to organize a counterattack. The Meison members, *kebele* officials and other possible targets were issued handguns, and given unlimited discretionary powers. *Kebeles* set up local jails where they could detain suspects without charge or trial. The streets of Jijiga became ominous. The hyena was out of the cactus's belly, and the sun itself refused to rise.

For their part, the Meison roamed the streets of Jijiga picking up pretty girls under the pretext of obtaining the background analysis of a suspect. These young women found themselves locked in a Meison member's home until the "case was solved." Women who did not co-operate were variously raped and tortured, and sometimes transferred to prison to serve an open-ended sentence. Some were killed.

Male suspects were often sent directly to prison, where

they would remain until the individual responsible for their arrest decided otherwise. The legal system was in a state of paralysis and the police were reduced to the role of voyeurs, watching the machinations of the new regime. Those who were arrested had no form of recourse. They were at the complete mercy of Meison cadres.

I remember being rounded up with hundreds of other youngsters suspected of distributing pamphlets and painting anti-government slogans on the walls. When two members of the local Meison party were executed later that day, the government wanted vengeance and targeted our prison. At 3 A.M. I awoke. I heard two army trucks and a Jeep pull into the compound. The prison was an old converted warehouse and the trucks could be heard backing up to the door. Dozens of soldiers armed with machine guns leaped out of the trucks and lined up before the door. Two officials and four Meison cadres walked stiffly into the crowded jail, their faces hard and inscrutable. Suddenly the jail was a sea of frightened visages. Who among us would sleep our last night in the hyena's belly? We were lined up, our countenances desperately practising anonymity. *Do not see me, not me.*

The cold faces of the cadres broke with pleasure. They were God-like and vaudevillian at once. They walked up and down the aisle of men, passing the closed silhouette of a man, only to turn back and extinguish that man's momentary relief by ordering him onto the truck. The theatrics of death played themselves out over and over again that night, until the aisle of prisoners no longer practised anonymity. The dwindling line of men were tired, very tired. We resigned ourselves, waiting for the play to end, not caring whether we would exit to the truck and death or return to our cells, until that moment of survival instinct took over and the tired resignation rewrote itself into terror.

So you see, while I stood in the line growing bored at the play, I could hear the terrified cries of the other men chosen for the truck and knew in an abstract and even casual way that those cries could be, would be, mine, if the tired waiting ever stopped and the cadre pointed his finger at me. It was a knowledge all the men shared.

When all was done, some twenty teenagers were led from the prison, screaming and pleading for their lives. Some were political prisoners, some were pickpockets, some were thieves, and all were going to die. Any one of them could have been me.

By MID-1976 it was impossible for any youth who was not embraced by the Meison to walk the streets of Jijiga. Imprisonment and torture were the norm, and execution was always imminent. The reprisals for killing individuals in the Meison were so severe that people questioned the wisdom of the campaign. Members of the EPRP and their sympathizers wanted desperately to arm themselves, but it seemed impossible. For one thing, membership in the EPRP had grown quicker than its resources. Secondly, the usual sponsors of war in Africa had already taken sides: the Soviets were backing the military junta; the Arabs were arming the Eritreans, whose policies differed from EPRP's; and the Americans were preparing the deposed feudal lords for a return to power—while at the same time attempting to fill the void created in Somalia by the recent withdrawal of Soviet forces.

It was not only what one did that constituted a crime now,

but what one refused to do. It became illegal to abstain from participating in government-initiated meetings and rallies—a crime punishable by an open-ended imprisonment. Failure to expose one's past reactionary deeds (before someone else exposed you) and failure to practise criticism and self-criticism at the local *kebele* were considered proof of a person's ongoing commitment to criminal activity. Failure to expose other reactionary elements in the community was a crime of reticence.

THRUSTING BRASS

W HEN IT FINALLY dawned on me that it wouldn't be too long before I was done away with, I decided to join one of the many armed insurrections in the country. Some dissenters sought asylum in neighbouring countries. Others found it prudent to stay home and wait it out. My good friend Wondwossen and I decided to enlist with the insurgents in the southeast— the "Western Somali (Ogaden) Liberation Movement"— because we had a common enemy in the junta and the front operated close to Jijiga. We were barely eighteen.

W ONDWOSSEN AND I were separated in age by three months. I was the older. While growing up, however, he looked much older than me, being at least a foot taller most of the time and having the appearance and composure of an adult by the time he was twelve. His father was a military officer who was driven about town by a military chauffeur. Wondwossen's father was so highly decorated that the stars themselves seemed to flow over his shoulder. Wondwossen's mother, Mrs. Aster Tekle, had been born into an aristocratic family. She was driven by the same chauffeur, whether she ventured out to shop or to visit her friends and relations. Two additional men in army uniforms served the family. One guarded the main gate of their home and the other ironed Wondwossen's father's uniform until the khaki outfit was so stiffly starched that it could stand alone.

Wondwossen was a prayer child. He was born after years of prayers to all the known saints, the good spirits and the *Adbar*, and after a small fortune was spent on medicine men and fortune-tellers. It wasn't that Mrs. Aster Tekle had been cursed with barrenness. She already had three healthy, beautiful girls whom the neighbourhood admired. She had even given birth to two boys, but both had died in the crib; the boys did not seem to have the will to live. Mrs. Aster Tekle needed a holy man who could talk to the unborn and the dead in order to find out why she could not raise boys.

There was never a shortage of such holy men in Jijiga, who found it much easier to communicate with the unborn and the long dead than with the living. After all, the ones who existed between the different universes had nothing to fear or hide. The unborn and the dead are not afraid of loansharks, who chase the living from dusk to dawn; they do not run from the police, because the police don't chase after what has not crossed their path; and they haven't slept with someone's wife, and so are not worried that there is someone lurking in the shadows to cut off their penis.

Mrs. Aster Tekle found the right holy man camped under the bridge at the end of town. He was on a long journey to Madagascar. Nobody knew where Madagascar was, but it was where all the travelling medicine men headed. We thought that strange place must be less than two hundred kilometres from Jijiga, because they were all back in town within a month or two. It was a rare opportunity to come across a wandering holy man. They were the most sought-after because they had the most up-to-date knowledge about the dead and the unborn. They charged a king's ransom for their services, but everybody knew the money was not for their own personal use. It was for the spirits they served. The wandering holy men lived on prayers.

Mrs. Aster Tekle was asked to bring a three-year-old female sheep, five kilos of clarified butter in a sealed tin container and a box of choice *ood*. The holy man lit one of the *ood* sticks, took a pinch of the dust of the dead from a pouch about his waist, and sprinkled it on the *ood*, while raising it high above his head to draw the spirits closer. Then he closed his eyes for a full hour as he wandered in spirit between the universes. Mrs. Aster Tekle shuffled in her seat, feeling ill at ease, wondering what the spirits were communicating to the bearded learned man.

"Your marriage is cursed," beamed the holy man, suddenly opening his eyes. "Someone on your husband's side of the family has thrown a spell on you not to raise a boy." Close relations often cursed one another this way, to prevent inheritors. It was a common practice especially in the northern highlands, where farmland is a communal property and each boy born to one or another family in the community is seen as a threat, since he is entitled to a share of the land when he grows up. Mrs. Aster Tekle, however, was not a farmer. It must have been out of sheer habit that someone cast the spell on her. Mrs. Aster Tekle sobbed, for this lone old man had confirmed to her what she had always suspected, that her enemies were her husband's relations.

"But," the wise man added with a learned confidence, "the cure is not out of reach. You will soon bear a boy and when you do, let everybody think that it is a girl. Never divulge this secret to anyone, including his father. On his fourth birthday, throw a big party, alert all the neighbours, the gods and the spirits to attend the occasion, and announce its sex. Nothing will touch that boy again."

A year later, Mrs. Aster Tekle gave birth to a healthy child. Curious neighbours, friends and suspicious relatives were invited for the naming event, at which Mrs. Aster Tekle insisted on picking the unusual name Kutu for her daughter, a name that does not betray the gender of the child.

On Kutu's fourth birthday, the family organized one of the most memorable events in the city. All of their neighbours, acquaintances and relatives, the local authorities, and the good and bad spirits were invited. Some four hundred guests, twenty-two street dogs, seven stray cats and five famished eagles came to attend the party. The tent they erected in the compound for the event was overflowing with guests, and many had to stand out on the street. The food, from seventeen different menus, was dished out until even the street dogs said Enough. Drinks flowed like water. People did not know what the occasion was, so they drank to their own health until they became hopelessly sick. Finally, when the guests thought that this would be the one mystery Jijiga would never solve, Mrs. Aster Tekle appeared with Kutu in hand. Kutu was dressed in boy's clothes, her hair trimmed short.

Mrs. Aster Tekle asked the audience for a moment of silence. Struggling with tears of joy, she revealed the secret that she had held under a tight lid for four long years. "Kutu is a boy," she announced, standing on the highest platform in the compound. The news was repeated twice, but the only reaction heard from the audience was the shattering of glass, as cups fell from their hands and broke into thousands of pieces.

Nobody moved. Older women who had spent their tender years struggling against insurmountable odds to bear a boy, only to deliver countless daughters, shed silent tears. They had been cheated by the gods and the *Adbar*, and they were unforgiving. The young, unmarried girls saw justice in this little drama, for now they knew that they too could beat fate at its own game.

The silence hanging over the crowd like suspended rainfall suddenly broke. The guests were drowned in enchantment. They cried, embraced each other, laughed and stumbled through the crowded tent in sheer jubilation, stepping over a kitten and two roosters whose bodies had all but melted into the colourful floor cover of green grass and wildflowers. They were happy because the evil spirits had been deceived. No one could touch this boy, for a four-year-old is beyond the reach of the baby-snatchers.

And so Wondwossen, once Kutu, was again introduced to us, this time as a boy—a fact we refused to believe until he removed his shorts and unequivocally confirmed, once and for all, what his mother had taken such pains to hide. For many years that followed, we teased Wondwossen, calling him Kutu to make him cry. Eventually, he came to laugh it off.

Heartened by her success, Mrs. Aster Tekle attempted to have a second son. She successfully conceived and delivered a boy when Wondwossen was five and, like his older brother, the new boy was announced and dressed as a girl.

Sadly, he did not live long enough to see his first birthday. Many concluded that the evil spirits had finally cottoned on to the ruse.

THOUGH WONDWOSSEN lived farther away from my home than the other boys of my acquaintance, he turned out to be the one whose company I always kept. All of my memories of childhood adventures and of wild behaviour are inextricably caught up with memories of Wondwossen. Whether I found myself at war with Mr. Alula, the Morality teacher, or caught in an endless struggle with the kingdom for advocating land reform, Wondwossen was always by my side.

As children we built our toys together. We built cars and airplanes that neither rolled smoothly nor flew, out of scraps of tin that we meticulously flattened, cut and shaped. We would make slingshots from elastic bands and wooden handles and venture out together at dusk, hunting doves, lapwings, cuckoos and cranes as they returned to the city from their flights abroad.

When we grew older, we sought happiness in the most daredevil adventures. We sneaked into restricted military compounds, crawling through barbed-wire fences, carefully treading the thorny fields, avoiding the land mines scattered along the camp's perimeter to prove our own invincibility. Sometimes, we were caught by the military police and subjected to severe physical punishment. The lesson—that life was an entrapment to the young, and bliss to the dying—was not for us, but for the world around us.

Wondwossen and I set out hiking to the mountains and other far-off places we had been advised never to set foot in, dodging the scattered fire of Somali nomads, never imagining that we would later fight side by side with them.

Wondwossen and I did things together with so little fore-thought that we would be hard-pressed to say which of us had initiated any particular action. The decision to join the front, however, was both conscious and simultaneous. We both believed that we were doing the right thing. Wondwossen, unlike me, had a lot to lose. His father had been one of the few high-ranking military officers spared by the junta, and by the logic of the new regime the father could be held responsible for the crimes of his son. Wondwossen joined the war because he firmly believed that by doing so he could make a difference in the lives of many people, especially those who had been for-gotten by the government and the world.

Once we decided to enlist with the guerrillas, we had to figure out how to raise enough money for the task ahead with-out alerting anyone. We needed a sizeable sum to pay the smugglers for safe transport to the insurgents. We also had to buy some items for personal use—sleeping bags, canteens and the like. Wondwossen sold his Seiko watch for one hundred and fifty birr (about seventy dollars), a little over half the orig-inal price. His gold necklace fetched a little more than two hun-dred birr. I sold my Peugeot bicycle for seventy-five birr and some auto parts for fifty-four birr. We gave the two smugglers a hundred birr per head, which left us with two hundred birr altogether.

We did not have many supplies to purchase, only a sleep-ing bag, a water canteen, a few bags of sugar and a pair of sandals that the smugglers insisted we purchase. Although the journey would take place after sunset, and our trek was to take us through the territory of several warring tribes, the smugglers did not want to take any chances. The sandals, they assured us, would make it impossible for anyone to follow us.

The sandals were manufactured locally out of old car tires. The design of the shoes was ingenious. One could not tell, from the imprints on the ground, which was the front and which the rear of the shoe. Merely by coming upon our prints, a hostile tribe could not tell whether we were coming or going. To perfect the deception, we were instructed on the proper use of the sandals.

To an experienced tracker, footprints are personal diaries. The tracker can read the age, gender, living conditions and other particulars of an individual merely by examining the trails left behind: a steady stride distinguishes the young man from the old, who leaves behind faltering footsteps; the feminine footprint is delicate; a city dweller tends to walk with his toes turned outwards, because of the stiff leather shoes that deform his feet; running leaves a deeper toe print, and a hurried gait leaves a prominent heel stamp; a bulky person, as well as someone carrying a heavy load, leaves deep footprints, but the load carrier is distinguished by the occasional criss-crossing of the left and right tracks—zigzagging under a heavy burden can cause the individual's left foot to fall to the right of his other footprint.

We would be trained to lift our feet neatly above the ground, without dragging our heels, and land each squarely on the ground. Wherever possible, we were to cover our tracks by walking on rocks and weeds.

In addition, I brought along a few bundles of herbal medicines from Mam's treasured collection. Whenever she visited her relations in the highlands, Mam brought home a supply of roots, bruised leaves and ground seeds. Her uncle was a medicine man who carried in his memory generations of knowledge about the medicinal properties of herbs and roots. The knowledge had been passed from the father to the eldest son throughout time. Mam's uncle would later initiate his son, who would in his turn initiate his son, as soon as he felt the premonition of death.

As a young boy, I was fascinated by the strange behaviour of my mother's uncle and his eldest son as they set out for parts unknown in the small hours of the morning completely naked. They always came back before sunrise with full bags, but I was never able to discover the kinds of plants that they gathered, as they would bruise the roots and leaves before they returned, rendering them unrecognizable.

Once, when I was a little older, though still a boy, I mustered my courage and asked the old man why it was necessary for him to go out naked when he collected the herbs. He answered that you have to be one with nature before you can earn her trust enough that she'll let you in on her secrets. He reflected for a moment longer. "It's like nursing an infant. The only way for a mother to share a soul with her baby is to cuddle the naked soft skin of her young against her own flesh as she breast-feeds him. Otherwise, how is she different from a feeding bottle?"

Throughout the last day I spent with my family I was agitated and uncommunicative. Mam was quick to notice that I did not eat much of my meal and that I paced up and down like a caged tiger. On the afternoon of my departure I could not meet anyone's eyes. Just to keep myself from tears took all the energy I possessed. At one point Mam asked what was bothering me and I nearly vomited. An inexplicable sense of guilt had risen up in me suddenly. In the end I left home without saying goodbye. I knew full well that I might never see my family again, but I reasoned that if I stayed home it would not be long before I had joined those beneath the sod. The revolution was eating Ethiopia's children at an alarming rate.

A RELUCTANT GUERRILLA

T HE TRAIL the smugglers chose for us was a familiar one. Wondwossen and I had spent many Saturdays running up and down this beaten track in search of adventure, but the oppressive darkness, the twin, blinking lights that sprang up all around us, and the unfamiliar songs of the night made it look and feel alien. The smugglers tried to help, explaining to us which pair of shining eyes belonged to which animal, and the meanings of the howls in the darkness. They reassured us that no animal would go out of its way to stalk us, except perhaps the human animal. It was the only beast to be feared in the wilderness.

Once, while travelling alone under the breathtaking terra cotta of the dying sun, one of the smugglers had seen a bale of hay ahead of him. It was the end of the harvest season, and the harvest was very good that year, so he did not think much of it until he noticed the heap of grass moving. A bundle of hay left outdoors overnight is not unusual, but a bale moving on its own is uncommon even in Jijiga. Abdi quickly rolled the reels of oral history that had been passed to him through hundreds of generations but found no reference to a beast hiding behind a bale of grass. No such apparition had ever, to his knowledge, attacked a peace-loving nomad. He decided to move on.

With each measured step the nomad took, the bale of grass changed its shape until it became alarmingly clear that it was not one but two lions, a couple, lying side by side as they watched his thin frame emerge from the purple horizon. The beasts did not seem particularly excited to see him, but they didn't take their eyes off him, either. Abdi dropped the stick that all nomads habitually carry, to convince the lions of his peaceful intentions, and moved on, without betraying his alarm. The nomad was only ten metres from the couple when the lioness became threatening and restless, appearing eager to pounce on him. But luckily for Abdi, the king of beasts was in no mood for war and convinced his mate, with a few guttural reproofs and a nudge, to leave the young man alone.

Abdi earned his living smuggling humans out of the country and bringing in contraband goods from the neighbouring countries of Djibouti and Somalia. Once, when he was travelling with his fellow smugglers through the desolate mountains, one of his friends looked up and saw a lion sitting on a bare rock, casually watching the nomads. The lion was perfectly disguised, blending in with the greyish rocks and dying grass, and it was a matter of chance that the smuggler noticed him.

Instead of heeding what his ancestors had drilled into him and leaving the lion alone, the man raised his rifle, aimed clearly at the beast and fired. He missed. The lion disappeared. No one thought much of this little incident until hours later, when they were crossing a narrow alley. They were walking in single file along the belt of the treacherous mountain when a tortured shriek was heard from the end of the line. Looking back, they saw one of their men disappear downhill, carried by a lion. They could not tell if it was the same lion they had encountered earlier but there was no mistaking the identity of the victim—the man who had shot the rifle and missed. The moral of the story is that lions do not eat peace-loving nomads. If you are a nomad and you find yourself in the belly of a lion, rest assured—you are not nearly so peace-loving as you thought.

There was no moving bale of hay or vengeful lion on our trip. I did, however, discover just how ill-prepared I was for the task awaiting me. Unlike the Somali nomads guiding us, who seemed to flow like the wind, I had a difficult time crossing the mountains and hills. Halfway into the journey, I was suffering from a severe stomach ache and was barely able to walk. It was the miracle of Mam's bitter medicinal roots that put me back on my feet.

About eighteen hours after we left Jijiga, after rerunning many of my dreams, we finally reached the end of our journey. Beyond the next hill lay the rebel encampment. Unwilling to further imperil themselves, reluctant even to give advice as to how we were to present our hands to the rebels without being shot, the smugglers melted away into the hills. As our small troop debated the safest means of integrating ourselves with the rebels, one among us, I can no longer remember who, came up with the idea of waving a white flag—an idea most likely gathered from some grainy black-and-white Hollywood war movie. We had no other options. Wondwossen removed his shirt, which was stained with dust from our journey, and revealed a pristine white undershirt beneath, which he offered up for the mission. After a few minutes of scrounging in the scrub and brush, we found a suitable twig to which we tied our makeshift flag.

Though the way was clear and the day bright, our feet
were heavy and our progress to the rebel encampment was
slow. Ahead of us, a strange outcropping of mountainous
stone stood between us and the camp. As we approached this
monolith, hoping to share its view with whatever lizard had
slid out of its crevice to sun itself on the wide hot expanse, we
were ordered to halt by a voice that seemed to issue from the
rock itself. Half a dozen men then appeared from behind the
stone, wielding a variety of rifles, all of which were trained on
our small group. We were instructed to toss our bags a safe distance from us, and undress completely. The youngest of the
rebel scouts, a boy about our age, was the first to lower his gun.
He smiled at our naked troop amicably, displaying remarkably
white, well-structured teeth. One of his canines was plated
with gold—the style of the day among wealthy Somalis—and
it lit up with the sun like a flare. He offered his hand, and introduced himself to us as Hussain. Two of the others followed
suit, lowering their guns and shaking our hands. The others
kept their distance, still training their guns on us.

Hussain and the two others led us to their group leader,
who reclined in the sparse, sun-dappled shade of a truck con-
tentedly chewing *chat*. Three of his lieutenants were in attendance. The leader spoke slowly. He asked us our ethnic group,
what our fathers did for a living, what we knew about the front
and why we had decided to join. He asked us many questions
that we had never considered, and which we could not find
answers for, concerning the local army movements and the size
of recent militia reinforcements. Finding our knowledge on
these matters so easily plumbed, he turned his attention
towards his three lieutenants, and engaged in an intense discussion regarding the type and extent of the new armaments being

airlifted to Jijiga, the possible involvement of Cuban and Russian forces in the conflict, and how these factors would influence the outcome. When the conversation waned, he noted our continued presence with surprise, ordering Hussain to take us off somewhere and watch over us, until he had made a decision.

Hussain was an enigmatic person. His father was an important political figure in Djibouti—a Somali-speaking city-state on the Horn of Africa that had once been a colony of France. As his father's only son, Hussain had been groomed for great things. He had attended the best school his homeland had to offer, and later had rounded out his education in France. He spoke French and English fluently, as well as Somali, his mother tongue. And yet here he was, on the front lines, a gun-slinging rebel.

Hussain had remarkably easy manners, was quick to laugh, and was animated in conversation and gesture. On long dull afternoons, when conversation grew sparse, people would eagerly seek his companionship. During those times, Hussain would tell ebullient stories of the people and things he had seen while vacationing in France. It's not that anyone believed a word of it, just that the sheer incredibility of it all was enlivening to the ear. I remember one instance in which a crowd gathered to silently apprehend the strange imaginings of his mind. He told the group of an invention called the microwave oven, an object that looked very much like a transistor radio, complete with a dial, but which was only meant for heating food. You placed your cold meal inside this box and a few minutes later your food emerged steaming hot, while the plastic bag covering it remained intact. Before the hour was out, everyone at the front had heard tell of this ridiculous idea, and wherever Hussain walked that afternoon, he was taunted by soldiers about his "magic box." Hussain simply laughed it off. Another time, he let it be known that there were countries in Europe where the government paid its citizens money because they would not work at any job. That story got him a reprimand from the leader himself. Such stories, although harmless lies in one context, become dangerous under different circumstances. The leader believed it might give rank-and-file fighters the wrong idea.

One day, when the afternoon was particularly long and hot, Hussain and I exchanged stories. He admitted to me that while growing up in Djibouti, he had believed that Amharas each had a short tail between their legs. He had heard many stories of the atrocities committed by Amharas, mostly untrue, and had formed a mental picture of the people capableof perpetrating such horrors. It was not until he had made his first trip to Dire Dawa, Ethiopia's third largest city, that he was shocked to find the Amharas were shaped like men. His surprise in finding that the Amharas were indistinguishable from his own people was eclipsed only by his surprise that no one treated him badly. In fact, staying at the most expensive hotel, spending his money lavishly, accompanied to his room by more than one local prostitute at a time, he earned a certain fame and admiration from the people who got to know him. When I met Hussain, he had not only wiped his childhood prejudices from his mind, but had replaced them with the strongest and fondest memories of his young life, memories that were inextricably linked with the Amhara people of Dire Dawa.

Far from revealing the inner workings of his mind, this revelation made him an even greater mystery. How could someone who had developed such a fondness for a people fight them in the battlefield with such unparalleled determination?

The rest of the rebels were simple to understand; they abhorred all things Amhara with a vengeance. Though Hussain shared in their ideals of a "Great Somali Land," which would embrace all Somali-speaking people in neighbouring countries under a single banner, he proved exempt from the nationalistic dogma that held one must degrade all others in order to uphold one's own.

Hussain led us through our first weeks. Like children, we had to be taught all over again how to sleep, how to wash our faces, how to relieve ourselves, and many other things that one takes for granted.

I received my first shock in field etiquette when I went out to wash my face. Hussain gathered us all together that first morning, and led us down a hill, towards some grazing cattle. He asked us to pick our wash basins. He knew we were confused, and he had already begun to cry with laughter, his gold tooth flashing with each rib-cracking laugh. When he finally composed himself, he offered to show us how it was done. Hussain carefully surveyed the docile herd, finding an animal that suited him. He circumspectly approached the cow and gently began to rub its hindquarters. The animal appeared to relax, raised its tail and let out a fountain of urine. Hussain immediately bent down, and splashed handfuls of the yellow liquid over his face. Still grinning, he invited us to do likewise. I was revolted, and refused. The rest, some hesitating briefly, others for longer, all with an eye on the cows' hooves, followed suit.

Wondwossen decided to prove that prudence did not mean avoiding risks altogether, but minimizing them. He attempted to draw his wash water from a camel, thereby advancing the breakthrough, while minimizing the risk to himself. While we stood by, curious, he stroked the camel's hindquarters, accidentally brushing the animal's knee in the process. All camels have an aversion to this kind of knee-touching intimacy. This camel reacted swiftly and violently, kicking Wondwossen in the stomach and knocking him a full six feet away. As we laughed ourselves silly, Wondwossen brushed the dust from his clothes and stood up uncertainly. All that was hurt was his pride.

A couple of days later, five of us were sent to fetch water. There were no rivers, lakes or wells within twenty kilometres of the base. During the rainy season, water had collected on various surfaces, but most of the local ponds were already running low—holding more in the way of tadpoles than water. It took us the better part of the day to find a fresh watering hole. The hole itself was easy to spot; we just had to look for the cattle, donkeys, camels and nomads who gathered en masse around the precious water-filled basin. Though we were all sweaty, and in desperate need of a drink, the guerrillas did not rush for the water. Binoculars were trained, strategic positions held and the area carefully studied for a full hour before it was declared safe.

The nomads were not in the least surprised to see us. They must have crossed paths with the rebels too often to consider them intruders. The nomadic men came over to greet us, extending both hands, and touching their chests to indicate that their welcome was heartfelt. We did likewise. The women and children continued at their tasks, washing themselves in the pond alongside animals that were drinking, rolling and urinating in the water. These were people who had never heard of disease-causing bacteria and viruses. They sickened and died only after they had learned about the existence of dangerous micro-organisms. Until then, they neither filtered their water nor thought of boiling it, and they lived long enough to be killed by drought.

After we had filled our containers with water filtered using some contraption the Somalis had obtained from their Soviet suppliers, we rushed back to the base and informed the front of our discovery. There wasn't even time for a bath, as it was growing dark. When we arrived, a large group of men was sent, with donkeys and camels bearing huge receptacles, to collect more water.

FOOD WAS SOMETHING I had worried about long before leaving home. It wasn't that I had a special liking for anything, so much as I tend to be particular about all things I eat. I had broken bread with Somali friends numerous times, and knew that our foods were, for the most part, similar. But I didn't know what to expect in the field. In Jijiga, when a dish is called Christian or Muslim, it refers to the meat that is used in the stew. Muslims, like Christians, offer prayers over the animal before slaughtering it. These few ritualistic words, uttered more out of tradition than conviction, are the most divisive. Christians and Muslims maintain separate abattoirs, butchers, meat-caterers, restaurants and kitchens, at a respectable distance from one another. The majority of the Somalis of Jijiga, like their Christian counterparts, are not fervent in their beliefs, observing the major religious events like Ramadan the way that even lukewarm Christians will observe Christmas. Even at these times Christians and Muslims commingle, sharing food (except meat) and festivities alike.

I had often wondered why such rituals were significant only when they involved meat, and not other foods, like festival bread, which is also prayed over before being broken. When I asked Mam, she replied that the meat, owing to the simple prayers uttered before slaughter, changed in texture, taste and delectable qualities. She had never touched Muslim meat, but was certain that it had an earthy, flat flavour to it. Mam claimed that she could tell a piece of Muslim meat from three metres, though I did not put her to the test.

Mam did not mind that I ate Muslim meat. She only warned me never to bring it home to her, and to scrub my hands cleaner than the cat before returning from such a meal. When I invited my Muslim friends home to lunch or dinner, Mother never alluded to our religious differences; she simply treated my friends as she would her own children.

THE MAIN DIET among the rebels was sorghum grain, soaked in raw milk, with, if you were lucky, a touch of unclarified butter and a dash of sugar. Occasionally, there was a piece of barbecued camel meat to share. Most of the foodstuffs were either bought from, or donated by, the nomads. It was the rebels' policy not to rob their own people.

Sorghum and maize are the two grains cultivated in Ogaden. Even by Ethiopia's standards, the farming is primitive. There are no yoked bulls or horses to open the earth before planting the seed; no weeding; no tilling the soil to aerate the ground once the seed has germinated. In Ogaden, farming is typically a one-man venture.

Shortly before the rainy season commences, the nomads begin to stake out their territory. Caravans of camels laden with all the worldly possessions of each nomad arrive at their staked lot. The women unload the camels and in a matter of minutes assemble their huts—slender wooden domes covered over with leather. Within a fortnight, the dusty fields of Ogaden, once barren and utterly desolate, teem with life. The landscape, once a dusty plain with nothing to relieve the eye, is dotted with intricately crafted "nomad helmets."

After the first rain, the clay dust settles, the ground cracks and breathes, and life begins to press up into the sun. These grounds are among the most fertile in Africa, and a mere twenty-four hours after the first drop of precious rain touches the earth, the land is felted over with green. The nomads emerge from their helmet-shaped huts, pointed stick in one hand, bag of seeds in the other. They walk their parcel of land, end to end, stabbing the earth with the stick, dropping a single seed and, in a barely perceptible motion, covering the seed over with their heel. For the next few days each nomad-turned-farmer repeats this unvarying routine from dawn to dusk. For as far as the eye can see, this strange halting dance is performed simultaneously by hundreds of stoop-backed men, peering earthwards, stabbing and scattering without pause. To the casual observer, it looks like the fields of Ogaden have been overrun by a colony of lunatics, all under the delirious influence of an identical disease.

The nomads remain with their crops until they are two feet high, keeping them safe from winged predators. Then, as suddenly as they appeared, they disappear from sight, domed frames neatly bound to the backs of camels. No trace is left of their residence save for the green fields. During the coming months, the domesticated plants will fight the persistent weeds and survive the occasional rolling assault of wild animals on their own. Shortly before harvest, the nomads return.

There is no communal effort involved in the harvesting of the plants either. Each nomad prepares his own storage bin, carefully digging a hole in the ground—a single small opening at the surface, and a deep protected belly in the earth. The bin is lined with wet ash, to protect the seed from insects. Then, after deducting a few sacks of grain for the market and his own consumption, the nomad stores the rest in this bulbshaped recess, sealing the mouth with a lid and covering it over with dirt.

Once again, the camps are gone, and the landscape reverts to its original condition. There is no trace of the previous occupants to be found. Dust quickly settles over the small mounds of earth marking the scattered bins that lie just under the surface, making them indistinguishable from the numerous molehills that ravage the land. A few months later, the nomad will return to dig up his stored grains. He will use his pointed stick and a couple of distant landmarks to establish the location of his bin, triangulating between them. After removing the first few inches of dirt, he verifies that he is not breaking into another's property; then he bails out the recess and fills his sacks with grain, leaving a scattering of seeds for the coming rainy season. For the remainder of the year, the nomad will live off his cattle, fervently reminding his God to bring rain.

AFTER WE HAD lived among the rebels for two weeks, a decision was reached by the leaders as to the status of the newcomers. The numbers of male and female refugees of all ages who were coming to the front had been growing at an exponential rate. The situation was already critical; normal activities had been halted, security had been compromised, and an urgent solution was needed if the rebel army was going to continue.

The organization tentatively picked some of the newcomers as potential members, and allowed others to remain with them while they secured a safe passage to Somalia, where they would remain as refugees. Whether or not someone was awarded a firearm depended on how well he spoke the Somali language, and how well he could recite passages from the Holy Koran.

Wondwossen and I had joined up with four other boys, natives of Jijiga. Three were local Somalis; one was from the Adere ethnic group; and Wondwossen was Amhara, like me. The others, excepting Wondwossen and myself, were all Muslims, though none of us practised religion. All of the group, except for me, spoke excellent Somali, and so our group was accepted by the rebels.

Each of us was issued a carbine rifle and two rounds of ammunition. The guns were very old and often jammed when they were fired successively, leaving us with a general sense of anxiety. Hussain had promised to get us replacements, but they had never materialized. Perhaps the matter was out of his hands.

The first three months of our existence at the front were filled with excitement and anticipation. We were constantly on the move and took part in a number of dramatic and daring actions involving army convoys heading south. We were not able to claim a major military victory, but that didn't matter much at the time. We were satisfied that we were able to settle some old scores with the junta.

Wondwossen and I were separated about four months after we joined the front. He was sent to the eastern highlands.

Approximately a month later, my group mounted an impressive mission against an Ethiopian Army training camp in Chinaksen. A week before D-day, the activities in our camp had reached a fever pitch. We had been told of the imminence of a mission, and knew it was serious, but only the top commanders were privy to the actual target and date of attack.

Chinaksen was an eight-hour walk from the recent rebel base. Before reaching the target, we had to cross several mountains and pass through dangerously open terrain. The day before the attack, many of the Somali rebels smuggled themselves and their rifles into town, unbeknownst to the Ethiopian Army. It is not unusual for nomads travelling in twos and threes to pass into any city in Ogaden, and the disguised rebels had hidden their armaments under a pile of firewood carried on the back of a camel, where no one would think to look.

On D-day, at about 3 A.M., the big guns were drawn closer to the army barracks, mines were dug into the road leading out of town, and we took up our strategic positions and waited for the signal. At the first sound of machine-gun fire and mortar explosions, the alarm bell in the training camp was sounded. Conscripts, dressed only in their underwear, ran from the dormitories in panic. Many held their clothes in their hands, dragging them across the dusty ground, as they ran about the compound to escape the fire. The guns were locked away in the depot each night, and those unarmed boys were massacred by the dozens. If a boy raised his hands in submission, this sad gesture was the last he would make. The guerrillas took no prisoners.

After the training camp was bombed, machine-gunned and burned, we walked downtown, shooting our guns in the air, at village houses and at the church. Then the Somalis among us began to hunt for dogs. They were still smiling from the pleasure of victory as they killed the animals. Not angry or twisted smiles, as one might expect, but smiles that would be appropriate during some festivity, smiles I had taken pleasure in on long afternoons, when Hussain told his fantastic stories. The faces of these men conveyed no hint of the brutality of their hands.

Within a matter of hours, a village that had once been considered an island of peace had been devastated. When we left Chinaksen, a terrible silence hung over the remains of the camp and the streets of the town.

My friends and I were silent on the way to the rebel camp. We reminded ourselves that these boys had been training to be soldiers who would one day be at war with us. But it was impossible to reconcile a future possibility with the terror marking faces that still bore the vestiges of childhood. We had watched them run for cover, terrified and half-dressed, only to be slaughtered. What had occurred defied all logic, defied our comprehension.

The dogs had become eerily quiet the moment machine guns and mortar fire broke the night, and remained silent even as the rebels hunted them with the same determination that had strewn the training compound with the bodies of the dead. Somalis, perhaps because of their faith, have always abhorred dogs. They refer to these animals as *Haram* (cursed) and do not own them as pets. Street dogs are not treated well anywhere, but in the Muslim quarter they are stoned, starved, and forced, through adversity, into showing their true animal nature.

AFTER BURNING DOWN the Chinaksen training camp, we retreated to the base. There was not a single casualty in the troop, and the success was considered a godsend. Once we had passed through the flat terrain, we relaxed and rested. I was very tired, and rested my head against a rock. Within a matter of seconds I was sound asleep.

What happened next sounded like a bad dream. I could hear torrents of machine-gun fire. People around me were running for cover, and someone was tugging my shirt. I tried to turn over and sleep on my other side when I felt a sharp jab in my ribs. It was Hussain, trying desperately to wake me. Suddenly reality hit me: we were at war.

The rebels panicked. We had been tracked by an elite Ethiopian Army unit stationed some thirty kilometres away, and it was our turn, disoriented and half asleep, to scramble barefoot for cover. But there was not much chance. Mortars, high-calibre machine guns and grenades ploughed the field. Before we could make out where the enemy was and where the shots were coming from, the heavens opened fire on us. Out of the blue horizon, four fighter jets headed our way; they dipped down, spread us with machine-gun fire, and on their way up dropped bombs on us that shattered the rocks and multiplied the shrapnel. I discovered to my horror that when someone you don't know fires a .50-calibre anti-aircraft gun at you, he actually means to kill you.

I attempted to run for cover but I tripped over my shadow and fell into a hole in the ground. Fine dust got into my eyes, ears and nose, and I could barely make out my surroundings. When I finally managed to find my legs, I discovered that the sky had fallen. It was now supported by the tip of the mountain, and hung down so low over my head that I could easily have reached up and torn a piece from the blue canvas.

The mountains shrank. Everything around me—the trees, the people and the boulders—shrank, gaining in width what they lost in height. It looked to me as though the Earth was slowly being drawn through the two huge rollers of a heavenly extruder.

I tried to move but the air had tangibly thickened. It had solidified around me into a thick gelatinous ocean, and I was unable to move. I tried to slice at that jelly with my arms and legs and managed a few painful steps, but quickly ran out of breath. I opened my mouth wide and bit a piece of that jelly, but it got stuck in my throat. I reached down for my canteen to wash it down with water, but I found my rifle instead.

When I looked up again, I was relieved to see that the sky had receded, the mountains had regained their reassuring majesty, and the wind was once more blowing weightlessly past me. I noticed some fellow rebels dashing for the impregnable cover of the mountain and followed their lead. Many did not make it. I was one of the fortunate few to find safety in a cave. The camp below was smouldering; human limbs were scattered over a wide range. I paused in the dark belly of the mountain to see if I had sustained any injuries. There were tiny nicks all over my body and a gash under my right knee, looking up at me, wondering whether or not to bleed. I grabbed some fine dust and sprinkled it on.

Those of us who survived did not wait to witness the end. After collecting our units and gathering our strength, we ran for the only place we knew, the current rebel base, some twenty kilometres away. That night, when the casualties were counted, over one hundred and forty were dead, more than fifty seriously wounded, and the remaining three hundred psychologically crippled. Hussain was among the dead.

Darkness shrouded the base. The next few days were spent in mourning; the easy confidence that had permeated the rebels had been shaken to the core. Some members defected, heading for the relative safety of Somalia. I was undecided— until I heard what had happened to my friend Wondwossen. He had been killed while fighting to take over the town of Gursum.

I was told of his death, casually, by the group commander as he was making the morning rounds. I was not sure that I had heard the commander right, so I asked him to repeat what he had said, but he just patted me on the shoulder, adding a few comforting words before resuming his daily duties. Hundreds of fighters were dying in those perilous days. To him, Wondwossen was just another soldier.

I WAS STUNNED. Unable to carry my weight, I sought a solitary corner at the far end of the camp and collapsed on the thorny ground. My mind was racing. My eyes blurred. I felt such a terrible heat in my guts that it seemed to me that I might melt down unless I removed my skin. I searched for my battered canteen and dumped what little water it held over my head.

When my vision finally cleared, I found myself staring into pictures of my childhood as they rolled across the blue screen of the heavens. I saw myself in Memerae's shed with baby oil all over my face; I saw myself with Wondwossen hunting birds with slings as they returned to town at night; building toy planes from scrap metal; injecting Mr. Alula's cows with the avenging fluid. Soon the blue sky flickered with a scene from my childhood in which the mistress of a mansion drenched me with dirty laundry water, tossed over the fence of the compound. I could hear myself being regaled with all sorts of names, but when I looked around I was all by myself in the midst of a desert. The mansion leaped from the sky and lumbered after me. There was nowhere to hide, no one to comfort me. With each step I took, I sank deeper and deeper into the scorching desert sand. When I was about to give up and let the building press me down into the sand, I heard a voice say, "Never give up."

I leaped up with a start, but there was no one around except a large lizard who lay sunning himself on top of an immense rock, staring at me with unabashed confidence. I said a few words of prayer for Wondwossen, then got up to join the group.

I took a few tentative steps towards camp when I heard what was unmistakably Wondwossen's voice repeat the phrase I had heard before: "Never give up." I turned around as though I had just been slapped. All that remained of my vision was an empty field. The light morning wind tossed a tumbleweed across the expanse. The lizard and the bare rock it had been perched on were gone.

THE LAST STRAW fell for most of us when crates of advanced Soviet weaponry began arriving directly from the Somali Army supply depots, and when officers from the Somali standing army arrived to organize and train the fighting personnel. The war was no longer being waged by the Ogaden tribe in an effort to create their own homeland, but by the government of

Somalia in an attempt to annex the Somali-speaking territories of Ethiopia. What that meant for the non-Somalis in the front was plain enough—trouble.

During the seven months of my tenure, the rebels had become less and less tolerant of non-Somalis, dispersing us throughout the various fronts so that no more than a handful of non-Somalis were left in any one group. When all the other fighters were supplied with the newly acquired AK-47 machine guns, we were only permitted to carry less threatening Second World War–vintage rifles. We were under constant surveillance. The atmosphere became unbearably stifling.

The newly organized front engaged in more battles in the following month than it had in the eighteen months since it had been dispatched from Somalia. Unlike the earlier easygoing days, we were sent on strenuous sorties. As more and more Somalis joined the ranks, as more tanks and artillery were acquired, the nature of the battles changed remarkably. Soon, all non-Somalis were removed from the fighting teams. We had become expendables, whose duty it was to spy on enemy movements, or fetch daily supplies.

Those of us who were not Somalis resented our change in position and started seriously rethinking the whole business. First and foremost, it did not seem right that we should support what had obviously become a Somali effort to annex part of our own country. We may have had a different agenda than the military junta ruling the nation, but our involvement in the Somali faction was no way of settling the difference. Secondly, we were aware that our present status as expendables numbered our days. We would either be killed by the Ethiopian Army while fetching water or be disposed of by the Somali rebels themselves when the time came. Death was inevitable and dishonourable, either way.

For days we thought about our options. Dissent is not tolerated in a guerrilla army, so we were secretive and never divulged our plans to anyone outside our small circle. There are no prisons in the field, no courts to try each case, just summary execution. Whatever we chose to do, we had to do it together and quickly.

We had two choices: either we had to trudge hundreds of kilometres to Djibouti and seek asylum—a dangerous trek across a hostile territory infested by both the government army and the Somali guerrillas—or we had to give ourselves up to the Ethiopian Army and await our fate. We were literally caught between the Devil and the deep blue sea.

After a long deliberation, four of the boys decided to head for Djibouti. A boy from Jijiga and I decided we would return home. We were acutely aware of the consequences of our action, but we had long since ceased to care.

APATHY IN THE FACE of continual violence is something someone who has never lived through a war cannot understand. Barely six months later, when my family and I were seeking refuge, travelling slowly on the road to Harar, the heat of mid-afternoon was broken only by the treble whirr of falling bombs and the sight of the dead. People had long since ceased to huddle under their limbs at the sound. They simply walked unflinchingly past the dead. Their frail limbs could not stop the bombs, their ears could not tell them where the bombs would fall. Death was random and continual, and people simply got on with what living was left to them: the long wait in line for a bucket of water, the preparation of what food there was to be found. People simply gathered about themselves, like rags, what life there was left, deafened and inured to the inevitability of death.

THE PLAN AND execution of our escape was quite simple. The six of us co-ordinated the times when we were outside of camp, searching for supplies, so that we would all be out of sight of the rebels at the same time. We left the shelters at around ten in the morning and met at the foot of the hill. The first couple of hours were the most critical. They would give us the time to get out of the army's reach. We dumped everything we were carrying in the bush, except for three good rifles, some ammunition and our water canteens. Then we ran, for hours, stopping only to catch our breath and help each other with the small loads we were carrying. About seven hours after leaving camp we reached a point where we had to part. We hugged each other and wished one another good luck, joking that one day we would meet again in ivory towers.

The two of us who were heading back to Jijiga had an eight- to ten-hour journey ahead. As for the others, there was no telling. It might take weeks or even months for them to reach their destination, if they reached it at all.

Going back to the same old enemy after having experienced a sort of freedom was an obvious failure. However, I managed to convince myself that I had, at the very least, fought in the trenches for something I believed in. Whoever first said that he had won a moral victory had probably, likewise, lost the battle. The one failure I could not bury was the fact that I returned alone, without my childhood friend Wondwossen.

As I approached Jijiga, I worried about how I would face Wondwossen's parents and my own mother, who treated Wondwossen like another son. The other concern I had was obvious. After all, my absence hadn't been a night out to paint slogans on walls or spread illegal pamphlets. We had fought the regime in a real battle, inflicting serious damage to the army. Who knew how many soldiers had been killed during the seven months we were with the rebels? Who could tell how many children had been orphaned, how many wives widowed? But it was too late to worry. Whatever the consequences, they were only hours away, and inevitable.

We arrived in the city shortly before sunset. I was very surprised to find that we could walk right down the main street without being confronted by the army or the police. For a major military base and a strategically important city, the local security was pitiful.

There were many refugees in town from the regions south of Jijiga, recently conquered by the Somali Army. A good number of them were boys of my age, not much better dressed than myself, carrying or dragging guns. We were tempted to toss our guns in a ditch and head home. It was possible that we could hide for a few days, and then slip out of town under assumed identities. But we considered the consequences. If our relations were caught harbouring fugitives, particularly rebels, the punishment would be as severe for them as for us. We decided to do the right thing, and headed for army headquarters.

On surrendering to the army I discovered that a person's worst fears are seldom realized. We learned that the government had already granted amnesty to anyone in the field who was willing to give up arms and return to civilian life. We were ecstatic, incredulous, and naturally suspicious. After all, how could one expect the same junta that had chased us from one end of the bush to the other to be so reasonable, even merciful? We were proven wrong for once, and did not mind at all.

I wondered how many lives would have been saved if we had known about the amnesty earlier. The news had been aired for months in different languages, but radios and newspapers were off-limits to rank-and-file fighters because enemy propaganda was considered the most dire form of warfare. Anyone attempting to smuggle newspapers or radios to the front was considered an enemy collaborator. Obviously, these rules served the intended purpose.

The day after we gave up, when they learned of our arrival, my mother, brothers and sisters, close friends and neighbours came to visit me. My siblings were too young to know what had happened; they only felt relief to see me at the army headquarters. They crowded around, jumping up and down, outshouting each other to tell me what they'd done while I was away. My elder sister, Meselu, was still in Mechara, some four hundred kilometres away.

Mam was a wreck, her eyes peach-red and her movements unusually awkward. She tried to ask many questions at once, but words failed her and I could not follow her meaning. When she finally composed herself and was able to speak in coherent sentences, she asked me, as I was afraid she would, about Wondwossen's whereabouts.

I felt a lump in my throat and could not answer. All I could do was cry. She knew from my face that Wondwossen was gone, that she would never again cast an eye on him. Mam straightened her back and became still, facing the blank white wall in front of her for a very long time. Her lips quivered. Her face changed colour. The blood vessels on her temples and forehead became swollen with anguish, and it seemed to me that they would burst and drown her face with red. Then, all at once, her face broke like a ruptured dam and the tears poured from her eyes. She cried for centuries, pausing once every few decades to wipe her nose with her handkerchief. No form of persuasion would ease her weeping. She stopped only when she ran out of tears. For years afterwards, when something brought Wondwossen to mind, she would cry as though it were only yesterday that he had been home to see her.

W E WERE DETAINED for two weeks for political rehabilitation, but otherwise were treated like celebrities. The prisons had been transformed since I had last been incarcerated. With proper sleeping quarters, regular meals, exercise and access to showers, they had the feeling of bootcamps. Our relatives were allowed to visit us as often as they wished. As we were released, they advised us of our newly acquired freedom, and told us we were free to go to school, to seek employment or to do nothing.

All signs seemed to indicate that the junta would remain in power for some years to come. The Soviets and their allies, the Cubans and others, were embedded in the country, and it appeared that nothing would uproot them in the foreseeable future. If I had any hope of helping to change the system, I realized, I had better resume my education. With the endorsement of the local cadre in charge of my case, I was permitted to join my former classmates in Grade 12, despite the fact that I had been away for most of the school year.

IN THE WEEKS after my return, the Somali government intensified its efforts to occupy all Somali-speaking regions of Ethiopia. Despite desperate attempts to save Jijiga, we were completely surrounded by the enemy and cut off from the rest of the country. There was no form of civilian transport arriving in or departing from Jijiga. Martial law had been declared, and every available truck, bus and airplane had been diverted to the war effort.

This was the third attempt by Somalia to take over Ogaden. The first two wars, waged in 1961 and 1966, were mere child's play compared to the latest efforts. In terms of armaments, deployments and casualties, the enemy's achievements were breathtaking.

Somalia had laid claim to the Somali-speaking territories within Ethiopia, Kenya and Djibouti since its inception as a modern state in 1960. Somalia considered these regions "lost territories," and justified her war effort as an unfortunate, but necessary, measure towards reclaiming her rightful provinces. Indeed, the Somali-speaking peoples of Ethiopia and Kenya had little in common with the people they were "forced" to live with. Somalis are one of the few ethnic groups in Africa speaking the same language, having identical cultural and religious institutions, even as they live under four different flags.

I lay awake many nights wondering if Kenya and Ethiopia had not heinously divided a unique people, forcing them to live separately. I wondered if liberal elements in the two neighbouring countries shouldn't strive to reunite the "annexed provinces" with their mother land, Somalia.

But the more I studied history, the more I questioned this view.

BOOK THREE: STORM

WINDOW ON HISTORY

N THE YEAR A.D. 1000, if you had strolled along the northern frontier of the Horn of Africa, you would have witnessed a human tidal wave moving inland, and wondered where it could have come from. You might even have glanced at your surroundings and surmised that these nomadic people had somehow crossed the bottleneck at the Gulf of Aden; the vast Indian Ocean was impossible to navigate.

Having crossed this bottleneck, the Somalis found themselves in one of the harshest regions on the Horn, with little to recommend it for human settlement. They immediately started elbowing their way south and, to some extent, west. By the turn of the twentieth century, they occupied the regions they currently inhabit. Their progress, however, was not without obstacles. The Somalis faced their greatest challenge from the Oromo people, who were the original inhabitants of these regions. They drove the Oromos from their traditional homes into the Ethiopian highlands at the turn of the sixteenth century.

The land occupied by the Somalis is, for the most part, an arid savannah—an endless steppe punctuated by acacia trees, huge anthills and the thick-trunked baobabs. Somalis are nomadic pastoralists, their favoured domestic animal being the one-humped camel. This beast is the hardiest of all animals. In the dry season, it can go without water for more than three weeks. Between rains, Somalis can be seen driving a caravan of camels for a week or more, without regard for political borders, as they search for water holes and grazing lands. They repeat this arduous task, without rest, until the rains come. The nomads themselves subsist, during this period, entirely on camels' milk.

Today, Somalis number between four and five million. Three-quarters of them are still nomads. They have a modern form of government, but it has little meaning for them, indeed, is of no relevance in their day-to-day life. Somalis pledge their allegiance to traditional chiefs, who have powers over matters that concern the group as a whole. The chief heads the clan. The clan is subdivided into patrilineal kinship groupings, which themselves are subdivided into smaller hereditary groupings. The *diya*-paying group is the smallest and most relevant to the rank-and-file Somali.

Diya means blood compensation. A *diya*-paying group consists of anywhere from a few hundred to a few thousand kinsmen. If a Somali has been wronged by another Somali, it is unlikely that he will go to the police or the courts for justice, preferring to lay the matter before his *diya*-paying group instead. This group makes sure that compensation is made for injuries sustained, or for a violent death. Compensation takes the form of camels offered to the victim or the victim's family.

Somalis have managed their affairs without outside

intervention for many centuries. They have cultivated a rich oral literature, an egalitarian culture and religious institutions that are centred around Islam.

Many of the present-day Somali problems have their root in the European scramble for African territories, not to mention Ethiopia's own imperial ambitions. The recent bloody breakup of the country into five different pieces, for instance, stems from attempts to force a fiercely individualistic, clan-minded people, through colonial influence, into the mould of a nation.

The three European powers who had a stake in the area were France, Italy and Britain. The British interest was exceedingly simple. They had a colony across the gulf, in Aden, which had a very strong naval base. This colony needed a reliable supply of meat for its army and subjects. As the main suppliers of meat in the area were the Somali nomads, what better way to ensure the continuity of its supply than to annex its source?

The British weren't greedy. They didn't wish to occupy the entire Somali holding, just a strip of land on the north coast of the region. They didn't send armies to quash the nomads, but negotiated their way in, setting up shop on the Horn in 1884.

The successful, low-cost entry of the English in the region gave the French ideas. Why not grab the port of Djibouti? The port was exactly what they were looking for—a short route to Europe, aided by the majestic Suez Canal, which had opened its gates in 1869. Like the British, the French negotiated a protectorate agreement with the dominant clan of the region, the Issa. In 1888, France set up camp in Djibouti, one of the harshest regions on the Horn. France would rule this port for the next ninety years.

The Italians were the last to arrive, but their prize was by no means smaller than the others'. Indeed, Italy had staked out for itself the longest coastal territory on the Horn, bordering the English possessions and running along the Indian Ocean. This acquisition, along with Eritrea—which had come under Italian rule a few years earlier—was considered the perfect launching point for a campaign to take the grand prize of them all: Ethiopia.

Menelik II, King of Kings of Ethiopia, wasn't ignorant of the threat posed by the European warlords in the region. However, he was a practical man. He knew that his armament was no match for the enemy's, and that his arms supplies were very limited. The number and quality of weapons delivered by French smugglers were hardly enough to put out a small fire. It certainly wouldn't do for his grand imperial plan—which entailed sharing in the spoils of the Horn alongside his European competitors.

Menelik was an astute politician as well as a warrior. He made friends with the Italians. He humoured them into sponsoring his participation in the Brussels General Act. In 1890, Ethiopia, as a Christian state, was empowered for the first time in history to import munitions legally. There was one small drawback, however. The Emperor was a little short of money. The Italians obliged by lending him four million francs, which he later repaid. They also granted him 28 cannons and 38,000 rifles. The armament was meant to be used to subjugate the pagans and Muslims occupying the lowlands—an aim that didn't conflict with the interests of the European warlords in the region.

Secure in his power, and armed with up-to-date weapons and trained fighting personnel, Menelik waged war on the people to the south and west of his kingdom. The Emperor's soldiers decimated the much inferior armies of the local people in short order, extending his sovereignty to regions never before conquered by an Ethiopian king. In ten short years, the kingdom had doubled in size.

By the early 1890s, Menelik was ready to stake his claim in the Somali lands. First, he dispatched a carefully worded letter to the British government, reminding this likewise Christian kingdom of his Solomonic lineage; that Menelik was a kinsman to none other than Christ; and that challenging his grand plan to extend his empire as far north as Khartoum, and as far south as Lake Victoria, would be tantamount to interfering with the wishes of God. Menelik's new scheme included taking more than half of the British protectorate.

"A deranged upstart," the British thought.

The moment of reckoning came when Menelik had to fight the Italians in Adwa. In 1895, Italy dispatched a strong force to the north, led by a highly decorated warlord, General Barateri. On March 1, 1896, Barateri decided to launch his attack on Ethiopia. He amassed his soldiers in Adwa, the capital of Tigre province. The only information the Italian general had about these formidable northern highlands was in the form of sketch maps. His forces were soon separated, and completely routed. The casualties numbered eight thousand Italian soldiers and four thousand Eritrean recruits by the time the rest of the Italian army beat a hasty retreat.

The unexpected and swift destruction of the Italian forces in Adwa sobered the British in the east. It was clear that Menelik was not, after all, deranged or an upstart. The British decided to smooth things over with this fourth power. Barely a year after Adwa, the British government dispatched a highly

regarded diplomat, Rennell Rodd, to amicably settle all outstanding issues with the now formidable Menelik.

The French outdid themselves. They advanced traditional
Franco-Ethiopian relations by redrawing the frontiers of their
new colony. They pulled back the borders of their enclave to
no more than one hundred kilometres inland. The sweetest of
all victories to Menelik came when the Italians dispatched a
special envoy, headed by Major Nerazzini, to bring the Somali
territory issue to an amicable settlement. The Italians demonstrated their friendly intentions by pulling back the frontiers of
their new colony to a mere 180 kilometres inland, significantly
short of Italy's claim before Adwa.

Menelik's new acquisition—Ogaden, home of the tribe of
the same name—encompassed an extensive tract of fertile
land. The population was less than a million. This land, however, did not fall under the interests of the Somali government,
as there was no such political body in existence. The Somali
government didn't appear until 1960, when Italy and Britain
relinquished control of their colonies, permitting them to unite
under a very feeble regime. The various tribes had always
administered themselves.

THE POWER BROKERS

SOMALIA'S AFFAIRS made a startling appearance in my young life one windy afternoon in October 1969. Another season of the Morality course was winding up. A year had passed since the first one concluded and, as this would be the last time the class would be facing Mr. Alula, there was an air of relief and elation among the students. The teacher, however, was as passionate and persevering as ever. Walking brusquely into the classroom with a grim look on his face, he announced that our neighbouring country was about to lose its flag. Somalia's independence was in peril.

I didn't know what it meant for a country to lose its independence, but wasn't so sure that the deprivation of a flag was such a bad idea. I wouldn't mind it one bit if I didn't have to stand stiffly at attention twice a day as the battered rag was hoisted up and down a decorated post.

Mr. Alula went on to explain that General Siad Barre, in a successful coup d'état, had assassinated the popularly elected president of Somalia the day before. Our teacher was primarily concerned that Somalia's former colonizers, Italy and Britain, might be on the alert and use the recent unrest as an excuse to march into our backyard.

This was even more confusing. Normally, an event that was so monumentally bad as to throw the almighty Alula into a glowing tantrum meant good news to me. Not that removing a president placed in office by the people seemed like such a bad idea. After all, as we'd been told many times before, God chose our leader for us. So, I asked myself, what was so hideous about knocking off a man deposited on the throne by erring mortals?

But Europeans marching into our backyard did appear alarming. Dad said that the one unforgettable blemish in our long and proud history was the occupation of Ethiopia, however brief, by fascist Italy. Questions quickly formed in my head but I did not dare open my mouth for fear that Mr. Alula might send me out to kneel on the gravel grounds, a brick balanced on my head. I decided to save my questions until I got home.

Dad was in an unusually good mood that night. He didn't think that the European powers would bother us, but thought there were a few things I should know about the inner workings of modern government in Africa. A coup d'état, Dad said, was more like *Tsewa*. A group of army generals form a pact to dip their hands into the government coffers. Power (the *Tsewa*) exchanges hands every five to ten years among the brothers in uniform. Opponents of the scheme are dealt with swiftly and mercilessly, but every now and then, civilians would be handed the helm to appease aid-donor countries. I remember thinking that a coup d'état was the most profiting and ingenious enterprise Africa had ever embarked on, one wherein everyone involved came out a positive winner. Except, of course, the faceless masses.

General Siad Barre, meanwhile, appeared to have carved out a destiny for the fledgling country. He proudly announced that Somalia would embark on a course of "Scientific Socialism," following the cue of that powerful nation, the Soviet Union. Barre believed that in a few years' time the national economy as well as the territory of the young country would triple in size.

Barre's aides did not share his enthusiasm, at first. "Siad," they said, "a country needs to have a proletariat class to embark on such a mission. We are nomads; there is not even a peasant base in the country."

"We don't need a proletariat class or a peasant mass. We won't do what the *gaal* [unflattering term for white man] says. Somalia will be a Communist nation like no other," the General declared.

And so, Siad Barre convinced himself, his aides and the Soviets that the revolution was not only timely but a long time in coming. The Soviet Union responded in kind, and economic and technical assistance poured in. Most important of all, the armaments that the West had been reluctant to deliver arrived by the ton. The Soviets trained and equipped a 20,000-man army—a staggering number for a country with a population of 3.5 million and no potential aggressors. The Russians delivered fifty MiG fighters (twenty-four of which were the most advanced supersonic MiG-21s), a number of Ilyushin bombers, 300 armoured personnel carriers and 250 medium tanks including several T-54 models—one of the most sophisticated in the Soviets' arsenal. Overnight, the Somali army became the fourth largest fighting force in Black Africa—as Siad Barre was well aware. On July 13, 1977, the General declared war on Ethiopia by dispatching a massive, brutal force to Ogaden.

The newly crowned Ethiopian dictator was completely overwhelmed by this sudden, although not completely unexpected, onslaught. The junta was already busy on a number of fronts. After the fall of the monarchy, most of the conquered peoples had picked up arms in order to break away from the central government. The army was engaged in battles against the Eritrean People's Liberation Front (EPLF), the Oromo Liberation Front (OLF), the Tigre People's Liberation Front (TPLF) and the Western Somali Liberation Front (WSLF). There were too many fires to put out for the few extinguishers at hand.

The traditional arms supplier of Ethiopia was the U.S. The Emperor's musketeers were issued First World War–vintage rifles, primitive tanks and a handful of F-1 fighter planes. The Americans trained the young officers in modern warfare. They taught them English and showed them how to starch their uniforms impeccably; how to properly salute one another in the street; and how to kick the ass of the Somali nomads who were making trouble for their Emperor.

Unfortunately, the nomads were now much better armed than the venerable Ethiopian Army. The nomads didn't starch their uniforms, because they didn't have any; they wore *sherits*. They didn't salute each other, because their tribal chiefs did not approve. But they kicked ass. They perfected their primeval practice of kicking ass, directing their collective boots (sandals, actually) at the ass-end of Ethiopia. The Soviets helped, because in their own country they had long ago kicked the monarchy off its throne and into an unmarked grave.

Ethiopia was desperate. The soldiers in Ogaden were running for their lives, tossing their cumbersome M-1 rifles in the desert, as they covered their rear ends with both hands. But the

Somalis were unrelenting. They wouldn't rest until they had driven the last Amhara out of Ogaden, out of Africa, out of this universe. There must be, they reasoned, a much bigger universe somewhere—one so large it could accommodate the overblown chauvinism and arrogance of the Amharas. The Somalis didn't know where it was, exactly, but then it was for the Amharas to find their own bearings.

The Ethiopians hated their vulgar and violent rulers in Addis Ababa, but they hated the Somali aggressors even more. A nationalism that had been locked and buried in a rusted vault at the death of Menelik once more showed itself. After all, a thousand-year-old pride was at stake. A glorious history was being rewritten by a people who didn't know how to write. It was too much for the old warriors to take. They hung their ploughs in the shade, kissed their families goodbye, and descended from the mountains to reassert their God-given rights.

However, times had changed, and the tide was against Ethiopia. The traditional allies of this Christian empire, the Europeans and Americans, were less Christian now (even if they never missed a mass), and far more embroiled in the East-West game.

The Americans refused to send arms. Only months after promising $22 million worth of fighting equipment, they were struck with second thoughts. It seemed immoral to support what was obviously a Communist venture. Americans hate communism, and fight it by supporting other Communists. The United States turned its back on Ethiopia, and offered its hand to Somalia. At the height of the conflict, on July 26, 1977, the Americans signed a friendship treaty with Somalia, promising to sustain the arms supply. The U.S. also encouraged the

Muslim countries of Egypt, Saudi Arabia and the Sudan to funnel aid to their cousins in the south.

The Ethiopian bigwigs confirmed the final divorce with the United States by closing down the U.S. military base in Eritrea, booking flights for the one hundred American officials and their families out of the country, and giving them four days to leave. The junta started looking for a new love.

The military junta sent emissaries to Turkey, Yugoslavia, China, Vietnam and Czechoslovakia to acquire much-needed arms, but in vain. In desperation, Ethiopia sent an envoy to Libya. The strongman of this oil-rich and vulgar North African state was already sending arms to the Eritrean rebels who were fighting to secede from Addis Ababa. Obviously, it would be a conflict of interest for Moammar Gadhafi to help Ethiopia. However, being a conscientious man, he couldn't say "no" to someone in desperate need. Gadhafi agreed to supply arms to Ethiopia. The weapons were in Tripoli, waiting to be shipped to the Eritrean rebels. But, Gadhafi reasoned, as the Ethiopian regime's need was so much more dire than that of the rebels, he would ship the weapons to the junta at once. He even scraped the bottom of the barrel (in fact, the barrel was full) and came up with a few extra long-range cannons, and half a dozen slightly used fighter jets. However, before he would sign over the weapons, Gadhafi wanted a small concession in return. Would Ethiopia help him to overthrow the government of the Sudan?

The military junta had already bitten off more than it could chew. It wasn't ready for a new war with its northern neighbour, and declined Gadhafi's offer.

Finally, help came in. The Soviets sent $100 million worth of arms, promising more would follow. The Soviets were still supplying arms to the Somalis: there were thousands of Soviet military advisers on that small desert strip. The Soviets didn't see any contradiction in arming both sides. After all, both Somalia and Ethiopia were socialist rookies, so the aid was obviously advancing the cause of socialism. Siad Barre was, however, a little confused by the actions of this venerable Communist nation, the USSR. Either Barre wasn't as well versed in communism as he thought, or this recent manoeuvre had been taught in one of the classes he'd missed.

Siad Barre felt the sting of betrayal only when the Soviets sent more arms to Ethiopia than to him. His nomadic instincts took over, and he kicked the Soviets and their Cuban allies out of his desert outpost, telling them to stay away until they had paid a *diya*. The Soviets didn't have far to go. They boarded the bus north, to Ethiopia. At the border they passed the last of the Americans, who were headed south.

In a short time, Soviet military aid to Ethiopia had reached an unprecedented level. Between May of 1977 and March of 1978, killing hardware worth a cool $1 billion to $1.5 billion arrived in Ethiopia. This was four times what the U.S. had delivered to the country in the previous twenty-odd years. In the month of November alone, the Soviets delivered such an overwhelming quantity of arms that not only did it make previous U.S. aid look like pinpricks by comparison, but it set a record in the annals of modern warfare. It was the largest long-distance airlift in Soviet military history! For Ethiopia, it was a time of reckoning.

Somalia intensified its aggression, attempting to pre-empt the Soviet intervention. It rallied all of its armed forces, including the police, the armed robbers and the smugglers, for a decisive victory before the Ethiopian Army could regroup. In a few short months, most of Ogaden fell. By late 1977, the war was being waged for the grandest prize of all: the cities of Jijiga, Harar and Dire Dawa—the third largest city in all of Ethiopia.

JIJIGA BESIEGED

JIJIGA WAS isolated and encircled. Besieged. Bombs fell relentlessly. Refugees from the conquered regions in the south littered the city streets, the parks and the public buildings. The country was under a state of martial law; all civil affairs were under the command of the army.

High-ranking military and government officials moved their families, chattels and pets to safer places early on. Anyone with the right connections could sneak out one or two members of their family, as long as it was not a boy or man who could bear arms. But very soon even that became impossible. Hospital patients who had been referred to better facilities in bigger cities for life-saving operations were denied permission to leave. "Jijiga should be defended until each man, woman and child has breathed its last," the high brass announced.

I roamed the city streets, taking in its new features. There were more guns than people, it seemed. I saw teenagers with AK-47 machine guns sitting on the hood of a Jeep slowly rolling through the crowded street. These school kids turned soldiers were veterans of one of the major wars in Africa. Several groups of militia were camped along the roadside; some men were cleaning their guns, others staring at the blue horizon.

A man in a Land Rover pulled up beside me. I noticed that its front tire was damaged, and that there were a few bullet holes in the sides of the vehicle. He asked me, with a far-off look in his eyes, where the next filling station was. I was leaning over the window to give him directions when I noticed the young girl sitting beside him, peacefully resting on his shoulder, her torn dress caked with dried blood. My mouth gaped and my eyes bulged. I hoped it was not what I thought it was. The man's eyes regained their focus and he turned to me, reading the horror so plainly written on my face: "She is my daughter," he said, unburdening his grief. "She was killed on the way here. I am taking her home."

"Where is home?"

"Dire Dawa."

"How can you get out of town?" I asked. "Even if you get past the soldiers at the gate of the city, I don't think you can make it much farther. From what I hear, every metre of the way to Harar is mined," I said, trying to make him see the danger.

"What difference does it make? I am already dead," he sighed, asking me once again the direction to the petrol station.

A friend of mine ran his father's tea room downtown. I went to visit him, to chat. The huge café was overflowing with human agony. I caught a glimpse of my friend as he ran at break-neck speed to serve water to one group and loaves of bread to another. They were not paying customers, but refugees accepting, graciously, the hospitality of the town. The war brought out the generosity in everyone. My friend noticed me in the crowd, and shouted over his shoulder for me to lend him a hand.

I picked up a tray and went to serve a lady with two kids. The kids were crying but the woman didn't seem to notice. I gave a loaf of bread and a cup of steaming tea to each boy. The boys grabbed the bread with pathetic haste, and started munching. I warned them that the tea was very hot and that they should wait until it had cooled off. The lady was still lost in thought, unconscious of all that went on around her. I offered her a loaf and a cup of tea. She raised her head to look at me, but her eyes refused to focus. I thought she was too exhausted from the trip to talk. I put the contents of my tray on her side of the table, asking her if there was anything else I could do to help. She shook her head, her eyes still staring at the vacant space between us. A man sitting at the next table beckoned to me.

"She lost three of her kids on the way. I think she is suffering from some kind of mental trauma," he whispered.

"How did it happen?" I asked him.

"Like everybody else she had to make a choice."

"What do you mean?"

"She had to catch a truck rushing to get out of town. She only had time to collect two of her kids, leaving the other three behind. No one was waiting for anyone any more; the Somalis were already in town."

I finished helping my friend and went out for a walk. The southern half of town, the Muslim part, was eerily quiet. I could've walked for miles without meeting a living soul. The shops were padlocked, and the compounds and alleys, where one would expect to see and hear children playing and

laughing, were as dead as a graveyard. Anticipating the outcome of the war and following their nomadic instincts, the
Somali residents had already left for Somalia. The gravel-laid
highway running through the centre of town, dividing it in
two, proved to be both witness to our heavenly allegiances and
a measure of where our hearts lay in this backsliding world.

The dark blanket of night did not hide the scars of the war.
No hyenas came to visit us during the night. Instead, gunfire
descended from the desolate mountains, convincing people
that the war was being waged in their own living rooms. We
made fortresses around our bedrooms with sandbags and
heavy stones, and slept under our beds. But soon we realized
that the enemy was not under our dining-room table, but outside. The deserted half of town was reborn each night to shoot
at us.

One exceptional evening, the gunfire was so overwhelming, and the bullets flying overhead so abundant, that pieces of
darkness fell from the night, tearing jagged holes in the night
sky. Light rushed in through the gashes from the other side of
the universe. The night repaired itself, plugging in the fissures,
but soon the Somalis shattered it with more colourful fire.
Tired of repairing itself every few seconds, the night decided
to shed its layers like a bulb of onion, removing a peel of the
dome with each bout of fire it received until, finally, the sun
was forced to show itself.

With the rising of the sun, the Somalis decided to call it a
night. But it was not a regular day that was dawning. The town
had closed its exits. Tanks, armoured vehicles and Jeeps with
high-calibre machine guns had sealed off the south end of the
town while soldiers in war gear flushed the enemy out of their
hiding places, killing them mercilessly. By noon, the enemy

within the city limits had been exterminated, but the soldiers were still furious. They rounded up the few remaining residents of the Muslim half of the city, lined them up against a wall and shot them dead.

Still thirsty for blood, the soldiers turned to the Christian part of town, looking for Somalis who had long since forgotten what they were. They found them. The soldiers took each one from his home, herding them all towards the police station. The Somalis were irritated that the soldiers should handle them so roughly, but were confident that, once taken to court, they would be exonerated of any charges that might be brought against them. They hadn't seen or heard about what had happened in the other part of town.

With each step they took, each inscrutable crowd they passed, each mournful face that peered towards them from the street, the prisoners became more and more certain that this was not just a case of mistaken identity. They never knew what awaited them. As they turned the last corner to the police station, they found a clue to their fate lying on the street, wrapped in red-tattered rags. The prisoners panicked, trembled. They turned to every civilian they saw, pleading that someone vouch for their innocence. "Ato Abraha, you know who I am—please tell these people that I am not a rebel. Aster, I attended your wedding; please vouch for me! Save my life," they cried. But few dared to intervene. The soldiers had already defied their commanding officers, the gods and their consciences, and no one could stop them now. The last Somalis in the city were lined up against the wall and savagely murdered.

A MOVING TALE

T HE FOOD had run out. The city of Jijiga slid to the brink of famine. The government decided to help. It announced, over national radio, that we should eat twice a day. People wondered where they could get the second meal.

Earlier, Mam had consulted the *Adbar*. She had seen the future written in the aromatic plumes of smoke rising from the *ood* and incense: the enemy would come riding a six-legged horse, chasing us from our homes and killing many of us. "Go out and purchase any canned food you can find," she told me. "Don't worry how much it costs." I purchased as many tins of sardines, beans, corn and pineapples and boxes of biscuits as I could find. Mam emptied the wardrobe, put the packaged food in it, padlocked the door and hid the key in her bosom, tied to the end of her handkerchief.

The school was still open, and so was every government office. Life went on, undeterred by the chaotic drama unfolding around us. I was writing the university entrance exam when the turmoil reached its climax. Huge cargo planes flew in and out of town every few minutes bringing in militiamen and armaments, then airlifting out the wounded and sick. Fighter planes flew in squadrons, one after another, brushing over the roof. Bombers followed their lead. The building shook with the noise of their engines; the Earth let out a tortured cry when the bombers unloaded the curse of napalm on her; but victory was elusive. The war had already been lost on the ground.

Orders to evacuate never came, but the necessity of leaving came to Mam, who shot out of bed in the small hours, one morning in early September 1977, rushing us all to get up and dress. I stumbled out of bed with bleary eyes, looking for things to take. The house that I had called home all my life, the only place I could walk through blindfolded, had, overnight, become strange. The architecture of the rooms struck me as odd; the bedstead, chest of drawers, dining-room table and chairs looked peculiar. I wondered how I had come to live in this place without ever really seeing it.

There were so many odd items in our house. A small table with one missing leg, which nobody used, stood beside the main door, confronting anyone coming in or out. It was one of Mam's many relics of the past. Once, I decided to lock it up in the storage room. It did not take long for Mam to notice that it was missing. "Where is the table?" she demanded, worried that someone might have thrown it out. I explained to her that I had put it away. She shook her head in sadness before admonishing me. "You kids of this troubled generation have no regard for things you can't make use of. Someday you might even throw me away," she remarked bitterly. "Did it occur to you that the table might have held some sweet memories of bringing you up? Go and bring it back."

There was also the incense burner with a chipped edge, the

broken piece carelessly shoved inside the ash. My sister Meselu broke it when she was about five or six years of age. She broke it on the same day she discovered that her hand was not rigidly attached to her forearm.

My sister had run into the room, crying, holding her arm high, telling Mam that her arm was broken. In her excitement, she knocked the incense burner, breaking it.

"My arm is broken," she repeated, sobbing.

Mam shot out of her seat, startled, believing that Meselu had indeed broken her arm. "How did you break it?" Mam asked, examining my sister's arm.

"I didn't," my sister replied.

"Then how did you know that it was broken?"

"See," Meselu demonstrated, flexing her hand up and down. "It is broken."

Mam burst out laughing. The neighbours who were having coffee joined her. For a long time to come, they would point at the chipped incense burner and talk about my sister's broken arm. Mam received many beautiful incense burners over the years as gifts, but she refused to give up the broken one.

I was spending a great deal of time selecting one item over another, studying each object in our home, when Mam woke me from my reveries. "Here, put your stuff in this," she said, handing me a corn sack.

While choosing what to take with me, and what to leave behind, I suddenly remembered the disoriented young woman with two kids that I had met in the tea room downtown only a few weeks before. I wondered how she would ever survive the dreadful decision she had been forced to make.

Mam shouted orders from the living room, hurrying us along. She was the only one who seemed prepared for the occasion. She had packed three large sacks, mostly with food-stuffs, but also with family photographs, pictures of the saints and some documents. Mam made me carry two of the bags, one on my head and the other on my back. Before closing the door of our home for the last time, she took one final look, her eyes moist with tears.

Outside, the crowd was frantic. Cars were blowing their horns and pedestrians stumbled over each other and swore. Each one of us was headed in the same direction—towards the unknown.

THE EXODUS

⸺

T HE ONLY road that exited Jijiga was located in a narrow alley between Mt. Karamara and Mt. Chinaksen. Karamara is the tallest of three mountain peaks surrounding the city. As a kid, I had spent many memorable moments with friends looking down on Jijiga from its towering height.

We passed through the dangerous alley without being molested by the Somali Army. Once behind the mountain curtain, the refugees were ordered, by the Ethiopian Army, to set up camp in the valley. The army hoped to reclaim the town before long.

There were no forests in this region, only a sparse population of acacia trees, promising little in the way of shade from the unforgiving sun. The valley was a natural passage for wandering packs of monkeys, hyenas and black lions. The monkeys of these regions are unlike any others in the country. They are immense in size, combative and stubborn. They are known to ram heavy boulders on passing cars, but their obstinacy and aggressiveness is best mythologized in a tale that Dad once told me about a remarkable battle between these beasts and a couple of black lions.

I̶t so happened that the monkeys were driven from their den by a herd of lions and moved to an area close to the town of Kocher. This region was rich in wild fruit and leafy plants, and was close to a body of water. The monkeys had just finished refurnishing their new residence and were organizing a house-warming party when their old enemies came knocking on the door. The party turned into an emergency meeting to establish what needed to be done with the intruders—a couple of black lions. Votes were cast. The majority were ready to fight. So the monkeys opened their trunk, dusted off their war gear and decided to meet the enemy at the front porch.

The lions couldn't believe that a mob of monkeys would actually fight them. Thinking it was a bluff, they resolved to teach these inferior creatures a lesson. But, though individually the monkeys were not strong, they were strong in numbers— there were upwards of four hundred of them. They nominated one of their rank as Admiral, and the Admiral drafted an immediate strategy. He announced that the plan of attack was very, very simple. "Surround the enemy and kill him!" he said.

Like so many other warriors who have lived and died in this pleasing but perilous land, the monkeys declared war. They surrounded the two lions, three rows deep. All at once, the first line of fighters leaped upon the backs of the black lions, scratching and biting them. The lions responded by breaking the back of each monkey they caught, but many escaped and rejoined the ranks, reinforcing the tightening circle. The monkeys co-ordinated their attack, sometimes leaping upon the lions from the front, sometimes from the back.

The war continued for three days, at the end of which dozens of monkeys, whose lives had been sacrificed in defence of their territory, lay scattered about the blood-soaked bodies of the two black lions. On the fourth day of war, the lioness died. The male lion lingered on, his back badly skinned, his mane rooted out. The monkeys offered the lion an armistice: he could go back home and they would forget what had happened provided that he submitted to the shaving of his head. He refused. The war continued.

By the end of the week, before either of the belligerents had accepted defeat, the local peasants raised the white flag. The stench of the dead animals and the flies they had attracted were quickly becoming unbearable, and the peasants dispatched a courier to the governor of Kocher, alerting him to the disaster unfolding in his jurisdiction, informing him that the effects of the war were being felt by the surrounding community. The governor gave the word and the police were ordered to finish off the lion and help restore order. Against all odds and in vivid contradiction of legend, the monkeys had won; the king of all beasts had been defeated.

LIKE THE MONKEYS, the refugees, uprooted from one home, were in search of another. West of the arid, lifeless valley in which they camped, there were hills that were farmed during the rainy season to yield a good harvest of sorghum and corn. But the exodus left Jijiga during the dry spell, and this area had been claimed by hostile weeds. Farther west of these hills lay the temperate climate of the eastern highlands—an area renowned for agricultural produce, for bananas, mangoes, papayas, oranges, cabbages, lettuce, red beets, sweet potatoes, *chat*, and many other types of fruits and vegetables. It was in this direction that we would ultimately head, towards Harar.

The city of Harar was only 120 kilometres from Jijiga, but it took us almost two weeks to get there. Those two weeks left an indelible mark in the lives of many. It would be remembered in history as a time when it rained upwards, for many would shed tears that they scooped up by the tips of their fingers and flung at the faces of the treacherous gods.

The exodus, however, was a triumph for teenaged boys who aspired to play cops and robbers. They were issued real guns with live bullets, and could shoot without asking their mothers' permission. I was given an M-1 rifle, which, I discovered, was more dangerous to me than the enemy. It was too cumbersome, recoiled too much when fired, and was almost as tall as I was. I dumped it in a nearby bush before walking over to a militiaman who had two Kalashnikovs. I borrowed one of them, with two clips of bullets. He reminded me to give it back to him before we arrived in Harar.

The guns we were issued were meant to protect our families from the various unsavoury elements in the jungle. The army did not expect the civilians to fight the war for them. The old rifles were useless as far as the invading Somalis were concerned—even the tanks were of no avail. The enemy fired long-range cannons at us. Their location remained a complete mystery. The only time the firing let up was when jets bombed the area in which their cannons were suspected of being hidden, but even this did not slow them for long.

Running into wild beasts was never a concern during the exodus; they had long since made a wide berth around us. On the day of the massacre in Jijiga, the hyenas severed their diplomatic relations with us, withdrawing their missions from all towns and villages. The lions made a proverb out of our carpet-bombing of the countryside, teaching their young that killing neighbours indiscriminately was the truest form of wild behaviour and that it was to be avoided. The elephants had come to regard the exodus as a threat to their lifestyle, an irresponsible squandering of natural resources, and vowed never to set eyes on us again.

The two-legged beast, on the other hand, was a constant threat. Truck drivers who cut through the treacherous Ogaden steppe in search of market outlets tell of "tire dealers" who stopped them in the middle of the desert and offered to sell them tires—their own tires. To rob someone, or to admit that one is being robbed, was considered rude by the nomads, so the whole business was conducted as a transaction in which one man sold something that the other man simply couldn't do without. Upon being offered the tires, an experienced trucker would immediately get down to business and pay the price. If the tires were too costly, one could always bargain. After all, the sellers were not unreasonable. They were often willing to knock off a few shillings or even take something else as payment, say, a few bottles of Pepsi-Cola and a bundle of *chat*. Once the transaction was settled, the customer would receive a guarantee that he would not be required to buy his tires again on the same trip.

Occasionally an inexperienced driver would refuse to buy his tires, despite the added persuasion of a loaded rifle that the dealer swung towards his face. Such folly would result in a nomadic tantrum for the dealer, who might demonstrate his determination not to let anyone walk away without paying for his merchandise by destroying all the tires on the truck, stranding the driver in the middle of the desert. Often the next truck would be a week or more in coming, and even then there was little one could expect from a passerby. The surrounding nomads were unlikely to lend a hand, as they knew that you had refused to partake in the traditional barter.

Tire dealers were the least of our worries during the exodus; among us, the ones driving trucks were the army, and the dealers were not known for selling military merchandise. Fear of bumping into Adal tribesmen, however, ran high.

YOUNG ADAL MEN have a special way of proving their manhood to their future wives. As their fathers before them and their children after them, these young men have to maintain the continuity of thousands of years of culture. A dowry is not enough.

The glaring eyes of countless stars in heavens are upon the Adal elders as they gather around a campfire to determine a young man's ability to support his future wife as determined by the head count of his cattle, his skill as a warrior and his ability to defend her and the community she lives in from an invading enemy. If the young man has already proved himself a man and has the trophy to substantiate his claim, the elders will pass judgment before the campfire is out. But if he has yet to pass the last hurdle, he will be sent away in quest of the indispensable credentials. The young man will not be accepted by the community unless he comes back with the trophy dangling from the tip of his stick, held high above his head for everyone to see. His homecoming will be announced by a bull-horn trumpet; children will receive him at the skirt of the settlement, singing and cheering, leading him to every doorstep so everyone can bear witness to the trophy, and agree to its legitimacy—the trophy being a penis of an enemy the young Adal has overpowered in an open engagement.

Unfortunately for the young Adal, the golden days are gone for good. Tribal wars are not so easy to come by, so the young man is forced to travel far from his immediate neighbourhood in search of his trophy. He rides the bus, hikes or steals a ride on a passing train, criss-crossing the country, coming dangerously close to towns and Christian settlements. Many young men spend weeks away from home, surviving on plant roots and wild animals, before they can claim success.

Not every penis is the right candidate. The victim has to be an adult from a different tribe, and the penis has to be of a convincing size. In cases where the penis could be mistaken for that of a boy, the bridegroom must skin the part of the pelvis attached to the penis, as well as the chin, so that the victim's beard can be offered as irrefutable proof of the trophy's legitimacy.

Young men of the Adal tribe often hide themselves in the brush by the highway waiting for accidents to happen, so that they can lay claim to the members of the victims. Truck drivers who stop in the middle of the desert to change their tires often end up losing more than time. Public transit buses on long journeys have to stop en route, and passengers who get off to stretch their legs and relieve themselves are sometimes relieved of their trophies by Adals who have hidden in the bush in anticipation of just such an interlude.

The state farms in the west (mainly in the province of Arussi) are often transformed into gruesome theatres during the marriage seasons of these infamous tribes. A good number of the daily labourers are ensnared either on the farm or on the way home from a night out, losing their lives or a part of them. No amount of education or admonition seemed to have any effect on these fiendish people until the late seventies, when the military junta let it be known that anyone caught carrying what was obviously not his own piece would face the firing squad, effectively throwing a monkey wrench into this antediluvian practice.

Under the circumstances, it was no longer safe for the Adals to use public transport to hasten the delivery of their catch, and so they were forced to negotiate the unforgiving desert on foot. Thus, by the time they returned home, the trophy was in such bad condition that they were required to prove they had not robbed someone's grave.

Young Adal men do not like the government.

DURING THE EXODUS it was necessary to travel as part of a group. Survival depended on numbers. Fetching food took more than one person, getting medicine took connections and finding out when the water truck would be coming before it became public knowledge took a reliable information source. Water was rationed and many would spend a full day in line, under the scorching heat, to get their daily supply. With more than twenty thousand refugees leaving Jijiga, the barest necessities of life were purchased by constant struggle.

I had a personal reason for wanting to associate myself with a group of men that I was not related to. I had seen people who stepped on anti-personnel mines lose their limbs, sustain pitiful wounds and still live, becoming a liability to their loved ones. In a journey where the clothes on your back felt like a burden, where food was an expensive rarity and basic medication was nowhere to be found, it would be selfish to expect others to care for you. I had resolved, early on, that if I ever ran into such a predicament, Mam would not be forced to decide what to do with me. I relegated the decision, unknown to her, to a group of young men whose animal instincts I could rely on.

The group that I belonged to consisted of a young officer from the infantry, also a native of Jijiga, and two boys I had known by sight as I was growing up. The four of us roamed together in the morning, giving vent to our boyish imaginations, pretending to be detectives in search of Somali infiltrators. In truth, we were scrounging for anything that could possibly be of use to our dependents. We hunted for flour, cooking oil, dried beef, Aspirin, bandages and anything else of practical value. Most of the time we bought the items, but sometimes we were able to trade them for some service we could deliver. Afternoons were spent in the shade, chewing *chat*, which besides being a mild stimulant was also a very good appetite suppressant. I would return to Mam and the kids with the morning's bounty and again before sunset to see if they required anything else.

I usually took my meals with my new friends, but sometimes ate with my family. The food Mam offered us was typical for the refugee camp: stale bread and a soup prepared from dried lentils or beans. There was seldom cooking oil, salt was a luxury, and the word "spice" raised eyebrows. If the soup appeared to be brown, it was because the water itself was that colour.

Meals became sacred to us. They required our complete and undivided attention. One's mind was occupied only by the sensation of each small bite of stale bread as it broke against the teeth, by the barely discernible taste of the watery soup. Meals became exercises in the subtle detection of small differences, today a tiny pinch of salt in the bean soup, another day the effect of a slightly better grade of water. Mealtime, however, never passed without disruptions from unwelcome visitors. Flies hovered above our plates. Vultures carved circles in the sky.

Flies had always been part of my life. The flies that I knew in Jijiga were shy creatures, timid, never keen on confrontation. They were never known to be upright citizens, exemplary subjects, but were nevertheless accepted as part of the family, every family. They slept on the family bed, used the family washroom and dining room, and partook in funerals. They never said thank you for the free meal they received, but at least they knew when to call it quits. You only needed to wink an eye and they were already gone. During the exodus, however, these winged creatures became so aggressive, so outrageously arrogant, that they had to receive a good spanking before they would so much as stretch a wing, signifying to me the change that everyone had to go through in order to weather the relentless storm.

Beetles and bugs could get into pots hung from the moon. They were a terrible nuisance, scurrying onto your plate, reminding you that even your watery bowl of soup had already been another's meal. Throwing out anything was unthinkable. Eating it while you knew full well that it had already been tasted was repulsive. But hunger demanded compromises. The beetles received a spoonful of the territory they had claimed and you worked to keep the rest.

However hard we compromised, food ran out barely days after we'd left Jijiga. We were still camped in the valley and hoping to return home, when the last cup of dried lentils was emptied into the cooking pot, the grain bag folded and placed in the storage sack. There was a flourishing black market for foodstuffs, but only the very rich could afford to purchase any of the items.

The army decided to help. It identified the perpetrators and profiteers responsible for the black-market monopoly on flour, cooking oil and salt. The guilty were brought out with their hands tied behind them so that the public could note that the enemy was also within. Most of them were familiar faces, merchants from the Gurage ethnic group who have earned a reputation as gifted entrepreneurs. It didn't come as a surprise to me that some unscrupulous merchants considered the present war to be yet another business opportunity, a once-in-a-lifetime chance to make a fast buck. I was even understanding. I asked myself: who would not be tempted to exploit the unprecedented opportunity that the exodus opened up for traders of consumable items?

But since I was one of the exploited victims, and since what I could and could not have determined whether I would or would not live, I was also enraged. I was glad that they were going to be shamed in public. What I bore witness to next was, however, something beyond my comprehension.

It was a beautiful desert morning, the air was still and cool and the sun had just broken over the cliffs. The valley we settled in was peaceful, as the bombers had rained napalm on the enemy holdings the day before. Just after dawn, eleven men were lined up against those mute cliffs and shot dead. They were the unscrupulous merchants.

Some thought that the execution was a noble idea. They believed, mistakenly, that other merchants would learn their lesson from the massacre and put a harness on their eternal greed. As it turned out, the markets dried up altogether. There was no flour to be had by anyone, no cooking oil, no dried beef—nothing. No one would admit to ever having been involved in selling foodstuffs. The ones who benefited from this drastic measure were the soldiers, who divided among themselves the confiscated goods, but after a short while, as the supplies were eaten up, even they became victims of their own poor judgment.

Two days passed and I had not had anything to eat. I chewed *chat*. The acidic juice of the leafy plant burned holes in my stomach, heart and spirit. I drank water to extinguish the fire building up inside of me, but the warm liquid stirred up something in my stomach and I felt terribly nauseated. I attempted to stand up but my head spun, my vision blurred and I could not find my legs.

I decided to quit chewing *chat* and guzzling water until I found something to eat. I sipped a bit of water from time to time and lay in the meagre shade of an acacia tree, puzzling out a food source. Hunger was nothing new to me. My guerrilla résumé was punctuated by episodes of hunger, thirst and want. What I could not get used to was the hunger inside of hunger, that brief moment of ravenousness that came after your stomach had falsely promised to go without food.

Looking around, all I could see were vultures and weeds. I wondered where the gazelles had gone, the antelopes and spurfowls. This was not the Ogaden I knew. It was a different realm, a place where humans had squeezed all of the vivacity out of the earth. For once, I wished I was a bird.

Not surprisingly, the hunger was particularly tough on my brother Henok, who at three years of age was the youngest of the seven children in our family. The boy cried himself to sleep, and after the second day of going without food it seemed that he would never wake up again. Mam soaked a piece of rag in water and squeezed it between his chapped lips. She told him stories, and promised him that very soon he would have all the food that he could eat, but he did not seem to hear.

I knew that I had to get the boy something to eat, and soon, or I would never see him again. Abraha, my officer friend, thought that he could help. He picked up his bag and went limping towards his fellow soldiers. Abraha had been exempted from his front-line duties ever since he had been wounded. He had recovered much of his health while still in Jijiga, but the war had left him with a bad leg and only three fingers on his left hand. He still served in the army, but in a much humbler position. He spent most of his days with us, his civilian buddies. The young officer had come to terms with the fact that life in uniform was no longer for him, and planned to go to college and pursue a civilian career as a teacher as soon as the war ended.

Abraha wasn't married, but his older sister had been widowed by the war, and she and her three young kids relied on him a great deal. While in Jijiga, he had visited the family quite often, helping control her two young boys with his army-like discipline. Now, he also had to see that they did not starve to death or wander among the minefields.

ABRAHA HAD BEEN gone a long time, because when I opened my eyes the sun was staring me in the face. The shadow of the tree had shifted. I decided to get up and stretch my legs, but I was so weak that I staggered and fell.

From the crowded distance, I noticed my officer friend emerge with the life-saving goods in hand. He brought along a large loaf of bread, three cans of corned beef and four bags of intravenous fluids, which, he explained, were saline water and glucose. He poured a portion of both fluids into a tin can, mixed this with a bit of water and gave it to me to drink. He then opened one of the cans, and handed me the odd-tasting meat. It didn't take long before my energy was restored and I was able to walk. The two of us took the remaining foodstuffs to Mam and the kids.

The loaf of bread attracted many eyes. I was stopped on the way by desperate mothers, some begging a piece of bread for their withering children, others offering me a sizeable sum of money. But I did not have much to spare. Mam shot out of her seat when she saw the staff of life and hugged me, her fragile body unsteady and trembling. While holding Henok's sleeping body close to her chest, she bowed and thanked the officer with an awkwardness I have seldom seen in her. I noticed that she had already lit a fire, and that a pot was hanging over it. I opened the pot. Mam snatched the lid from my hand and replaced it. But not before I saw what was simmering. The children were sitting around the fire, their eyes glazed with anticipation.

"It is weed that you are boiling," I whispered to Mam. "How do you know that it is not poisonous?"

"If animals could eat it and live, who says that we can't?" Mam argued, radiating the wit and confidence that I had always admired in her, undefeated even in these tumultuous times, when death was staring her and her family in the face. Mam reminded me of the story of "Resourceful Kebede" and repeated the fable to the kids once more.

ONCE UPON A time there was a young man named Kebede. He was a student who lived in Gonder. He travelled from village to village learning *kinae*. After ten years, he had learned all the *kinae* in the land and decided to go back to his home village to teach poetry.

A goat who had heard him read his *kinae* out loud every morning thought that Kebede still had a lot to learn. "Your *kinae* are good, but not as good as those of the blind monk who passed by here two days ago," the goat remarked.

Kebede thought that the angels had spoken to him. He got down on his knees and started praying.

"Praying won't help your *kinae*. Go and catch up with the blind monk before he falls off the edge of the world. You might learn something from him," the goat advised. Kebede realized that it was the goat talking.

"You can talk!" he said, surprised.

"Of course I can talk. What do you think I am, dumb?" the goat replied, clearly irritated.

"Why haven't you talked all these years?" Kebede wondered.

"Because I had never before heard such terrible *kinae* as yours. Everybody knows that goats love poems, and that they love *kinae* above all. Don't waste any more of my time, or yours. Go and catch up with that blind monk," the goat urged.

"Which way did he go?" Kebede asked.

The goat stood on a high boulder, raised his head high and indicated with his chin the direction in which the monk had gone. "That way, and hurry. He must be at the edge of the Earth by now," the goat advised.

Kebede quickly packed a small bag of clothes. He threw a

sheepskin over his shoulders for the cold nights, and found a good sharp stick for a weapon. He then locked the door of his hut and began walking after the blind monk. He walked for two days and two nights without rest, searching for the learned man. On his way he met many merchants, and each told him that the monk was still far ahead. Because the monk was blind, they offered, he could walk much faster.

On the third day, Kebede was too overcome with hunger to walk. He was also very tired, as he had not slept in two days. He stopped at a nearby hut, and knocked on the door for help. A young maid opened the door.

"Yes, can I help you?" she asked. Her eyes brimmed with pity as she looked at the stranger.

"May God be with you, ma'am, I am a student on a long journey. I need a place to stay for the night." Kebede bowed, pleading.

"A home is to be shared with God's children. Do come in, don't stand in the rain," the young lady offered. She gave Kebede a dry *netela* to wrap himself in and a dappled cow's hide to rest on. She then took his wet clothes and hung them by the fireside to dry.

Kebede was very hungry and hoped that the lady would offer him something to eat. But she did not. The night deepened. Hyenas howled outside and dogs barked. Kebede was going to spend another night without food, unless he was very clever.

"Ma'am, have you ever heard of stew made of pebbles? It's a new dish. Even the King has a taste for it," he said.

"Did you say a stew of pebbles?" the lady asked, unsure of what she had heard.

"Yes, ma'am."

"My, my, my. Living long is good. There is something new to be learned every day. Do you happen to know how it is made?" the lady asked, quite interested.

"Yes, ma'am. It happens to be my specialty," Kebede replied, smiling. As the lady nodded her encouragement, he walked outside, returning with five black pebbles, which he washed and dried.

"What I need now are two heads of onion," Kebede requested. And when the young lady brought the onions, he asked for a bit of cooking oil. Kebede peeled the onions, diced them and browned them in the cooking pot. He added some water to the pot and carefully placed the five pebbles in it.

"Pebble stew tastes better when it is spicy. Would you happen to have a dash of hot pepper and a pinch of salt?" he asked.

The lady fetched the spices from the back of the room, and sat down beside Kebede once more, watching the pot with great interest. Kebede added the spices to the pot. The aroma of the pebble stew was pleasing to the young lady, and she smiled.

"The King would never touch pebble stew without lentils or beans. It takes only half a cup," Kebede suggested. The young lady dashed behind the curtain once more and brought the lentils. She wanted to eat precisely as the King did, and her appetite was primed by visions of the King's guarded kitchen. She wouldn't have the pebble stew any other way.

Kebede washed the grains, before mixing them with the pebbles. He then lowered the heat and waited while the pebble stew simmered. Before long it was ready.

"All we need now is a loaf of bread or some *injera*," Kebede said.

The young lady was very eager to taste the stew of pebbles and she dashed behind the curtain once more, coming back with four large loaves of bread. Kebede emptied the stew onto a large plate and the two of them shared the meal.

The dish was unlike anything the lady had ever tasted before. She liked it exceedingly, and thanked the gods for sending her such a bright and resourceful young man, one who could teach her a skill that none of her neighbours had. The two ate their fill, leaving nothing behind. Except the five black pebbles.

The next day the young lady asked Kebede to marry her. She did not wish to lose this resourceful man to any other woman. The couple were married a week later in the church of Medhane Alem. One of the dishes served at the banquet was five-pebble stew.

And so, the resourceful Kebede had provided himself not only with dinner, but with a good wife as well.

THE EXODUS CLAIMED more civilian lives than military. A good number of people were killed or maimed when they stepped on anti-personnel mines that were buried under the roads and hidden on trails in the jungle. Many more were killed by the persistent cannon fire.

The cannons were predictable. They began slowly in the morning, ceasing altogether at lunch, while somewhere far away distant Somalis chewed on *chat*. The stimulant sharpened their senses; eyes were glazed and alertness heightened by mid-afternoon, bringing on a predictable fit of frenzied cannon fire around 3 P.M. The targets were initially military supplies and personnel, but eventually the cannon fire became random, landing anywhere inside the settlement. But people no longer tried to dodge the bombs; they merely continued with their daily chores.

About a week after we left Jijiga, as I lay in the afternoon shade, I was reminded by my friends that it was my turn to fetch water. No one likes to fetch water, as it often means standing in line for hours, waiting for a truck that may or may not arrive that day, and may or may not run out of water before your turn, making it necessary to return to the same line the very next day and go through the waiting process again.

When I arrived, the line extended for half a kilometre before me. I hoped that this would be one of those days when the army would arrive with a few trucks of water, making it possible to have a shower as well. The dark dust had formed a thin caked layer over my skin, and the colour of my shirt had long ago been rendered completely unrecognizable. As I ran over my petty calculations, gazing at the bright blue sky, I heard distant explosions. Looking at my watch I saw that it was 4:15. The cannons were right on schedule.

After I had filled my jerrican with water and balanced it on my shoulder, I staggered to find my way back through the confused crowd. Soldiers were dashing to and fro like mad. Women were shedding tears. Small crowds had formed here and there, watching the smouldering smoke. I realized that the Somalis had done significant damage this time around.

A crowd had gathered around the spot where my friends awaited me, so I pushed my way through. Nothing I had left behind remained. The Jeep was gone, the tree, my friends . . . surely I was lost. Then I realized that one of the shells had landed right inside our small bit of shade and all three of my friends had perished, their remains scattered over a large area, intermingled with ragged shreds of metal. I was not shocked. I was not angry. I did not cry. I didn't feel lucky for having survived, either. Strange as it may seem, I almost felt relieved for them, because I knew that wherever they now were it could not be worse than the life they had lately led on earth.

I took the jerrican to Mam. She had already been to the site and was visibly shaken, tear stains marking her dusty face. I had no words to offer her. I found some shade nearby and sat alone, watching as the dispossessed walked up and down, up and down. Everyone was carrying a gun—young and old, rich and poor, Muslim and Christian, the sick and the healthy—everyone. Stranger still, those who carried these guns were for the most part unable to afford a single meal a day. A bag of flour (ten kilos) cost forty dollars, a soldier's monthly salary, whereas ten dollars could get you a slightly used AK-47 machine gun. If you bargained with the seller, they might even throw in a hand grenade or two for free. Life in the camp was inscrutable and tragic.

On the night of the explosion, it rained for the first time in well over four years. Children had been born and raised without ever knowing the touch of rain on their faces. They were mesmerized, ecstatic. The sky lit up with fire and heaved and shook. And the children discovered to their delight that the heavens were not about to swallow them up or break their tiny bodies under a torrent of cannon fire, but would pour down on them water—dear, precious water.

It rained for hours. There was no shelter from the rain, but it didn't matter. The rain opened the people's hearts, brought out a faith in the Prime Mover that none believed they still possessed. The storm, although harsh and accompanied by hail and wind, was considered a very good omen. It was agreed by all that God had opened the heavens so that our sins would be washed away, along with the filth, the rot, the stench of the camps. The future had been remade into something bright, something clean and forgiving.

The next morning the settlement was eerily silent. There was no sniper shot or cannon fire. Dawn broke quietly for the first time in memory. It was as though the rain had affected the Somali soldiers with the same heavenly thoughts as us. We scrambled to leave the valley quickly, as soon as there was enough light to find our way. The effect of these sudden storms is often felt hours after they have stopped, when the accumulated rainfall gathers enough momentum to wash away everything in its course. It is not unusual for a storm in southern Ethiopia to sweep away loaded trucks and buses full of people like specks of dirt in the bottom of a tub.

That day the 20,000 of us walked until sunset, by which time we were out of sniper range. The flood had come behind us, sweeping across the valley, creating an insurmountable divide between the enemy and us. The rains had washed away the remains of my three friends and then built up into a huge force, which literally tore a chasm into the land between Jijiga and Harar, saving the lives of some 20,000 beleaguered refugees in the process. The next day we rested our sore bodies and ate our first decent meal in days. We were in the fringes of the highlands and able to buy fruits, milk and other food we had almost forgotten existed.

My youngest brother, Henok, had been coughing for days by then and had difficulty breathing. A knowledgeable nurse diagnosed him as having asthma, reassuring Mother that it was not life-threatening. She observed that since Henok was so young, the condition might even heal in time. Mother kept him warm by wrapping him with her *netela* at night and massaged his chest when he began to wheeze. Medicine was still days away.

Four days after the miraculous storm, we finally arrived in the city of Harar. Those four days were uneventful ones. No one was killed or seriously injured. We knew then that the rain had indeed been a good omen. It had written itself into the people as well as the land.

RETIRING SAINTS

H ARAR IS AN ancient city founded on the rolling
grounds of the eastern highlands, indented by
perennial brooks and streams, graced by tower-
ing trees. The green-carpeted hills, scenic valleys and mild climate of the old city made a lively contrast to the eternal dust,
scorching heat and barren countryside of my hometown.
Harar had better roads and a more advanced infrastructure
than Jijiga; the buildings were ancient, graceful and built with
the shortage of real estate in mind. But what made Harar strik-
ingly different from Jijiga, or any other town or village I had
been to, were the stone walls that had been built around the old
city, rendering it a fortress.

Harar had once been an independent city-state, home to
the Adere tribe, one of the two Semitic peoples who had settled
far from the northern and central highlands. The other Semitic
people, who had drifted away from their kinsmen, were the
Gurages. The Aderes, who at the best of times numbered
35,000, faced a great threat from the surrounding Cushitic
peoples—primarily the Oromos, but also the Somalis. In the

early sixteenth century, after the Oromos had been driven from their homeland by their Somali kinsmen and thrust into the eastern highlands and farther north, it became painfully clear to the Aderes that this human tidal wave would swallow and digest them as well. There was nothing more unacceptable to these proud people than being assimilated by a people at a much lower stage of civilization. The Aderes had never been warriors, but they were intelligent; they realized that to retain their unique way of life what they had to do was fence themselves in, creating an enclave formidable to an aspiring aggressor.

The stone walls they built around their treasured city were three metres high, broken only at four strategic locations where heavy wooden doors had been installed between the stones. The city opened and closed its doors, taking its cue from the honourable sun. The main gate stood facing the major street, a shout away from the city centre, which was a roundabout. The shops and trading places lined this major artery and the roundabout, each building shouldering up against the next. There were no empty lots in this ancient city, and no farms or green lawns either. The roads, roundabout and walkways were all lined with cobblestones.

The residential areas were immediately behind the business district. Here, the houses were mostly two stories high, built from carved stones, and whitewashed. Each individual property was fenced in, once more, with high stone walls, making the neighbourhood look like a wild honeycomb, each small cell separated by a shoulder-width walkway. The walkways ran into one another like a tangled nest of sleeping snakes, making it completely unfathomable, and impenetrable to an intruder.

Traders were welcome in the ancient city, as the Aderes

were merchants, but the visitors left for home before the setting of the sun, when the watchman announced the closure of the city gates, pacing up and down the busy streets, his customary words amplified by the hollow bull-horn dangling from his neck. No outsider was allowed to remain behind.

From time to time, a bandit would steal into town disguised as a merchant, and stay behind the closed gates of the city. Soon, however, he would discover his mistake. Unable to find his way through the wild tangle of city streets, the lone venturer would invariably be caught by the city guard. The Aderes are not violent people, they would never molest a trespasser. They simply placed him in a shelter, fed him and threw a blanket over his shoulders to keep him warm during the chilly highland nights; but to avoid his secret escape, they also provided their prisoner with shackles for his legs and chained him to a heavy post. The sun rose and the city opened its gates, but the intruder remained chained. As meal after meal and day after day passed, the intruder wondered what exactly was going to happen to him, and why he was being fattened up. He would discover his fate only when the Arab merchants came south, for at that point the Aderes unchained him, put him in decent clothes and sold him to the highest bidder.

Today, the old town of Harar is still an exclusive residence of the Aderes, enabling them to retain their unique language and culture in a massive sea of Cushitic peoples and self-righteous invaders. The business centres of downtown Harar are, however, shared by other entrepreneurs, and new settlements have sprouted outside the gates of the old city, extending the boundaries of the ancient city and multiplying the population four- or five-fold. The Aderes are, now, a minority within greater Harar.

WHEN WE FINALLY arrived in Harar four days after the flood, the city was bustling with activity. Thousands strolled the streets. The shops and businesses were open, the market full of merchandise. Had it not been for the distant grumble of cannon fire and the overhead singing of fighter jets, Harar would have seemed completely removed from the theatre of war.

The day we arrived in Harar, we caught sight of army ambulances dashing past us at breakneck speed as they headed for the hospital, and we followed their lead. Henok's breathing problem had become alarming.

In Ethiopia, hospitals have always been regarded with suspicion. Many will resist a visit so long as there is some alternative—whether it is traditional medicine, a holy fountain or the *Adbar*. It is only after all the bitter roots have failed to cure the ailment; after the holy water has gone amiss, refusing to wash away the sting of the evil eye; and after the sacred tree has failed to defeat the Devil, that the patient is sent to a sanatorium. It will then take a miracle to keep the individual alive. No wonder hospitals were reputed to be places of the dying.

We took Henok to Jegula Hospital. In its heyday, this institution had been the pride of the nation. King Haile Selassie had always regarded the city of Harar with fondness, and did everything he could to support it. He established the only military academy in the nation within its city limits; he gave his blessing to the American proposal to found the first agricultural college within a stone's throw of the city; and, when it became obvious that modern medicine was indispensable for an aspiring nation, he broke ceremonial ground for the foundation of Jegula Hospital. While he remained in power, the

King paid frequent visits to the hospital, wishing its patients a speedy recovery, and ensuring that his pet project didn't go awry. Regrettably, in the few years the junta had been in power, the quality of care given at the hospital, as with much else, had quickly plummeted.

I had seen Jegula Hospital in better days. I had strolled under the graceful eucalyptus trees lining the fenced compound; I had rested on its manicured lawns, appreciating the mature gardens; and I had slipped inside the building itself, leaving with a secret pride in my beloved city, in the extraordinary world that existed behind what was otherwise a very ordinary building facade.

As we walked in with Henok, I thought that there must have been some mistake, that we had taken a wrong turn. The building which I beheld might have been lifted from some devil's sketchbook. The wide green lawns I remembered so well were littered with human misery, the bodies of the sick and their families camped before a building scarred with years of neglect. Indoors, the cleanliness that had once tickled my pride had been replaced by utter squalor, the dirty floors checkered with missing tiles, and the corridors pervaded by the smell of something dead and rotting.

There was nowhere to register, and no one to turn to. Neither a waiting room nor a queue existed to indicate that something was being done. We saw several patients brought in on makeshift stretchers who died and were removed without having ever seen a nurse. Several nomads led camels through the gate of the compound, the patient balanced on one side, sacks of grain on the other; they could neither sell their produce at market nor hear the diagnosis of the ill. They, like the whole institution, and everything in it, were in complete suspense.

The only discernible activity came from the part of the compound cordoned off from the public. A number of military tents and army ambulances were in the lot. Indoors, what had once been a tuberculosis ward was now an operating triage and intensive care unit, run by the Cuban Army. No civilians were permitted in these areas, but as each truck and ambulance pulled in to deliver the war victims, a mob of local people followed. They ran behind the tent and peeked through the cracks, standing on each other's shoulders to look through the windows of the operating theatre. They had never seen a white man die before and would not pass up the bloody opportunity, even when the soldiers persuaded them with the butts of their rifles and the heels of their boots. They had to satisfy themselves that in death, the white man finally regained his human colour, very much like a piece of wood in a fire, which crackles and burns red for a short while, turning dark and sooty once again when the fire is out.

I was intrigued and saddened by their behaviour. In Ethiopia, as in many countries, people maintained a healthy respect for the dead. In fact, a dead person was often accorded far more respect than he or she had received while alive. In the presence of a casket, no one spoke out loud; whistling and playing music were taboo; laughing was wickedness; and above all, no one gazed upon the remains. What I had witnessed that sunny day was a mob that had broken free of the intricate chains of tradition, willing and keen to do what had always been forbidden—just because the context had been redefined, and the subject seemed alien, not looking or behaving like them.

Although I had never liked what the Cubans and Russians had done on the continent, and sometimes went so far as to wish them immediate death, it was sad to see their young men sacrificed for a people they hardly knew. Watching the wounded and dying, I couldn't help but think of their mothers who, so far away from the continent, were unaware of what had befallen their dear boys. I couldn't help wondering what went on in the minds of those young men on the stretchers as the final curtain fell over their brief lives. Did they pass into oblivion confident that they had advanced the international spirit of Marxism-Leninism?

As I was engrossed in my own thoughts, I felt a soft touch on my shoulder. When I turned around, I was confronted by a beautiful woman in her late thirties. She was grinning, confident that I would recognize her immediately. Disappointed, she pursed her mouth and raised a single eyebrow, asking, "What is the matter, Nega? Don't you recognize me any more?" She removed her oversized sunglasses, pulled off her nurse's cap and shook loose her hair. I recognized her immediately—the infamous Kibret. I called out her name; we embraced and kissed. She, too, was a newcomer to Harar, having recently been transferred from her home town of Addis Ababa. Kibret had once lived in Jijiga, where we had been neighbourhood friends. I apologized for taking so long to recognize her, and reminded her that I had never before seen her in a nurse's uniform.

Kibret was a striking woman who possessed a tall and slender hour-glass figure. Even the starched white anonymity of the uniform she wore could not erase her graceful curves. Anyone who knew Kibret, even for a matter of minutes, would be witness to two remarkable facts—she was a fashion cultist, and would sleep with any man who had a title.

Kibret was the first woman in town to wear a miniskirt—

long enough to conceal her sex, but no longer—and a murder-
ous shade of red lipstick, soon named for her by the other
women of the town. She invariably wore high heels, precarious
stiletto spikes that bore her lithe figure over rough dirt and
gravel roads alike—her hips cutting curves like a snake as she
sauntered past a group of men. Quite conscious of the effect
she had, Kibret would stop and swiftly turn her head, catching
the boys staring after her, before flashing a smile and resuming
her majestic gait.

Kibret had a reputation as something of a celebrity hunter.
She was always in the company of one of the big shots in
town—today it might be the police chief, tomorrow the army
general. If a new civil servant was sent to work in Jijiga, and if
he had any rank at all, you would be sure to see him escorted
through the streets by Kibret.

All this, of course, was a kind of hobby for her. She had a
much softer side as well. While in Jijiga, Kibret had fallen in
love with my good friend Wondwossen. For a few months,
they had been inseparable. As she was twice his age, their relationship quickly became the talk of the town. Wondwossen
and Kibret strolled the streets of Jijiga, utterly immersed in
one another, seemingly unaffected by the baffled looks of civil
servants and the disapproving stares of the general public.
Though she was insulted and taunted at every turn, and even
berated by her boss at the hospital, she remained adamant,
believing that her personal life was her own affair and that sacrifices should be made for love. As mysteriously as it had
begun, the affair ended. One day, Kibret simply refused to
see Wondwossen again, and would not explain, either to him
or to us, his friends, why she had undergone the sudden
change of heart. It would take weeks before the slow machine

of talk revealed the truth to us. Wondwossen's father had offered her a choice—highlighting the correct answer with a gun to her head.

I explained Henok's problem to Kibret, who looked him over, then reassured Mam that she would see that he received the medicine he needed before the day was out. She led me inside to look for a doctor, but there was none in sight. We decided to wait at the nurses' station, where half a dozen nurses giggled and chatted.

I paced up and down the corridor, trying to find some order in the chaos that surrounded me. A few doors down from the nursing station, I came across a male nurse carefully stitching a gash on a patient's forehead with a hooked needle. The patient, a woman, was the victim of domestic violence. The stitching was being done without any anaesthesia. Her face contorted with pain. As I watched, I developed a great deal of admiration for the woman. The nurse pricked her forehead with the needle, wound its steel curve through her skin and pulled it up. He had repeated the procedure twice, and was piercing the lips of the wound a third time when the woman shrieked. Undoubtedly, he had been careless with the needle, I said to myself. He put the needle down and rolled up his shirt sleeve, after which I expected to see him comfort her. To my amazement, he gave her a hard slap instead, first on one cheek, and then the other. He barked at her in warning: "If you keep on screaming like that, I will walk out of here and the flies will take care of it for you." Then he looked up, noticing my presence for the first time. "Get lost," he told me, "or I will give you your due." I decided to walk.

The adjoining room was full of languishing patients, milling about dazedly and waiting for something to happen.

The sole nurse in attendance toyed with her ballpoint pen. As the day was hot, the ink in the tube had rushed to the tip, threatening to spill out. She casually removed the tube, placed it inside the centrifuge machine and turned the motor on. Satisfied with the result, she replaced the tube inside its sheath and put the pen by some papers on her desk. Then, she became aware of an imperfection in her fingernails, clipping one and filing another. Finally, it dawned on her that there were patients in the room, waiting for her attention. "Next?" she called.

I returned to the nurses' station, where the number of nurses idling about had increased to ten. It was noisier than the local market. Bells were ringing on the board from the nearby ward, but they fell on deaf ears. One of the bells rang continuously, finally getting their attention. A female nurse rose from her chair angrily. She pulled the broken handle of a broom from beneath her desk and strode towards the ward. As soon as she entered, the seven bedridden patients pointed at the man responsible. The nurse stood over his bed, eying him, as if to confirm his sin. As soon as he confirmed her suspicion and began to attempt to explain himself, she started beating him in earnest with the broom handle. He cried, pleading for mercy, but she was unconvinced. She stopped only after the fourth brutal whack, warning him that next time it would be much worse. On the way out I heard her muttering: "They eat excessively, and when they get constipated they give us a headache."

I told Kibret what I had witnessed, thinking that the hospital authorities should know. Although physical violence is often tolerated, and even condoned, I believed that a bedridden soul should be exempt. Kibret was surprised by my ignorance. Apparently this practice was as old as modern medicine in our nation. She took me on a tour of the maternity ward, to better demonstrate how refined and theatrical the entire practice had become.

As we watched, a woman in her early thirties was wheeled into the delivery room, where she was transferred to the operating table. A single blue sheet, stained with the blood of previous patients, had been hastily laid beneath her. There were three nurses in this room. One fiddled with a needle, a bowl and a flickering lamp—the hospital's only sterilization equipment. She was attempting to fish the needle out of the hot metal bowl with a tiny tong. Having failed repeatedly, she grabbed the edge of the bowl with a piece of cloth, tilting it to the side, thereby drawing the steaming water away from the needle. She then grasped the needle between forefinger and thumb, dropping it on the dirty linen when her finger was singed. Afterwards, she fetched a syringe, affixed this needle to its tip and administered some kind of medicine to the patient.

Soon after, the doctor made his entrance. After a hasty conference, the doctor and nurses began to work on the patient. The doctor absently fiddled between the patient's legs, hidden from view by a square of linen spread across her knees. A few minutes passed before labour began in earnest. Overwhelmed by the pain, the woman shrieked wildly. The head nurse coolly responded: "You should have thought of that before lifting your leg." The same nurse followed her pronouncement with a solid whack to the woman's head with the side of her hand. The other nurses followed suit: whack, whack. If I hadn't been incredulous before, what occurred in the next moment would have rendered me so. A hospital worker casually strolled into the room, in order to pick up the dirty linen. As he did so, he watched the performance of the nurses, and on his way out gave the patient one last slap himself.

The doctor continued his absent fiddling, indifferent to all that occurred around him. The patient screamed again, and was rewarded with another series of blows to the face. I blanched and turned away. I had seen quite enough for one day. A few hours later I came across the mother in the corridor, as she was being wheeled to her room. She was proud of her new delivery, a beautiful baby girl, and offered a weak smile. Her face was a mess. She had a black eye, a swollen lip and a wound on her cheek.

Kibret had finally spotted a doctor and sprinted after him, presenting her diagnosis of Henok. The doctor slapped her on the ass, pulled a writing pad from his pocket and scribbled some small words. As we thanked him, Kibret leaned over and whispered something in his ear that lit up his eyes and seemed to erase all the fatigue lines from his face. I could see his eyes following her as we made our way farther along the corridor.

The hospital pharmacy was better stocked than any of the private ones, and far cheaper, as it received its supplies from foreign donors. When Kibret and I presented the prescription to the pharmacist he muttered something about supplies being low and only emergency prescriptions being filled. Kibret sent him an icy glance, and told him that this was an emergency. Reluctantly, he slowly walked to the shelves, returning a few minutes later with the precious medicine.

As Kibret filled out the necessary forms, I read the label on the bottle and noted that the medicine had long ago expired. I pointed this out to the pharmacist, who told me that the numbers meant nothing, but that if it were important to me, he would be happy to erase them.

Kibret insulted him, calling him a bribe slave as she passed through the swinging door that had separated us from the pharmacist. A few moments later she returned with two bottles of fresh medicine. The pharmacist was fuming in anger and threatened Kibret with all kinds of retaliations. But in vain. Having laid the hospital director, the chief surgeon, the head gardener, the chief cook and the master plumber, Kibret was the most powerful person in the establishment, and he knew that very well.

WE STAYED IN Harar for over a week, stationed in a refugee camp along with thousands of others. Mam was planning to take us to her birthplace, the town of Asebe Teferi, where many of her close relations still lived. Her mother owned some property in town and would give us a place to stay.

Asebe Teferi was about three hundred kilometres west of Harar, and though the route was unaffected by the war, it was almost impossible to procure a bus ticket. Many beleaguered refugees were trying to get out of town, and most buses and trucks had been appropriated by the army to move troops and supplies. While we waited for a miracle to lift us from the camps of Harar, I was imprisoned in a blind roundup.

It was as if all the intervening years—the war, the amnesty, the long trek to Harar, two years of my life—had been instantly erased. A Meison cadre in town had been killed by EPRP members and the regime was out for revenge. Suddenly things had returned to how they had been before I joined the Somali liberation movement, before Wondwossen's death. Every youth who walked the streets was arrested, and some were even taken from their homes. By the end of the day the various prisons and jails were teeming. I was caught while walking downtown, along with two friends. No one asked us for identification or proof that we resided in Harar. As refugees, we were unlikely to have known the victim, even if it was assumed that we were likely to have bumped him off. But this was considered a minor detail. We were loaded on a truck like a flock of sheep and sent to the detention camp.

The regime had already announced that suspected EPRP terrorists would be dealt with very severely. Suspects were detained longer; fact-finding procedures, otherwise known as various forms of torture, had been refined; and the ratio of so-called terrorists executed to cadres killed had risen significantly. The Red Book set a goal of a hundred terrorists done to death for each comrade killed.

On the first night of our imprisonment, about ten suspects were randomly selected from our ranks and shot to death in the prison compound. We could hear the machine-gun fire from our cells. Their bodies were later laid out in the streets for the public to see. No one, not even members of the immediate family, could show grief for the deceased, for that would be treason of the highest degree. The relations could claim the remains of their loved ones at the end of the day, for an inconspicuous burial.

The following night we were bracing ourselves for what might well have been our turn when the father of one of the boys in prison came to see us. His father was a highly decorated military officer from Jijiga who had won the admiration of the chairman of the junta, Colonel Mengistu Haile Mariam, for his bravery on the northern front. He had recently been promoted to general and had been sent to lead the Mechanized Brigade in the south.

The general considered it treasonous that his only son should be sent to jail while he was putting his life in jeopardy so that others could live free. He flew from the front not only to secure the release of his boy and the children of his comrades, but also to get revenge. He wanted to show these spineless civilians who was in charge.

The confrontation between the hot-tempered general and the cowed Meison cadres was quite something to watch. The general had brought along two truckloads of soldiers, armed with machine guns, keen to dispatch anyone at the wink of their patriarch's eye. They disarmed the cadres and the *kebele* officials, and brought them before us for interrogation.

Initially, the cadres made an attempt, though feeble, to stand up to him, arguing they needed more time to consider the matter. After all, they said, when lives are in the balance things must be carefully thought through and one should not assume that they killed people who were only randomly rounded up. The general swatted aside their arguments like drowsy flies. He ordered the release of his boy, the children of other soldiers and finally everyone from Jijiga and the other towns from the annexed area. He took down the names of the cadres, promising them that it wouldn't be the last time they'd hear from him.

Mother was waiting in the compound when I was released. As she cried, she felt my body like a blind woman, to make sure that I was not injured. Despite the anxiety and shortage of food in the prison, we had not been tortured. In fact, as we waited to see who among us would be chosen to spend the night in the hyena's belly, we had longed for the good old days when all you could expect of prison was the "helicopter," the "spread-eagle" or the "pilgrim." But those days were gone for good.

Mother appeared to have aged a great deal since we'd left

Jijiga. I don't know how old she was then, but she couldn't have been more than twenty years older than me, which would have made her about forty. Mam was like most Ethiopians: she would cite a historical benchmark when asked her age. Typically, if asked how old she was, Mam would respond that when the Italian fascists invaded the country and when her father took up arms against them, she was five years old. The war itself lasted about five years, so one could figure out her age with a likely margin of error of two or three years.

Father had been less clear about his age. His benchmark was a remarkable flood that had destroyed part of his home-town, at which time he lost his wisdom teeth. Assuming that there was a record of the flood, this case poses a daunting prob-lem—how does one establish the average age at which a Chris-tian male from the eastern highlands loses his wisdom teeth?

FOR THE NEXT few days Mam, the kids and I set up camp at the bus station, attempting to buy tickets to Asebe Teferi. Bus sta-tions in Ethiopia are open laboratories for social dealings. It is here that new products are tested, and fresh schemes plotted and launched. Masculinity is demonstrated by fist fights, and sweethearts sought. Long before the hummingbirds of Africa announce the break of day, and well after sunset is marked by the crane's swift flight past the terra cotta line of the horizon, the bus terminal is alive with furtive gestures and desperate schemes.

Each morning children as young as five leave the clinging warmth of their blankets before dawn to earn a few birr in the tumult. Thermoses filled with steaming coffee dangle from hands as frail as the bones of a bird. On each head is balanced a massive basket heaped high with various fruits, sweets and deli morsels. The children come to the terminal unaccompanied by adults, carefully avoiding the rabid dogs that plague the early morning streets and beggars who would not hesitate to rob them of their produce if the opportunity presented itself.

The bus terminal offers these children no more security than the streets. The adults they serve—passengers, coolies and bus drivers—do not see them as innocent victims of rampant injustice and the poor social conditions that plague the country, but as willing accomplices of these forces. These children can expect to be shortchanged at every opportunity, robbed of their merchandise by adults whose height gives them the advantage, and beaten without the slightest provocation. They are regarded with suspicion by the very society that has brought them into existence—as though their lives required justification.

Not unlike these children, inner-city sheep and goats leave their barns early to scavenge a living from the refuse and litter scattered on the grounds of the bus terminal. Here, these domesticated animals are engaged in a desperate bid for survival, stealing and fighting at every turn. There is no shepherd to watch over them, except perhaps a canny instinct that these animals have developed over time, alerting them to the precise moment in which to snatch a banana from a fruit stand; just when to make that surprising leap onto the sill of a window and escape from a speeding truck; and how to avoid those shady characters walking slowly backwards into hidden places, some small morsel in hand—luring them to certain death, with the intention of slaughtering and taking home that precious meat.

Bus terminals also house those that are considered the most loathed and feared members of society: beggars, thieves and the insane. The only lunatic asylum in Ethiopia is to be found in the capital city of the nation, far too long a journey for most. And since the mental hospital offers little more in the way of therapeutic treatment than the bus terminal, even those living nearby dump their demented relations at the station. Besides, people passing through the terminal are happy to contribute to the quick recovery of the insane by beating them, dousing them with cold water and giving them "Spotting Therapy"— an early form of electric shock treatment in which a gang of hoodlums ties the lunatic to a utility pole and burns his skin with cigarette butts.

As in many cultures, beggars are despised. They are living reminders of an uncertain future, of what could happen to many "respectable" citizens if that next paycheque doesn't come, if the marriage ends, if the gods call home the family's breadwinner. Beggars are not violent; in fact their job requires them to be more refined in their manners than the average person. They are quite entertaining and are expert at understanding the human heart. No two beggars beg the same way—the rhythmic narration, the heartbreaking melody, the subtle reminders of a coming judgment day are wound into performances that rival the national theatre. Learned at an early age, these eerie arias are passed from generation to generation with unparalleled respect for copyright.

There are variations on this age-old tradition. While waiting for our ticket in Harar, I witnessed a most original and enterprising school of beggars. The troupe consisted of a dishevelled couple and a well-dressed woman. This seemingly respectable lady casually strolled throughout the terminal, watching for possible victims, typically wealthy women travelling alone who had recently lost a loved one. Mourning families signify their loss in the clothes they wear. A woman dressed completely in black, for instance, is likely to have lost a very close member of her family in the last six months. If her dress and *netela* are only trimmed in black, it is likely that she is past the immediate six-month period of mourning. If she wears her regular dress with the *netela* upside down, and the head-wear to match, then she is probably remembering a distant relation who passed on a long time ago. If one end of the *netela* is tied at her waist, the light fabric draping low behind her, and the other end is carefully folded around her shoulders, she is just coming from a funeral.

As I watched, one of the troupe, the well-dressed woman, approached a mourning lady, greeted her sombrely and, in a low tone that expressed her respect and sympathy, asked about the woman's recent loss. The stranger gave her detailed information on how her six-year-old boy was afflicted by the evil gaze of an unknown *Buda* on St. Michael's day, becoming delirious and feverish for two days, before suddenly succumbing to the illness on the third. The two women shed tears together, and parted.

A few moments later, a dishevelled couple could be seen begging in divine melodies, pausing here and there, before casually stopping before the lady in black. They expressed their humble sympathies for the dead, and urged the lady to cease her mourning. They implored her to give thanks to a kind God that had seen fit to bless her with the beautiful daughter that still accompanied her. The girl, about three years in age, clung to the hem of her mother's *netela*, watching the exchange. Without missing a beat, the beggars related their own tragedy, telling of the sudden death of their six-year-old son, who had been afflicted by an unknown *Buda* on St.

Michael's day. They told her of his last delirious days, sweating like a candle in the sun, before he passed away on the third day without saying goodbye.

The mourning woman was stunned. She raised both hands to her mouth to stifle a scream, her dazed eyes shed tears and her frail body trembled. She had never expected to share her most private torments with such a down-and-out couple as this. The beggars, if they noticed any change in her demeanour, didn't let on. They continued to relate the details of their tragic existence. While grieving for the loss of their son, they continued in tandem—one voice taking up the narration when the other was too overcome with grief to speak. They railed against the gods, saints and good spirits for their misfortunes, only to be suddenly reminded of how much worse their lot in life could be when, a few months later, their beautiful three-year-old daughter was snatched from them by a pack of wild hyenas.

The mourning woman was overcome with hysteria. She wailed in utter despair before losing her balance and falling to the ground. When she finally regained her senses, she found herself cradled in the arms of the two miserable beggars. A crowd, four rows deep, gathered about the trio and stared. Lying on the ground of the bus station, among the chaos and litter, her small daughter clinging to her arm, suddenly it all made sense to her. These two strangers were not beggars at all, but angels in disguise, who had come down to Earth to deliver a warning. They had arrived in time to save her and her daughter from the wretched misery that had engulfed the family after the loss of her son. She opened her purse and emptied its contents into the laps of the couple, and was glad to do so.

We were finally able to obtain our tickets about a week after I was released from jail, thanks to a fairly sizeable bribe. Once aboard the bus, it would take us five hours to get to our destination.

The road to Asebe Teferi is carved into the mountainside. Our journey occurred during the wet season when the hillside was sodden with rain and fell away beneath the most practised of steps. The narrow gravel road, which could accommodate only a single vehicle at the best of times, was, therefore, the only means of travel, and was shared by men, cattle and wild animals alike.

As the bus passed by farms and villages, neighbourhood dogs would bark and give chase, attempting to sink their teeth into the bone-dry rubber of the bumpers. Children often joined with the dogs, snatching at the back of the bus, hanging precariously from its cargo ladder and back end. For most of these kids, the surreptitious moments spent dangling from the backs of passing buses would be the closest they would ever come to riding in an automobile.

About forty-five minutes into our trip, we reached a scenic region where the houses clung to the face of the mountain on one side of the road, and distant villages dotted the green landscape sixty metres below us on the other. Shepherd boys occupied strategic posts high on the cliffs, very much like a defending army prepared to launch an attack on a hostile convoy. The driver pulled over to the side of the road, lifted a duffel bag from behind his seat, and called the boys down.

They recognized him immediately, clambering down the cliff face like wild monkeys descending on some unexpected bounty, arms extended before them, laughing and charging ahead of one another. When they reached our driver, some shook his hand, others bowed and kissed his fingers; all stood around with an undisguised air of anticipation. The driver took the time to inquire about their health and well-being, how this or that boy's mother fared (despite the fact that he had most likely never met her), then opened his bag and dispensed his gifts of sweets, toys and soccer balls. They were happy beyond words and jumped up and down with glee. The driver's face was transformed with pleasure. He asked the children if there was anything he could bring them from town on his return trip. They could not think of one.

I was touched by this display of generosity, by the spectacle of this angelic character who made a difference in the lives of poor shepherd boys. When I couldn't restrain my curiosity any longer, I walked to the driver's seat and asked him why he was so kind. A shadow fell over his face. In a serious tone of voice he admitted to me that he had no choice. Perched high on the cliffside, stones at their feet, the kids could really damage buses.

The shepherd boys' skill in using slingshots was surpassed only by their mountaineering genius. Although this highway was the main artery connecting the southern regions with the nation's capital, it saw only light traffic, and the frequent travellers were easily identified by the boys. The prudent commuter paid a simple toll.

Before long we stopped in Kulubi, where driver and passengers alike made sacrifices and offerings in recognition of St. Gabriel in delivering us safely to this point in our journey.

KULUBI IS HOME to the largest and most celebrated church in the whole of Ethiopia. At the time of its construction—it was a ramshackle hut, initially—there were already two churches within twenty kilometres dedicated to the same saint. Many considered it irresponsible to build a third one within a stone's throw—as it only added to the confusion that St. Gabriel had been experiencing lately. Everyone knew that after the addition of the second church St. Gabriel's miracles had begun to diminish in size and frequency; and that prayers and pleas directed to one saint, at the same hour and from two separate locations, had ended in disaster, for the requests of the two parishes were too often mutually exclusive. One parish might pray for rain in their village, for the crops, while another living close to the river might beg the saint to keep the rain from falling, in order to keep the water level low as it passed through their village. One man might ask the good saint to keep his bee farm prolific, while another asked him to care for his horses—resulting in bees that multiplied quickly before falling dead from the sky, as bee stings were fatal to horses. Often enough, it was the absolute number of the requests that resulted in disaster. So many parishioners had begged him for boys, and so many for girls, that he lost track of whom to grant the requests to—sending a dizzying number of variously gendered children to all who were capable of bearing young. Adding a third church of St. Gabriel within shouting distance would only compound the problem, the parishioners argued, and sent a delegation of elders to intercede on their behalf and aid the people of Kulubi in finding another, sympathetic saint.

After much lobbying, the elders agreed to meet with the representatives of Kulubi in the half-finished confines of the new church. Outside, villagers slaughtered a healthy bull, serving the choice parts to the elders—raw. An abundant supply of *tella* and *arake* was placed inside the church with the two parties—to help the elders see the light—before the doors of the church were padlocked, and a guard was placed outside the door to make sure that no one wandered off before a sound decision was reached.

The elders spent a day and a half locked inside the latest church of St. Gabriel, trying to find an appropriate replacement saint, one who would look after the people of this village and the properties of the community without further diminishing the miracle quotient.

St. Michael was immediately ruled out. People could not forget what had happened to the church of St. Michael in Jijiga. Though it was by far the largest church in Ethiopia to be named for this saint, it hadn't withstood the hardships that were sent to test it. Founded generations before, the church occupied a sprawling tract of land in the heart of the city, fenced in with high stone walls and iron gates. Several houses shared the compound with the church; some were used as preschool classrooms, some as homes for the monks, and still others as tombs for the local rich.

The church had been repeatedly burglarized over the years, and had once been demolished by Somali invaders, generations in the past. Recalling these sad omens, the priests of Kulubi reasoned that the locals would have no faith in anyone who was unable to care for his own home.

St. Peter was ruled out because of his poor performance in a small village nearby. He had not intervened when half of the villagers had been wiped out by cholera, and he stood by in silence as a school of locusts descended upon the valley, destroying the crops and causing famine. As if that were not enough, St. Peter neglected to bring rain on time. In fact, half of the parishioners attending the church of St. Peter had lost their faith so completely as to revert to the *Adbar* for their most pressing needs. They now went to church only for baptisms and funerals.

St. Joseph was eliminated without argument. It was common knowledge that he had fallen from favour with Christ. Very few churches had named themselves for this saint to begin with, and those that had quickly repented. Many of them had gone so far as to change the paintings that graced their church, so as to make their small temples unrecognizable to their former patron.

When one of the visiting elders suggested that the new church be dedicated to the Virgin Mary, the priests of Kulubi were insulted. They knew that only large cities could afford the luxury of naming a church for Mary—it was a sign of deference and respect to honour Christ's mother that way. In the city, parishioners were able to take their most desperate prayers to a neighbouring church, dedicated to a saint known for actually performing miracles. Besides, it was unmanly to pray to the Virgin Mary. Only women in labour directed their prayers to her, in hope that she would view them with sympathy. In any case, St. Gabriel would easily deliver far more in the way of miracles.

Needless to say, the deliberations did not end amicably. The priests of Kulubi could not be persuaded to take up any other patron saint for their church and the visiting elders expressed their displeasure by refusing to recognize the new church and threatening to petition the Archbishop for an injunction.

The subsequent rise to fame of the Kulubi church of St. Gabriel was nothing short of a miracle. The local farmers were the first to reap the benefits of St. Gabriel's patronage. The prayers of the people of Kulubi were swiftly answered— whether they prayed for rain, a good harvest, twin calves, the death of a neighbour or the birth of a child. Year after year, the size and extent of the pleas increased, and St. Gabriel did not waver—the rains came on time, the harvest was abundant, the people were prolific, and many enemies fell dead through the intervention of St. Gabriel, who granted all requests but the most sinful. In return, the church received generous sacrifices in the form of bulls, cows, sheep, goats, grain and even gold. In less than two decades, the poor cottage had been replaced by a majestic building whose cathedral dome was inlaid with gold and marble. Nothing of its like had been seen in the region before.

No one was more surprised by the achievements of this church than its poorer cousins, the two original parishes of St. Gabriel. Many theories were advanced to explain the spectacular success of Kulubi, but the most popular one, by far, had to do with its location. Because the church was on higher ground, and was therefore closer to the heavens, prayers offered from its confines could of course be more easily heard.

In the past, churches had been built at ever-increasing altitudes, though the results were mixed. The church of Debre Damo, for example, was built at the tip of a precipice so high in the heavens that its spire is often hidden in clouds. The land on which the church is situated is so small that storks avoid it entirely for fear of running out of runway; and the cliffsides are so steep that mountain goats shy away from them. The only access to this church is by climbing a slowly swinging rope that is hung from the church's entrance.

The parishioners are all trained in rope climbing from an early age. By adulthood, most are expert at mountaineering. This training, however, doesn't guarantee a safe sabbath. There are numerous stories of pendant parishioners losing their grip and falling to the parched earth below, twisting an ankle, breaking a rib or even fracturing a skull. But the parishioners are aware that such accidents are the Devil's deeds, and refuse to be deterred from attending mass. They wipe the blood from their brows, bind their broken ankles and reach for the rope yet again. Once on top, the crippled parishioners are congratulated by many others who have lost an eye, a tooth, an ear or a limb in past endeavours, and are hailed as heroes and heroines of the day by priests who, since the wee hours of the morning, have been inhaling fumes of the seraphic fig, also known as marijuana, to elevate themselves to an even higher plane of awareness.

For decades the parishioners of Debre Damo kept their zeal, and attended mass without faltering. Then they realized that they were being short-changed; that their efforts did not guarantee the deserved reward. They did not have far to look for evidence—the nearby Church of Lalibela was standing proof.

Even though the roof of the building is at ground level, the Church of Lalibela is an impressive structure in the shape of a crucifix, carved from a single rock. In order to find the church, one would have to know exactly what to look for. And yet it delivered just as many miracles as its rival church of Debre Damo, without the attendant injuries. At one time, pilgrims would travel hundreds of kilometres in order to partake of the church's generosity. Sacrifices were made at its doorsteps, and warriors crossed mountains to seal a pact of peace in the shadows of the temple. The Church of Lalibela fell out of grace only when it was discovered that its miracles could be reproduced at a nearby shrine, at much less expense to the parishioner.

WORD OF KULUBI'S success got out; people from all over the country started directing their most pressing needs to that distant land, shaming their home-grown churches. The bedridden prayed for a day in the sun, the crippled begged for a life without crutches, and mothers petitioned on behalf of demented children. St. Gabriel of Kulubi obliged; miracle after miracle unfolded. And the legend started growing as fast as the wealth of the Lord's House.

On St. Gabriel's Day, which is celebrated on December 28, some three hundred buses filled with pilgrims descend upon Kulubi, while thousands of others trudge in on foot from nearby towns. The vast domain of land surrounding the church, which once seemed to swallow her in its awesome expanse, becomes a hive of human worship. Those whose prayers have been answered by St. Gabriel of Kulubi come forward to tell of the power of the saint. Standing on platforms, each announces the miracle that has transformed his or her life. A middle-aged woman, tears streaming down her face, displays the child she has borne after years of fruitless marriage; a fragile-looking man, delirious with joy, raises a limb, once withered, that has been healed by prayer. A long list of miracles follows throughout the afternoon, as those who have journeyed so far bear witness to their attainments.

At night the celebrations intensify. Barbecued meat,

offered freely as a form of sacrifice, is sampled by all. Alcohol flows freely. And the recipients of St. Gabriel's largesse lose themselves in a world of passion.

Our next stop was the town of Hirna. Midway between Harar and Asebe Teferi, buses and trucks travelling between the two cities pause for food and refreshment at one of the many restaurants this town has built in response to the traffic, most of which serve delicious, affordable meals, at an uncommon speed of service. The morning and evening hours in town are slow. Activities pick up at about eleven o'clock, reach a climax at one, and wind down by three in the afternoon. Within this time frame, one can see men running from their buses to lunch and drinks at a restaurant. After lunch, these men mount forays to the local hotel for a quick act of coitus with a local prostitute, before running, at breakneck speed, back to the bus.

No sooner had our bus started to roll out of town than some of the passengers began to moan, and show signs of distress. These newcomers to the bus were peasants from deep in the mountains who had seldom had an opportunity to ride any form of vehicle. A family of three, two rows behind me, were the most pitiable. When they first boarded the bus, their six-year-old boy was all smiles, full of anticipation for their grand adventure to Asebe Teferi. As the vehicle rolled out of town, he leaped up, counting out trees as they passed us, before weakly staring into the distance as his head began to spin. He collapsed almost immediately. His mother picked him up and laid his head in her lap, before doubling up over him. She pressed her shaking hands to her ears, to block out the rumbling sound of the engine. Minutes later, the boy's father leaped up, struggling to open the window. Before he could figure out the mechanism, he had thrown up on the glass. The conductor cursed up and down the aisle, and made the man clean up his mess before he would open the window for him. Before returning to his seat at the front of the bus, the conductor lit a stick of *ood* that smelt like a sickly mixture of wildflowers and manure, and handed it to the man.

Silence descended on our bus. After a long and quiet journey we came to a stretch of road about two hundred metres long. Ahead of us, I could just make out the dark outline of an object that lay lifeless in the middle of the road. At first, I thought it was an old spare tire that had fallen from a truck. As the bus came closer, I saw that the object was moving, lazily coiling in on itself, before raising its head to stare at our party. It was a six-metre-long rock python.

The bus came to a halt about fifteen metres in front of the animal. The passengers got out of their seats and rushed forward for a look. Many encouraged the driver to simply run the snake over, but he refused. In the past, the driver had come across a wide variety of wild animals, and was wary of confrontations. While driving a Land Rover in the western province of Arussi, for example, he had come upon a pride of lions sunning themselves lazily in the middle of the road. It was, as now, the rainy season, and the only dry land to be found was the macadamized road. He did everything he could think of to discourage them: he revved the engine, honked the horn, banged the doors. Finally, desperate to pass, the driver decided to gently nudge the pack from his path with the nose of his car. The herd's reaction was swift. The lion mounted the hood and shook the vehicle through and through with casual swipes at the windshield. The lionesses and their cubs leaped onto the back of the vehicle, and began to slowly waltz over the burlap sacks of maize that he was carrying. It took a few terrifying minutes of erratic driving to shake the beasts from his pickup.

The snake, however, did not take much persuasion to relinquish his possession of the highway. It caught sight of an animal in the bush and its hunger overtook its lethargy. We managed to resume our journey, and a few minutes later we arrived safely in Asebe Teferi.

AN ALIEN ADBAR

SEBE TEFERI snakes along the edge of the main highway that links the city of Harar with the capital city of the nation, Addis Ababa. Asebe Teferi is a melancholic small town whose drab conditions are accentuated by the black roads, laid with crushed basalt rocks, that lie at the foot of a dark mountain chain adorned with the same black, shiny stones.

Most of the buildings in town were made of wood and mud, topped with old and rusted corrugated metal sheets. The houses, which had long since shed their paint, were ranked on the mountainside, where they desperately clung to dead cliffs. Generations of neglect were written into the faces of these derelict buildings. The walls had shed their meagre mud linings, and a few of the buildings tilted to one side or another, making it as dangerous a proposition to stand in their scant shade as to live inside them.

The main business in town was the hotel and restaurant service industry, which catered to the equally wayward peasants and truck drivers. The peasant would bring his wife along to market, and at the end of the business day, would share the booze and festivities with her, celebrating the fruits of their labours. They would stagger through crowded streets, completely oblivious to their surroundings, doing the town until the city announced the closure of its doors. Then they would help each other mount their horses and head for home. They didn't always succeed in getting home at night. Many of them would fall off their horses before crossing the mountain, spending the night in the bush while their horses calmly grazed nearby. Robbery was unknown in this region.

In normal times, the neighbouring farmers used the town as a staging area to ship local agricultural produce to larger cities, and the market was continually busy. Hundreds of peasants came in with donkeys laden with various goods and returned home with textiles and other items that they could not grow on their own farms. At night the market was transformed. The abandoned market stalls became a violent theatre in which drunken peasants let fly machetes at each other's throats. Peasants were known to bear their grudges for generations, so there was always someone a farmer wanted to bump off. It was simply a matter of finding him.

When the opportune moment presented itself, the peasant would ambush his foe, hack him to pieces, then fall into despair and attempt to cover his trail. But relations of the victim would be quick to identify the assailant. One always announced one's enemies to family members, warning them that in case of an "accident" the individuals on the list should be held accountable. Peasants didn't go to police or the courts for justice. Blood called for blood.

The perpetrator knew the rules. He packed a gun and headed for the forest. After some months had passed, the turmoil would die down. Then elders would be sent to the victim's family, establishing compensation—blood money. The assailant would sell his cattle and a portion of his land to settle the debt. Then he would go on with his life, keeping a watchful eye on the son or brother of the man he had done to death. He might live to die of old age, but not all of his sons or brothers would. It was an endless cycle.

MAM'S MOTHER HAD owned three houses in the town before the junta took office. She lost two of them and a few others in another city during the revolution. Nevertheless, she did have a roof over her head, and was willing to share it with us. We were given the use of one of the two bedrooms and seven of us had to rough it together. And we felt lucky, for renting our own house was impossible: there were no vacancies in the whole country, and even if there had been we couldn't have afforded it. It was the one area in which connections were of absolutely no use.

The barest necessities of life were bought with constant struggle. We had to stand in line for hours to purchase a bottle of cooking oil so dirty that light would not pass through it; we had to travel to the farmer's door in order to buy eggs, milk or vegetables, since the shops were empty of everything; and we had to wait outside the city limits in order to buy a load of firewood. It was a time when everything, except human life, was in short supply.

TO MAKE THINGS easier on Mam and everyone else, I left town within a few days to live with some relations in Kuni, a rural

town less than half an hour's drive from Asebe Teferi. One of
my younger sisters went to live with our eldest sister Meselu,
who held a teaching position in another rural town called
Mechara, about two hundred kilometres from Asebe Teferi.
Both Kuni and Mechara were located in the highlands. They
shared a temperate climate, lush vegetation and dense forests,
and were criss-crossed by streams and rivers.

Kuni could not have been more different from Jijiga. In
Kuni there was no electricity or running water, and the "outhouse," which was no more than an open field, was in the backyard between the banana plants and coffee trees. When I was
growing up, Mam would send me here on vacation, and one of
my chief pleasures as a child had been the freedom this sort of
life lends. I would tiptoe through the jungle, carefully watching where I planted my feet, looking out for wild animals that
might have overslept in the bushes, until I found a convenient
nest where I could carefully lower myself down—clutching a
nearby coffee tree—and begin negotiating with nature. What
could be more natural? The only hitch to this form of outhouse
was that you had to remember to bring along toilet paper each
and every time. I received a fiery lesson in botany when I happened to mix poison ivy with some familiar leaves.

My relations in Kuni were very reserved people, soft-
spoken, sparing, and more mild-mannered than any people I
had ever come across. They not only abhorred profanity and
swearing, but also frowned upon giggling, back-biting, name-
calling, idleness and a whole array of lesser sins. It looked to
me as though they led their lives within the narrow and suffocating confines of two timeless cultural icons: the Holy Bible
and the *Adbar*.

As time passed and I got to know them better, that

peaceful facade was lifted. Once I was invited to witness the execution of a project intended to discourage monkeys from overrunning the cultivated farm. The plan was centred around the watering troughs at the narrow clearing between the farmers' holdings and the adjacent forest, which was densely populated by centuries-old trees and was so dark inside that I found it too frightening to venture in. Among other animals living in the jungle, there were no fewer than three different types of monkeys, ranging in size from rabbits to mammoths that weighed in at several hundred pounds. The water troughs, I was told, were for the huge monkeys.

After generations of living with and fighting against nature's creatures, the peasants had catalogued the behaviours displayed by the beasts they had dealt with, behaviours which they mercilessly exploited to their own advantage. They had, for instance, noted that the big monkeys always washed their faces before drinking from a pond or river. And so, the peasants fouled the water in the troughs with chilli peppers and waited in the shade of the corn fields for the drama to unfold.

The monkeys don't often keep to a schedule, so the peasants took turns keeping a vigil around the spice-laden water. After having waited for only half a day, their prayers were answered. A small number of monkeys (I was told that they were all males) came out of the forest, walked up and down the narrow clearing and after convincing themselves that all was safe and sound, let out a series of sharp wails. As if by magic, countless others gushed out of the silhouettes of the trees, some carrying babies on their backs. They made their way to the watering troughs.

Those who washed their faces became maniacal as the chilli pepper seared their eyes. Completely blinded, they pushed at each other, jumping and falling. During the confusion, they accidentally tipped the watering trough and spilled its contents onto the surrounding grass. Now even those who had not yet washed their faces became soaked by the perilous liquid as they scrambled, hand and foot, over the slippery grass. As they rubbed their eyes in disbelief, they too became blinded.

The peasants waited a while longer, until the hysteria and maniacal cries of the monkeys became unbearable. Then those mild-mannered, reserved and sparing country folk pulled out their machetes, spears and wooden clubs, and started working on the pack, beheading them, amputating arms and legs, stabbing and clubbing them until the green fields turned red, and there wasn't a live monkey left in sight.

I was so disturbed by what I witnessed that I threw up on myself. When I got home that night, I refused to eat. Neither could I sleep. The next day, I was given a jar of holy water to drink and wash my face with. I was also given some bitter medicinal roots. When I felt a little better, I was teased about what was perceived to be unmanly behaviour. I was told that boys as young as five were encouraged, every growing season, to witness the extermination as a form of initiation.

Indeed, the sons, like their fathers, had come to know the feeding habits of their prey, and the boys carried out their own bloody projects, targeting the tiniest monkeys. One project revolved around a wooden shack that they had built to trap their tiny visitors. It was a small hut made of wooden planks, with gaps left between the boards. There were no windows in the miniature building, only a door that slid up and down. A single rope, which held the door up, was fastened to an ear of corn that, in turn, was nailed to the ceiling plank.

A generous amount of corn was spread in the shack, and the door was left open—an invitation for the visitors to entertain themselves. There were no men waiting in the shade, and no suspicious activity in the area, for fear it might scare off the shy little creatures.

The pack of monkeys made its entrance into the dining room after careful observations of the area. Once inside, they fought each other, snatching at corn and carrying on until the feed was almost depleted. At this point, one of the industrious little creatures looked up and noticed the ear of corn nailed to the ceiling. It snatched at the corn, thereby freeing the rope, so that the door slid down its slots to the ground. The monkeys were now prisoners with no means of escape.

The next day, the boys returned, armed with spears and pointed sticks and, like their fathers before them, started the carnage. They poked and stabbed at the helpless little creatures through the wall slats until the entire pack had met a bloody end—all in the name of a good harvest.

I'd always liked those little mischievous creatures. As a child, I used to ask Mam to bring me a monkey or a young gorilla when she returned from a trip to the highlands, but she never did. During summer holidays here I preferred playing with animals to the neighbourhood kids. There was a domesticated monkey that I was particularly fond of. I would give the animal a looking glass, which it anxiously grasped in both hands. The monkey moved its head from side to side and up and down, watching as the "other" monkey imitated its every movement. Then, while still holding the mirror in both hands, the monkey would swiftly move to see the back of the stranger. Despite the disappointment, it never changed its pattern of behaviour.

Sometimes, I set the mirror before the rooster. I would scatter some feed just in front of the looking glass and watch as it rushed towards the grain. But before the rooster could eat, it would catch sight of its twin, and fighting would ensue. The rooster was never willing to share the feed with anyone else. But every time it gave the prospective thief a blow or two with its beak, the intruder fought back. The rooster would jump high to leap over the trespasser, but the other would jump as high—making it the most frustrating encounter the rooster had ever had.

The serene nights of the countryside were typically punctuated by the barks and howls of dogs. Every household kept one or two pooches, which they released within the compound during the evening. The folks understood what various intensities and frequencies of barking portended, and when the occasion warranted, the head of the family would step outside to ensure that everything was in its rightful place. By far the most ominous sign was when the dogs did not bark at all, for an eerie silence was unmistakable proof that big cats were in the neighbourhood.

If the quiet persisted, doors would be heard opening, as neighbours alerted each other to the possible threat and tried to determine what sort of big cat was in the area. Each species had its own brand of deterrent. Once it was known that there were lions nearby, for example, the peasants would light torches and march towards the suspicious area, yelling and uttering brave words—more to keep up their own fighting spirit than to scare off the king of beasts. The lion would melt into darkness and disappear upon seeing the torches, lest a stray spark light upon its mane, setting it ablaze. In the very rare instance that cheetahs or leopards invaded the sleepy village, on the other hand, the solution was simple. As soon as their presence was perceived by the neighbourhood, the men would arm themselves with solid sticks. Cheetahs as well as leopards are very much like dogs—they bluff, but if you stand your ground, the legendary sprinter quickly gives way.

During an invasion by wild cats, one or two cows, bulls or sheep would invariably be lost. The peasants minimized their losses by slaughtering any animal that they found maimed but alive for the shared consumption of the community. The dead were discarded. Eating the carcass of an animal that was not prayed over while still alive was considered unorthodox, a taboo, though wild game, shot from a distance, was exempt from this rule.

SHORTLY AFTER I settled in Kuni I was surprised to learn that I had passed the matriculation examination, with distinction, no less. I was to report to the university at once, for there were a limited number of openings in the faculty and immediate registration was necessary. It was October 1977, and the semester had already begun.

When I told Mam that I had passed the examination she was overjoyed. Mother had always held education in high regard. When my sister Meselu decided to become a teacher instead of going to college, Mam did not disguise her disappointment. Now that the future seemed so bleak, it was more important to her than ever that I pursue my education. Her hopes lay not in her own life but in those of her children.

If Meselu had lived nearby, I would not have thought twice about boarding the bus. Mam was confident that she could manage by herself and even joked that if I were to die that very moment the family would not join me in the grave, but would keep on living. But for the moment I wasn't sure if I could leave the family in such a distraught condition. I had just about decided to pass up the opportunity to enter university when an event that was otherwise outside the affairs of my family persuaded me to do otherwise.

In Asebe Teferi, the underground guerrilla units of the EPRP were more active than elsewhere in the province. There was a strong peasant base around the city that provided a great deal of support for the party. The forest cover in the areas nearby furnished a formidable hideout for those on the run. Furthermore, there were a number of armed insurrections in the region—the Oromo National Liberation Movement, for instance, was expanding rapidly and was actively recruiting new members. The culmination of all these factors was that the EPRP guerrilla units there maintained a vigilance more extreme than anything I had previously encountered.

I used to look in on my family at least once a week. One day, as I visited Mam, one of the local members of the Meison party was grazed by a bullet, apparently fired by a member of a guerrilla unit. He was not seriously injured, but was visibly shaken. He came out of the hospital the same day and joined a manhunt for his assailant. No one, including himself, was sure of the identity of the attacker, but everyone was convinced that it had to do with the EPRP. The search was being conducted from door to door. Any place where a human being could conceivably hide was being searched.

They found me at my grandmother's house. The cadre, who had been born and raised in the city, recognized that I was from out of town. He gave me a chance to explain myself and spent about fifteen minutes listening to me and going through my documents. Normally a question or two would be enough for one to be labelled as reactionary or identified as a comrade, for it had long since been established that one could only be on one side of the fence. The fact that we were refugees must have appeased them. In those days, there was a good deal of sympathy in the region for victims of the war. I must admit that I have played that part up more than once to save myself from blind roundups. It worked again; the cadre decided that I could live.

I felt extremely fortunate for having survived this last brush with death, but knew it would be only a matter of time before a similar incident happened. Late in October 1977, knowing that my refugee status would only hold water for another month or two, I packed a bag and headed to the university in Addis Ababa, where I hoped to become lost in a faceless crowd.

SEVEN MONTHS
OF DARKNESS

ADDIS ABABA is a city that has the emperor at its heart. It expands outwards from his palace, fanning west and east. There exist two distinct nuclei to the city, like the twin chambers of a heart, each pumping life into the vast sprawl with the rising of the sun. One is named Merkato, the other Piassa.

Piassa is the legacy of Italians, who made a brief appearance in Ethiopia half a century ago. It has that unmistakably European touch—narrow winding asphalt roads lined with cafés and restaurants and Western-style buildings carved out of the surrounding hills. Piassa, however, is very small, a mere hyphen in the vast text of the surrounding countryside.

Compared to the sophisticated brevity of Piassa, Merkato exists with the explosive insistence of an expletive. Cranky Fiat taxis fight for what little room there is with wild-eyed donkeys and men urinating in the middle of the boulevard; barefoot hawkers outshout each other for the attention of bewildered customers, abusing them when they get no response; angry peasants wield machetes at any Gurage merchant who attempts to defraud them; and fastidiously dressed pickpockets make the rounds, levying taxes from unsuspecting newcomers.

Indeed, when I was in the city, theft was one of the three towering vices—prostitution and violence being the other two. The most helpful advice I was given before leaving home was to be on the lookout for these human vultures. In Addis Ababa, bags are clutched to bosom, jewellery is tucked out of sight, pocket knives are held at the ready. On a single trip from Merkato to the university campus, I witnessed six successful robberies and nine failed attempts.

While waiting for a transfer bus, I saw a young lady waving for a taxi. There were very few of the old Fiats around, and too many passengers, eager to escape the neighbourhood. People shouldered up against each other, shouting and shoving until the crowd had consumed the sidewalk and half of the road. The young lady seemed out of place; with grace and restraint, she raised her hand every so often to announce her destination and the fare she was willing to part with. One driver slowly trolled the road, ears perked, looking for a tempting deal. He pulled over a few feet away from her to pick up two passengers headed for Piassa and one for Arat Kilo. The cabby needed one more passenger. He reversed the car—running over one man's foot and just missing a stray cat—to ask the young lady if she was willing to walk half of her trip. She declined, deciding to wait for another cab. It was a fateful decision.

Unbeknownst to the young lady, the small suitcase so carefully planted at her feet had been noticed by the vultures. They slowly circled, waiting for another cab to pull over and the driver to begin bartering with her. The lady was desperate and her frustration was obvious. Unable to meet the fare suggested by the cabby, she gave up and decided to start walking. But when she reached down for her suitcase, she clutched only a fistful of stale air.

I saw the robber walk calmly away, the small suitcase tucked inside his oversized coat. I wanted to do something, but the robber's partner read my mind. He lingered behind, and flashed a foot-long knife at me from inside his jacket. I was persuaded to mind my own business.

The poor lady fell to the ground screaming, pulling at her hair and beseeching the gods and the *Adbar* to intervene. She pulled at the tattered clothes of passersby, begging for help, pleading with merchants to intervene and telling the world that the old, moth-eaten suitcase held her only worldly possessions, and that if they would only give it back to her she would never again set foot in that part of town. Her pleas, of course, were in vain.

When my bus finally arrived, it was full. A sea of human faces peered out of the windows at me, one huge creature with thousands of dark eyes and countless small mouths. The doors yawned wide, but no one emerged. I considered waiting for another bus, but given what I had just witnessed, I decided to squeeze in, becoming part of the hideous beast.

The bus smelt of generations of sweat and unrequited sex. Men rubbed their crotches against the rear ends of women in front of them. They breathed on the backs of the women's necks and made lurid remarks. The women played dead— there was nowhere to go. Instead, they lowered their heads and prayed.

Just as I was beginning to lose myself in the din, the lewd murmurs and deafening noise of the engine were shattered by a ten-year-old boy who cried out that his mother had been run over by a speeding truck in Merkato that very morning, leaving her only son an orphan. He was now lost. Someone had placed him on the bus, but he didn't know how to get home, or, for that matter, if he would ever get home again.

Some of the passengers looked at the boy askance, others with sympathy. All were distracted by his plight. When the bus pulled into the next station two of the boy's friends got off first. One of the boys left with two purses, the other with, among other things, a pair of earrings that he had snatched, almost as an afterthought, from a girl at the front of the bus, savaging her earlobes in the process. No one intervened.

I was still reeling from the shock of the brazen thievery that infested Addis Ababa when I was confronted by yet another repulsive fact: the rampant sex trade.

The practice of prostitution in Ethiopia is as old as the country itself and as prolific as unanswered prayers. There remains some prejudice against prostitutes, but no more than that harboured against Catholics. In Jijiga, ladies of the evening confine their practice to bars and restaurants. The prostitutes are all waitresses—and the waitresses are all prostitutes. The bars and restaurants are located at the town centre, so the obtrusive presence of these working girls on the day-to-day life of the sinful populace is less pronounced. The only time that disgruntled housewives are forced to acknowledge the threat posed by the beautiful, young and exotic-scented competition is on Tuesdays.

For generations, men had convinced their wives that they contracted gonorrhea while sitting on a chair recently vacated by a patient. The priests agreed. But times had changed. It was now clear that the cause of this dreadful disease was the "early water" that prostitutes used to wash their private parts. This water was carelessly tossed out into the streets by hundreds upon hundreds of prostitutes each morning. Men, walking over such water, contracted the disease. Housewives demanded that the government create new policies to protect them from "early water." They demanded immediate results. But the government had decided to peer under the skirts of the working women instead. The only economical way of controlling the devastating effects of gonorrhea was to make weekly hospital checkups mandatory for prostitutes, and Tuesday had been legislated as a perfect day to accomplish just that. Decent women stayed away from the hospital on Tuesdays, so no one would think that they showed their private parts to complete strangers.

The health officer in Jijiga was the most conscientious and the hardest-working man in town. His job didn't end at the hospital. Each night he made the rounds, list in hand, looking for young women who had failed to appear at their checkup. In a single night, this officer collected hundreds of birrs in fines. He then put the money away in a safe place—where the government couldn't find it. After all, he reasoned, if the government felt that money was owed to it, then it should damn well make the rounds itself!

The health officer in Jijiga was not insensitive, nor did he judge those men who slipped, under the cover of darkness, into the bars to have a private moment with one of the girls. But then again, he was one of them. Every night the health officer would walk from bar to bar, looking for new arrivals and sampling the merchandise.

In Addis Ababa, the sex trade spilt over the bounds of bars and restaurants. Office secretaries, schoolgirls and married women alike indulged in the wayward practice. It was an overtime job, an extracurricular activity, a way to feed one's children. The government turned a blind eye; the health officer was told to keep an eye on reactionaries instead; and wantonness was officially recognized as the most affordable form of democracy—the only form of public intercourse, in fact, that didn't send the regime into one of its violent tantrums.

It even helped the tourist trade. Arab men clad in desert garb and bathed in oceans of whiskey staggered from hotel lobby to hotel lobby in search of a peerless pimp. They had generations of lust to quench, for at home they were forbidden to even talk to a woman, or see her face, let alone admire her sensuous ass. They wanted them young and old, fat and skinny, with dark skin or green skin, with large breasts or many breasts, and the pimps obliged.

Schoolgirls were persuaded to cut classes so they could earn a fast buck. Baby-faced teenagers with angelic smiles, their mothers' warnings still ringing in their ears, giggled and dilly-dallied in the back alleys of the big hotels until they were picked up by some unkempt, bow-legged animal. They broke the seventh commandment, not merely for earthly desires, but also for the grandest cause: the motherland. The girls needed a new pair of Levis and the junta needed some more munitions.

I wished I had been born in another universe.

ADDIS ABABA UNIVERSITY was the only institution of higher learning in the country. It had once been known as Haile Selassie I University in honour of its founding father, the deposed emperor. After the revolution, like many other institutions with names that recalled the bygone era, it shed its imperial skin.

The university had four major campuses spread out across the capital city, offering a sober and pleasant contrast to the surrounding ruckus. The main campus was centrally located on a high plateau, surrounded by important government and foreign offices. It was fenced in by three-metre-high stone walls manned by security men in beige uniforms, the university insignia on their jackets and caps. The university was no older than I was, but it appeared to have matured faster, earning the respect of many in the process.

The student dormitories, cafeterias and all other amenities were located on campus, and their services were free. There were no tuition fees, let alone boarding or lodging expenses. Even the blankets, bedsheets and toilet paper one used were issued at no expense to the student. To make sure that there was no mistaking the nationality of those involved in designing and building most of the university, the various gadgets and fixtures within them had the "American Standard" imprint on them. There were three red-brick, four-storey apartment buildings for the men. The women had a smaller building and a few detached houses. Men and women lived in separate residences, but managed to steal into each other's quarters for quick and discreet acts of coitus.

There was a grand library on the main campus. It was a very modern hexagon, enclosed by six-metre-high glass, which, to the horror of the school officials, the highland birds refused to acknowledge as a legitimate wall. The architecture and construction of the building had long been the wonder of the town. It was obvious that the hands responsible had issued from another universe—that it was not something a two-legged, short-tempered and plain-skinned creature, such as a human, could either conceive or compose.

The library was named after that famous fallen American president, John F. Kennedy. A statue of the young man, shoulder-high, was placed in the building's small lobby. His famous quotation—"Ask not what your country can do for you, but what you can do for your country"—was engraved on a metal plate. For the emperor to dedicate this remarkable building to a foreigner was, indeed, a noble gesture, high in the white clouds, and had very little to do with the fact that Mr. Kennedy paid for the building.

The main campus was graced with flowerbeds, water fountains (although seldom splashing water), exotic trees and carved stones, each deliberately placed by careful hands. The lion was everywhere. One couldn't go from one building to another without bumping into a full-sized statue of this venerable animal. There was a sense of divine permanence about the Administration Building, which sat facing the main gate. Its columns were cathedral-like; its stairs were carved from expensive stones; its banisters dwarfed the railings of a respectable bridge. The ceilings were high and painstakingly decorated, and huge chandeliers looked heavily down on the mortal souls who were permitted to walk beneath them. It had once been a palace, the original home of Menelik II, King of Kings of Ethiopia.

I TOOK A DORMITORY room on the main campus. My classrooms were in the science faculty, at Arat Kilo, four kilometres away. There were dormitories, a cafeteria and other amenities at Arat Kilo, but I chose to stay closer to the people I knew, students from my hometown. It wasn't that I longed for familiar faces and reassuring smiles, but that I felt I needed to know where they were and what they were up to, as the times required.

For the young and free-thinking youth of Ethiopia, 1977 was an exceedingly ominous year. Addis Ababa was shaken by a political tremor, and threatened to erupt with a ferocity of biblical proportions. The sun shone, but the sky was dark; the wind blew, but nothing moved. Many stayed indoors. When they ventured out, it was with the painful knowledge that they might never again see the light of day. It was a time when many young people simply vanished into thin air.

Army trucks and Jeeps were everywhere. Hostile soldiers wearing war gear were perched on these death traps, one leg hanging over, ready to pounce on anyone betraying fear. The trucks coasted downhill, engines shut off, to sneak up behind unsuspecting citizens. Militiamen peered into the face of each passing youth, reading his political aura, looking for signs of betrayal.

Many were picked up and thrown into the back of a truck. No one asked questions. If one was innocent enough to warrant release, it would be established in a week or two; so why hurry? In the meantime, it was safer to stay off the streets, out of the revolution's way.

The jails and prisons were teeming with panic-stricken children whose parents didn't even know their whereabouts. Such information was given out only on a need-to-know basis, and, the junta argued, the family members didn't need to know. I feared the jails in Addis Ababa even more than I had feared the war I had left behind, as there was no one in town to come looking for me.

Since the *kebeles* were ready to dispatch one across the bourn at the slightest provocation, I kept an eye on my hometown boys, making sure that I was not being sold out. I lived like a distraught gazelle on an East African steppe. I had to know where the lions were before risking settling down to graze, or taking the tiniest and most casual of steps towards a drying water hole. I sought them out with every breath. I searched for their scent. I stood facing them, watching their every move, while nibbling at a blade or quenching my thirst. That was nature's cruel interpretation of living in harmony—and harmony was what I needed most.

I shared a dormitory room with three other boys. Two of my dorm mates were from Jijiga, and the third was from Addis Ababa. The name of this other boy was Asfaw, but he preferred being called Alex.

Alex was something of an oddity, like those objects that every violent flood sweeps along its exacting course, only to spit out later, intact. He had survived the revolution's tidal wave for three tumultuous years without ruffling a feather, and vowed to stay on high ground, not smearing his delicate cowboy boots, until the storm had subsided. Alex thought little of anyone else, and held young radicals as the lowest of the low. He harboured an innate contempt for revolutionaries and their obnoxious ideals and considered the revolution a misconceived conspiracy, organized by barefoot peasants and half-witted militiamen to rob him of his imported hippie life.

Alex seldom spent the night in the dorm. He rarely came to school at all. The university was too modest for his grand ambitions—he was on his way to America. He had two sisters and a brother in that rich country, and they had already found him a good university. It was only a matter of time before he said Adios! He assured us that even as he spoke his father was looking for the right palms to grease, so his son could get an exit visa. He had already bribed half of the military bigwigs, and had only to cover the rest. Of course, by the time he had finished, he would have to start over again, because the first palms would once more be dry and parched. It was an endless cycle, but, Alex assured us, he was a man of endless means.

Alex dressed and walked like an American. He even spoke like one. Alex's English had an unmistakably American accent, a clear indication that he had been born on the wrong side of the Atlantic. Alex knew the names of all the American states and their capital cities. He knew where to find the tallest buildings in that vast country, the longest bridges, and the trendiest shops and nightclubs. He knew America better than the Americans, which pained him all the more since he was the one condemned to live in Ethiopia, not the Americans.

Alex was the only one in town who could speak Amharic that the Duke of Edinburgh could easily follow without his humble translator butting in. When talking about his weekend, for instance, he would say:

ቀዳሚ Piassa ሄፒ ነበር I met a girl ምን የመሰለች ቆንጆ ልጅ። Jolly Bar ወሰድኳት። cappuccino እና cake አዘዝን። ከዛ Ras Hotel ወሰዶ አገባኃይኳት። we made love for six hours!

Alex occupied the bunk bed above me, but since he seldom spent the night in the dormitory, I used his bedsheets as spares.

I WALKED THE four kilometres to the science faculty twice a day. With each trip, my chances of disappearing into the unknown became more statistically significant. School had started in September, and by November, barely days after I had arrived in the big city, the political volcano that had long been rumbling beneath us finally blew its top. The calamity was beyond anyone's wildest imagination. The streets, public parks and market stalls were littered with the open-mouthed dead.

The bullet-riddled bodies of children, with notes describing their contrived crimes carelessly pinned to their tattered shirts, greeted us every morning. Their crimes were ill-defined. The tags always read the same: "This was a reactionary! The Red Terror Shall Flourish!"

I watched on the common room TV as the chairman of the junta gave his public address on November 12, 1977. He explained: "The Red Terror was launched to curb the ever-increasing White Terror being waged on us by the EPRP. . . . In the preceding year alone over a hundred government officials and officers were done to death by this underground terrorist group." The *kebeles* were urged to be merciless against reactionaries, to intensify the "Red Terror."

Beginning in September 1976, the underground party, the EPRP, had intensified its campaign of terror against government officials. The bullet-riddled bodies of *kebele* administrators, political cadres and teachers in the junta's ideological school were left in public places. The government denounced the action as the "White Terror." Mass imprisonment and torture followed. Some were done to death in places where the terror was most severe. When nothing seemed to help, the junta decided to conduct a nationwide cleansing campaign— anyone who could not readily produce a badge of allegiance could meet with a swift and immediate death. The "Red Terror" was born.

I was used to seeing the dead. I had partaken in wars and seldom shuddered at the sight of mutilated remains. Murder itself is not repulsive, only the lack of justification for it. When society deems carnage justifiable, it organizes a parade to celebrate the occasion, heaping praise on the murderers, addressing them as crusaders, martyrs and patriots; it engraves their names on expensive stones and lays their remains to rest in public places, weaving their achievements into the national anthem and placing their likeness on our currency. No one would pause to reflect on what these idols of ours had actually done to claim our respect.

I was no different from my fellow man. What caught me off guard was not the mere sight of the bullet-riddled bodies of children, but the very arbitrariness of it. I knew that those boys and girls were no more guilty of any crime than I, or indeed millions of others.

Life-and-death decisions were now being made in the local *kebeles* and peasant associations. The old judiciary system with its various codes and canons had been put on the shelf—it no longer applied even to common criminals like pickpockets and arsonists. It was the *kebeles* who decided what punishment fitted each crime, and how justice should be enforced. There was no written law to guide them in this difficult task, but that was a mere detail.

The Red Terror had been waged in many urban centres and some rural areas, but it had never played itself out in so stark and gruesome a way as it did in the capital city. Here it reached a horror surpassed only in the darkest days of Nazi Germany and, perhaps, Stalin's purge of 1937. During the seven months that the "Red Terror" was in full bloom, all crimes serious enough to warrant a jail sentence were punished by the firing squad. An estimated 100,000 political opponents of the regime were dispatched across the bourn by the time the meat-mincer finally stopped whizzing.

Justice was swift. From the time of detention to execution

a mere twelve hours elapsed. The mayhem was public. The regime did not deny it. After all, the proof was out on the streets for everyone, including the foreign diplomats, to see. But the world outside kept its silence, as no one's economic interests had been compromised, and the most vocal opponents of the regime had been either done to death or made to rot away in various dungeons. And so the campaign was allowed to run its full course, coming to a halt only when it ran out of fuel.

For the first few days of the campaign I was tortured by what I was forced to see. I struggled hard, day and night, during classes and dreams. But, after a while, even this form of death became commonplace. It lost its potency. Throughout the carnage, I attended class.

One day, I saw a young mathematics teacher being followed by three Meison cadres in a Toyota Land Cruiser. Across the street from the campus gate, the young man got out of his taxi, paid the fare and was about to cross the road when he noticed the off-white truck that had been tailing his taxi. The Land Cruiser was one of countless identical vehicles bought by the regime for its various cronies. The young man realized what was transpiring, and knew that he was doomed.

The cadres jumped off the truck before their driver had a chance to put the brakes on. They shouted orders at the bewildered mathematician. They told him to raise his hands high above his head, and freeze in his tracks. The young man didn't oblige. He started fiddling with a charm that was hanging from his necklace, while walking backwards. The cadres were quick to realize what the young teacher was up to. They refused to be cheated of their prize catch now that it was so teasingly close. They yelled more orders as they took some measured steps towards him, their AK-47 machine guns trained on his chest.

The young man's hands shook, threatening to fly from his wrists, but he managed to untie the small capsule in time. He bit into it, infuriating the cadres, who tossed him in mid-air with a torrent of machine-gun fire. I hoped the cyanide killed him first.

An old lady who was walking in the firing line was an unintended casualty. I, along with a few others, hit the black tarmac in time. We lay still, faces down, hearts pounding so hard I thought the asphalt would crumble beneath us, waiting for permission to test our legs. The cadres were talking among themselves, unaware of us at their feet. What seemed like hours passed and I was still on the ground. Cars sped by, and pedestrians changed their routes. A long black limousine ambled down the tarmac. I was surprised that the driver had the courage to slow down. When it was three metres away, the dark-tinted rear window rolled down, and out of the corner of my eye I saw the head of a white man with a well-tended goatee. He was from the U.S. Embassy, a block away. The cadres showed scant interest; world opinion had long since lost meaning for them.

The cadres boarded their Land Cruiser, leaving the dead and the terrified on the ground.

ONE TUESDAY, I left class early and dashed to my dormitory to drop off my things before going out to meet a friend. Alex was lying on his bed, fully clothed, his cowboy boots still on. There was nothing unusual about that. I said hello to him, but received no response. *That* was unusual. I tried again, but he kept mum, staring at the blank ceiling. It looked as though he was on some kind of sedative. I decided to leave him alone.

When I returned to my dorm after dinner, Alex was still in bed. He hadn't moved an inch from his previous position, and was still staring at the blank ceiling. My two other roommates were already there, suspended in a rapt silence. Alex's disease weighed down on all of us. I nudged the boy to cheer him up a bit, but got no response. I asked him if he'd had anything to eat and if there was anything I could do. Still no response. I felt very uncomfortable being in the same room, and decided to stay out until bedtime.

When I returned at eleven o'clock, I didn't look up to see how Alex was faring. The cowboy boot dangling from the edge of the bed told me that he was still suspended in a comatose-like state.

The following day, after lunch, I made a conscious decision to return to the residence and find out about Alex's mysterious disease. I couldn't get him out of my mind that whole morning. It was an awkward thing.

We wanted to inform Alex's parents of his mysterious condition, but no one knew where they lived. We knew that the school officials wouldn't care to intervene. Thousands were actually dying a step away from the campus gate; why would they care about someone playing dead at the government's expense?

When I returned, there were two exotically dressed and perfumed young women, an elderly lady and a distraught old man inside our room. They were Alex's family, come to see how their dear boy was faring. They told us what had befallen him.

Two days ago, Alex had been ambling about his neighbourhood as usual, oblivious to the war that was raging around him and looking for a promising date. A *kebele* official who harboured ill feelings towards the haughty young man saw an opportunity to exact revenge: he made a quick detour, bringing his Land Cruiser around to accost Alex. He wanted to know what Alex was doing out on the street at nine o'clock at night; if he had clearance from the local cadres regarding his political background; and what his latest contribution to the revolution had been.

The *kebele* official already knew all the answers, of course, and Alex was escorted to the local *kebele*. However, there was a slight diversion. The angry young cadre decided to place Alex, unknown to other *kebele* officials and his family members, among the twenty-eight youths to be done to death that night.

At four o'clock in the morning, the usual dreadful army truck pulled up inside the *kebele* compound. The door of the crowded jail was thrown wide, and soldiers stood shoulder to shoulder on either side of the door directing the condemned youths to their seats on the truck. As they fired the engine, the gates of the compound were unchained.

Before the rear awning of the green canvas cover had been buttoned down, a *kebele* official glanced at the doomed young men and caught sight of a familiar face. He looked closer at the boy. "Aren't you Asfaw?" he asked. The boy, who was too shocked to cry or talk, nodded. "What are you doing here?" the *kebele* official asked. It was a silly question, but a ray of hope for the terrified young man.

The *kebele* official, who had always been on agreeable terms with Alex's family, went looking for the individual responsible for this error. Finding him, he vouched for Alex's innocence. "I know this kid like one of my own. I practically raised him. He's not into politics. In fact, he wouldn't recognize a political thought if it slapped him right across the face."

Alex was freed, and taken home by his guardian angel. His family was ecstatic that their dear boy had been given another lease on life. But, there was one problem: how were they going to keep him alive? The two-legged hyenas roamed the neighbourhood at will. They walked from door to door at very odd times of the day, searching every possible hideout, looking for their next victim. Alex had to be kept out of their sight, but where? That was when his mother thought of the university campus. It was still a safe haven for many.

Alex would have weathered the storm, at least for another few months, had it not been for his suddenly unhinged head. The family decided to take him to see an out-of-town medicine man, far away from the killing fields. When we bade him goodbye, he no longer recognized us. I still don't know what became of him.

We DID NOT REMAIN immune to the outside turmoil for long. The fragile peace of my first semester on campus had been the result of our collective anonymity. Students came from all over the country seeking safety. Now, that anonymity had become a desperate commodity. The curtain fell for many when their hometown *kebeles* sent lists of "suspects" to the Meison headquarters in Addis Ababa.

Soon, Meison cadres in progressive suits (similar to the Chinese uniform) could be seen walking stiffly into our classrooms, dormitories and cafeterias, picking out "suspects" with an exaggerated, almost theatrical show of force. Days were spent in terror, and the nights were no easier. Late in the evening, or early in the morning, when the bars and nightclubs closed, the students' dormitories became the last stop for cadres, who, having drunk themselves into a stupor, would break into the residences checking for signs of conspiracy. The washrooms were their first stop. In the unlikely event that there was not a single slur against the regime already written on the grey walls, the eager cadres would think nothing of scribbling a few incriminating imputations of their own.

The theatrics of life and death followed. We could hear their raucous name-calling from inside our rooms as doors were banged with the butt of a gun. Everyone on the floor was made to stand in the corridor, wearing nothing but underwear. We were then ordered to expose the reactionaries responsible for the graffiti in the washrooms. Our silence was proof of what they had always suspected: a conspiracy. Everybody knew that the university was a breeding ground for reactionaries.

Most of us escaped these incidents with slightly bruised pride, as we were made to clean the washroom walls with our toothbrushes or tongues. A few individuals went back to bed with bloodied noses.

Now and then, they took one for the road.

By MID-1978, THE "Red Terror" reached its climax. In Addis Ababa, between one hundred and two hundred youths were done to death each night, their remains left under the blazing sun until dusk settled over the horizon. Families of the victims lined the roadsides in tormented silence, making sure that their loved ones were not abused in death as they had been in life.

When it was time to remove the remains from the deserted streets, they followed the garbage trucks carrying the remains to the city morgue. There they stood in line to settle their bill at the cash register. They had to pay twenty-five birr for the bullet that the junta had advanced them to dispatch their loved one. Only then would they get the remains.

The junta was not insensitive. The unclaimed remains were kept in the morgue for another day, in case some tardy relations showed up. Only after a forty-eight-hour period of grace did they toss the remains outside the city limits. Addis Ababa's suburbs became a movable feast for countless hyenas and vultures.

A MOURNFUL GHOST

HE REVOLUTION was a very worry-prone mother; she kept close tabs on her children. She might not pack lunch for you, but she wanted to know how you spent every hour of your day. If you expressed a wish to go anywhere in town, she wanted you to carry a proper identification card with an up-to-date photograph issued from your local *kebele*. If you wished to go anywhere out of town, no matter how close, an additional travel document was necessary. This document explained why you were taking the trip and how long the trip would last. The expiry date could not exceed six months; otherwise the devoted mother-revolution would suffer a panic attack. And if, God forbid, you desired to travel to one of the restricted cities, like the ports of Assab and Massawa, then you'd better have a pair of strong wings—a simple *kebele* document would never do.

Roaming the countryside at will, as in the old days, was considered a bourgeois thing to do; communism had no place for such freewheeling. Where you went and what you did was everybody's business. *Did you say that you were planning to go to town this coming Saturday, to see your hairdresser? That might be all right, but first visit your* kebele *to fill out a triplicate form stating your intentions clearly; the original is for your file in the* kebele, *the yellow copy is for the local cadre, and the pink one is for your own records. If there is no ulterior motive involved, and your intended hairstyle is in complete conformity with the spirit of the revolution, you might be issued a day pass. And you had better see your hairdresser, because it will be noted in your record. By the way, an Afro is a no-no—it is evidence of the corrupting influence of American imperialism.*

When the school year ended, students were issued internal passports that allowed them to return home for two months of vacation. With my internal passport and a recommendation letter from the university, I went to the bus terminal to purchase a one-way ticket to Asebe Teferi, where I would spend the summer with Mam and the kids. I got out of my taxi and carefully treaded to the ticket kiosk. The ticket agent, an elderly man, glanced with tired eyes at the documents I presented to him, telling me without looking up to return early the next day and stand in line. I rented a hotel room close to the bus terminal and set my alarm clock for 3 A.M. As an extra precaution, I requested the front desk attendant to wake me as well, greasing his palm with five birr for the favour. Then I went to bed early.

When I finally arrived at the bus station the next morning, my eyes sleep-red, I was surprised to see that the line was already a light-year long. Upon closer inspection I noted that it was not composed of the usual travellers, but of homeless beggars. Cardboard-box shelters were strewn in a ragged line that extended willy-nilly to the ticket kiosk. At around 5 A.M., the beggars were given a few birr and relieved of their waiting duties by the real passengers, who flashed mischievous smiles at the ragtag end of the line, where I, and other less ingenious passengers, stood. Fortunately for me, a second coach was ordered and I was able to get a seat.

We were to make a stop about one hundred kilometres past Addis Ababa, in the city of Nazareth, for breakfast. On the way, the driver stopped periodically to pick up passengers, until every seat in the bus carried twice the designed capacity, and the aisle was a sea of human faces. When the steamy insides of the bus were so full that not a single limb could be moved or eye blinked without disturbing a ring of neighbours, the driver made the extra passengers sit on the rack on top of the bus. We must have offered a strange sight to passersby. Dozens of sweaty faces pressed circles into the dirty windows while a tangle of bodies, hooked by one or more limbs to the precarious seats on top of the bus, jolted and swayed with the uneven road, like an angry nest of snakes. Shortly before we arrived in Nazareth, the driver divested the bus of all these extras, returning our bus to its natural freight so that he would not be fined by the traffic police who waited at the gates of the city. These extras wandered into the city in ones and twos looking no better for their ride than if they had journeyed the full hundred kilometres on foot. Later, the driver and his assistant would divide the extra fares between them.

The bus pulled into a large restaurant in Nazareth called the Gion Hotel. The driver announced that anyone thinking of visiting any of the other establishments nearby would risk missing the bus, and after the morning's experience few passengers needed further persuasion. I joined the others and filed into the crowded restaurant. My mind was still thick with the heat of the bus when I thought I saw a familiar face.

I had almost passed him by when something about the man stopped me in my tracks. We stared at each other across the crowded restaurant for what felt like an eternity, as the realization of his identity slowly struck me. This was one of the rare moments when I saw Wondwossen's father in civilian clothes and it took me a while to put a name to the face. The man had changed considerably. His hair was thinning and what was left of it was almost uniformly grey. Gone was the imposing figure he cut, and the purposeful gait that I admired. I suspected that he, like many other officers, had been relieved of his job in the army. Whenever a battle was lost on any of the countless war fronts, the chairman of the junta always found a sacrificial goat. The lucky ones were sent packing; the unlucky paid with their lives.

I was staring at the man, not knowing what to say, when he finally broke the silence. He spoke casually, remarking that I had grown up, his words passing over me like the warm desert wind. Then he asked me what I had been doing since we left Jijiga, and I told him that I had been studying at the university. He fell silent for a while, sighed deeply, and muttered, as though talking to himself, "Wondwossen would have been a college student, too."

What might have seemed the most casual of remarks to anyone who overheard the conversation threw me headfirst into the past. I relived all those years spent with Wondwossen and wept. Wondwossen's father put his hand on my shoulder and tried to calm me, but something had broken and the tears would not stop.

There was so much I wanted to know about Wondwossen's family. I had always wondered how his mother had fared. After all, he was a prayer child and losing him, in his prime, must have left an indelible scar in her psyche. I wondered how his sisters had managed without him. Wondwossen was a jewel to his siblings. They loved and protected him. I remembered how, whenever he ran out of pocket money, all he had to do was ask one of his sisters, who would be eager to help. If he longed for a neighbourhood girl locked up behind the chain fence of her family residence, one of his sisters would always manage to reach her somehow and deliver his love letter.

I also dreaded encountering his family members. And so today, to be confronted with a ghost in this unexpected place and at this uncertain time, at a period in my life when I despaired of ever putting the past behind me, was too much to bear.

When we finally parted, in a painful silence, I saw Wondwossen's father remove his glasses and wipe his eyes with a handkerchief. Indeed, every man has his breaking point.

AN ENFEEBLED SUN

—————

T HAD BEEN almost a year since I had seen Mam and the kids, and I didn't know what to expect. We'd exchanged letters from time to time, but one couldn't say much in letters, for fear of having them intercepted. My anxiety was mounting as I got off at the bus terminal. I headed up the hill for home, passing street dogs fighting over bare bones and children running around in tattered clothes. The year I'd stayed in Addis Ababa had magnified the poverty of the town.

Turning the last corner, I felt a lump in my throat. Passing by the open door of the kitchen, I saw Mam sorting out split lentils as she prepared the day's meal. Tentatively, she raised her head to look. Realizing it was me, she dropped the woven plate on the ground, spilling the pinkish seeds across the dirt floor. I ran towards her and fell into her embrace. We must have been crying loudly, because neighbours gathered at the door. I kissed each one of them, and then my siblings, who soon joined us. When the hullabaloo subsided, I noticed that Mam had lost a considerable amount of weight, her eyes were sunken, and her cheeks were hollow and pale. The children were so badly dressed and so emaciated that one could easily have mistaken them for waifs. Our new home was not much better than when I had seen it last.

I soon learned that my younger sister Almaz was in jail— the victim of a blind roundup. After lunch, I went to visit her, accompanied by Mam. The detention centre was a large camp, fenced in by barbed wire, but the sheer number of children crammed together made it look like an undersized playground. A guard notified Almaz of her visitors, and she came running. We hugged, kissed, cried and laughed all at once. She must have been used to her surroundings, because she wanted to talk about many things, but I was apprehensive. A guard could easily decide that a visitor should stay. Promising to visit her soon, we left her standing at the fence.

I liked Almaz a great deal, but she was much too rebellious. Once, while still in Jijiga, a boy from her school, emulating the adult men he had seen, attempted to show his appreciation of Almaz's beauty by slapping her butt as she walked past him. Almaz was stunned. She couldn't believe that anyone had dared violate her in this way, let alone this skinny boy. She grabbed the boy, who quickly became incomprehensible with shock, and dragged him forward by the collar. When he attempted to resist her, she let go—causing him to fall back into the dirt. Almaz then mounted him and started punching him and pounding his head into the ground. A huge crowd gathered, but everyone was far too amused by the turn of events to be of any help.

When the boy got over his initial shock, he kicked Almaz from his chest. She fell on the ground, and as the boy attempted to run away, she grasped a handful of fine dirt and tossed it in his eyes. She had completely blinded him; he was now at her mercy. Fortunately for the boy, a man who was passing by intervened on his behalf. Almaz was finally held back, though the sheepish boy with tattered shirt and bloodied nose would have preferred it if she had killed him outright. Indeed, after the incident, he became the butt of his friends' jokes, a broken young man who would have needed divine intervention to regain his dignity.

When Almaz returned home that day, she was hailed as a heroine by Mam, who believed, despite tradition, that all women should follow Almaz's example. It was a good thing Dad was out of town. At the time he was stationed in the town of Kabri Dahar, some five hundred kilometres to the south, coming home only three or four times a year. Almaz knew little of him, though she would soon experience his crude interpretation of discipline.

On one of those rare occasions that our father was home, Almaz happened to break a neighbour's window. Dad considered the whole episode to be quite unladylike and impudent. He instructed her to go into the backyard and select a branch for her punishment.

When disciplining us, Dad would tell us to choose the branch that we deserved. It was his interpretation of democracy. The whole business was very tricky. We had to weigh the pros and cons of each branch, so that it was not too hard, for obvious reasons, yet not too flimsy either, so that he didn't use the belt instead, which would have been by far the most painful. After carefully trimming the leaves from the branch, we would hand it to Dad, grip first.

Almaz's reaction was to stand erect before Dad, staring into his eyes. Mam, knowing Almaz's disposition well, held her breath, arms folded to her chest. We, the children, rose from our seats and pressed our backs against the wall. After what seemed an eternity, Almaz appeared to acquiesce, and left for the backyard.

As soon as Almaz had stepped out of the door, Mam started pleading with Dad, begging him to forgive Almaz, who was, after all, only thirteen. She argued that Almaz was unfamiliar with Dad's ways, as he had been away for most of her childhood. Dad was unrelenting.

A few minutes later, Almaz made her grand appearance. She strode up to father, and dropped a leaf the size of a butterfly in his ashtray. She stood defiantly before him, head high, hands at the waist, staring right into his eyes. The silence was deafening. Mam put her hand to her mouth to stifle a scream. We retreated farther into the corner, away from the line drawn between Almaz and Father. Dad's mouth had gone slack with astonishment; his eyes bulged. When he composed himself, he leaped from his seat to strangle Almaz, but before he had passed around the huge dining-room table to where Almaz stood, she was gone—she had disappeared from the room, and was running from the compound.

She spent the next two days with her godmother, the landlady next door. On the third day, Mam and Almaz's godmother organized a group of four elders to intervene. The elders spent most of the afternoon behind closed doors with Dad, while Mam, the neighbours and a few close relations waited anxiously outside, hoping and praying that Dad would relent.

After many agonizing hours, the door to the living room opened. One of the elders stepped out and asked Mam to enter. The elders had established that Almaz was obviously under the influence of the Devil. What else could have made her so

outrageously defiant? They advised Mam to take her to a medicine man before she was permitted to re-enter her home.

The next day Mam took Almaz to a renowned medicine
woman who lived in the Somali-speaking part of town. In her
incense- and *ood*-scented chamber, the woman interviewed
Mam alone, before admitting Almaz for a cursory examination.
The medicine woman peered at Almaz's palms and eyelids,
then grabbed a handful of coffee beans from a container beside
her, piling them on the small table in front of her. The medicine woman asked Almaz to split the roasted beans into two
piles by running a knife through them. Quietly, the medicine
woman counted each pile of beans, making a mental note.
Almaz was asked to split the coffee beans twice more before the
medicine woman was able to establish, unequivocally, what
was the matter with her.

"Your daughter has crossed the path of the Devil at the
garbage dump during the high sun," the medicine woman pronounced, addressing Mam, who was sitting in the dark.

It was well known that humans had to take care to avoid
the dump site during the high sun, the time between midday
and three o'clock in the afternoon when the devils came out of
hiding to feast on rubbish, sing and dance on ashes, and mock
the gods. Those who had business in the area gave the dump
site a wide berth, never once looking at the dump, no matter
what was heard emanating from its confines. If you so much as
glanced at the garbage pile during this ominous time, the devils
would slap you across the face, twisting your features beyond
recognition.

No one had actually been hit by one of these devils—but
that was because no one had ever been foolish enough to look
at the dump site, even when the devils called them by name. If

you heard your name called, you had to recite aloud the long-established sacred words, while speeding up your pace. Almaz had clearly ignored these fundamental rules.

The medicine woman recommended sacrificing a rooster. It has to be a *gebsima*, the holy woman pronounced—a unique type of fowl, black, with white grains evenly sprinkled on its shiny feathers. Although a common sacrifice, *gebsima* roosters were hard to come by. Mam and I spent half a day in the market without success. We then walked from home to home, asking over the fence of each compound if anyone was willing to sell a *gebsima* rooster. Twice, Mam had to decline, because she suspected that feathers had been plucked out of the rooster to make it look like a *gebsima*. Once, Mam was very irritated because a woman attempted to sell her a black fowl that she had splashed with white paint; Mam exposed the fraud by spitting on the feathers of the rooster and rubbing it with her fingers. But before the day was out we'd found the fowl, with the acceptable height of comb and of the right age—which Mam was able to establish by the length of the spur on the rooster's feet.

Almaz and Mam went back to the medicine woman with the rooster in hand, and the fifteen birr in cash, which, as the lady required, had been wrapped in a clean white handkerchief by a veritable virgin. In her unique language, the medicine woman prayed over the rooster, and handed it to Mam along with a *kitab* for Almaz to wear around her neck. The *kitab*, a small leather pouch containing a holy fetish to ward off the evil eye and diffuse the effects of the Devil, had to be worn until adulthood. Only the medicine woman knew what was inside it. Attempting to open the tightly stitched pouch to peek at its contents would immediately void the potency of the medicine—so its secrecy was held in great reverence.

Dad refused to slaughter the rooster, as he was still mad at Almaz. Since the Bible forbade women to slaughter animals, I, the next oldest man in the family, had to take over the job. The rooster was slaughtered at the entrance of the main house, and Almaz was made to walk over its blood.

Dad didn't forget the humiliation that Almaz had caused him. A few days later he once again attempted to bring her into line. This time, however, he didn't ask her to fetch a branch. He grabbed her by surprise and had unbuckled his belt before she realized what he was about. Almaz bit his hand and fled the compound. She didn't return until Father had left Jijiga, a week later.

AFTER MOVING TO Asebe Teferi, this same disposition earned Almaz the respect of neighbours and acquaintances alike. She once confronted a man who drank himself into a stupor, nightly, before beating his wife. The man was old and frail, and though his wife was far younger and stronger, she had never dared to protest his abuse. Almaz, wild as she was, couldn't stand to hear the woman's cries any longer. She knocked on the door of their house one night, and when the man stepped out she grabbed him by the collar and shook him up, promising to break every bone in his body if he raised a hand against his wife again. Her admonition not only sobered the man, but stayed his hand. She had, in a single stroke, solved decades of feuding between the couple, becoming a legend in the process.

THE OVERALL environment in Asebe Teferi was, all things considered, much less tense than before. The people did not have that same look of tightness about the face and neck as they walked through the streets. One could see youngsters strolling about the roads, some of whom were even dressed fashionably. It seemed that most of the threatening political opponents of the regime were dead, in exile or rotting in prison, and the going was good for those in power.

A few days after I settled in, an old friend of mine, Tesfu, called on me. Tesfu had been my high-school teacher back in Jijiga, but because of his youth and political convictions we were more like buddies than student and teacher. I told Tesfu that in the four days I had been home I had ventured out just once, to visit my younger sister in jail. The memory of my last encounter with the Meison cadre was still fresh in my mind, and I did not want to take any more risks.

Upon hearing this, Tesfu laughed out loud and assured me that things were not as they used to be, that the storm had finally subsided. He told me about a number of people we both knew who had been imprisoned when I left for Addis Ababa, but were now free and reinstated in their previous jobs. He also told me that there were no more executions—political rehabilitation was now in vogue. Reactionaries were now enrolled in Marxist-Leninist re-indoctrination programs, where they were encouraged to practise criticism and self-criticism, then baptized as full-fledged comrades. They were even allowed to mix with the general population, their past sins ostensibly forgotten. To make his point, Tesfu invited me out for a drink and introduced me to a number of people, some of whom I was certain belonged to the Meison party. To my surprise, Tesfu had also become a member.

Tɛsꜰu Rɛmiɴdɛd Mɛ of another lost soul: a European adventurer who had gone astray in the Nile Delta. Fatigued from walking in the desert for many, many days, and burned by the unforgiving African sun, the young man sought solace in the Nile River. But he had the presence of mind not to jump in the river before finding out about the condition of the water. He consulted a shepherd boy sitting on a boulder. "Are there any sharks in this part of the river?" asked the European.

"No," answered the shepherd.

The European took off his clothes and dipped into the refreshing water. He swam, carefully avoiding the tree trunks and bushes carried by the majestic Nile. The shepherd boy threw the stranger a glance from time to time as he brushed his teeth with the chewed end of a twig.

Completely refreshed, the European came out of the water. While drying himself with his shirt, he decided to unload what had been weighing heavily on his mind for quite a while. He casually walked up to the shepherd boy. "Excuse me," the European interrupted the nomad's daydream. "Excuse me, but how can you be so sure that there are no sharks in the river?"

"Simple," answered the shepherd boy, radiating generations of wisdom. "There are no sharks where there are so many crocodiles."

Uɴbɛkɴowɴsт тo Tɛsꜰu, the Meison's days were numbered. The military junta had been cultivating its own brand of party for a long time. Barely a year after my encounter with Tesfu, the Meison would be outlawed.

I maintained irreconcilable differences with the military junta, because I was convinced that Ethiopia had no future under their leadership. In less than five years our country had been reduced to lawlessness; the legal structure had been completely destroyed; and the cultural and educational institutions had been transformed into propaganda machines.

The confiscation of private businesses during the revolution had made the country taboo for foreign as well as domestic investors. The roads remained unrepaired, the school buildings unfinished, and the hospitals had deteriorated because the West refused to lend us money. What little money the government was able to generate was spent in stabilizing its precarious position. Ever since the junta had taken power, the defence budget had steadily increased, until by the 1980/81 budget year it swallowed a staggering 51 percent of the year's US$835.8-million budget; education and culture (the regime's euphemism for propaganda) was allocated 13.2 percent of the budget, whereas agriculture, the backbone of the nation's economy, received a meagre 2.9 percent. Meanwhile, the real income of manufacturing workers had been heading down at an average rate of 5.5 percent per annum.

I realized that the nation was in a transitional stage and that some downturn of the economy and standard of living was to be expected. The problem facing the country was, however, not a temporary setback but a fundamental one. The high brass had misread the label, and given the wrong dose of "Scientific Socialism." What the junta overlooked was the fine print stating that Ethiopia, which had a largely underdeveloped economy, was in the "National Democratic Revolution" (NDR) stage identified by the mature socialist nations as the first tier on the road towards "Scientific Socialism." During the precarious NDR stage, both capitalism and socialism were supposed to be fostered under the watchful eyes of the revolutionary state, whose job it was to regulate them and set limits on the level of private investments.

Was there anything positive about what the junta had done, a weary reader may wonder? How about the land reform, which had obviously liberated millions of peasants from the clutches of greedy feudal lords?

The land reform was, indeed, the most courageous of all the measures taken by the junta. I remember shedding tears of jubilation that the sacrifices that we had made were not completely in vain. I was awed that such an ancient and arrogant feudal structure could be dismantled in a single, brave stroke. With many of my peers, I held my breath, expecting a massive reaction from the deposed landowners, and we sighed in collective relief when it failed to materialize. The peasants had won the war without shedding a drop of their own blood; the prize was laid at their bedsides, served up for them on a silver platter.

Why, then, three years after the fact, did the peasants still wait to celebrate their victory? Why did so many of them openly protest that while the old feudal chains may have been broken, they had been replaced by much more refined ones?

The land reform granted the peasant a "possessory" right of the land he tilled up to a maximum of ten hectares. He was the sole owner of the fruits of his labour. He paid no excessive tributes and did not have to shine the boots of the junta. But there were some minor hitches.

With the old feudal lords gone, the administration of rural lands fell into the hands of the twenty thousand peasant associations that sprang up all over the countryside to serve the seven million former tenant families. The peasant associations distributed the land, politicized the peasant and, when the motherland called, armed and mobilized him. But the land grants were not as generous as was initially thought, and an average of 1.5 hectares was allotted to each family.

The peasants' grievances were not so much with the shortage of land as with the uncertainty surrounding their allotments. The peasant associations continually subdivided and reallocated parcels as newly eligible young peasant families came forward, making it difficult for the peasant to develop his lot. Why would he spend his time and money on building terraces, fertilizing his fields and digging water reservoirs if someone would soon take the land away from him?

Leaders of the peasant associations were quick to realize the potential their offices had, and soon became corrupt. Monies changed hands for bigger and better parcels, and grudges were settled by assigning a bad lot to a neighbour in disfavour. It was not uncommon in the highlands for a single peasant family to be assigned and reassigned tiny pieces of land scattered all over the landscape, making it immensely difficult to look after their crop. There was no way to appeal the decisions of the peasant associations.

The peasant had to cope with another obstacle: the socialized market. Peasants were required to sell, at a bare minimum, fifty percent of their produce to the state-run "Agricultural Marketing Corporation" (AMC). Naturally, the AMC set the price. The balance of the produce could be sold at the local market or consumed by members of the peasant household, but roadblocks, checkpoints and other methods halted anyone from smuggling grain into the cities. I vividly recall having to walk through the jungle to bring Mam a few kilos of grain from Kuni, a mere half-hour drive from Asebe

Teferi. Prices in Kuni were as little as one-fifth of those in Asebe Teferi.

Collectivization of the peasant holdings—pooling the land, draft animals and farm implements—was meant to overcome the inefficiencies of small farms, taking advantage of the benefits of larger-scale operations. They developed in stages. In its final form, a collective farm would abolish private ownership of land altogether, and income would be distributed among the farmers based on labour contributions. Unlike state farms, which are owned and operated by the state, collective farms are the property of the farmers in the group.

For an Ethiopian farmer, to help out a neighbour in need is as primeval an instinct as sharing a feast with him. But collectivization had nothing to do with helping neighbours; it was an alien culture that had set itself on a collision course with the treasured attitudes and values of the peasants. Collective farms removed ownership of land and tools from the individual's reach, and made them properties of the community. They made it impossible for the peasant to walk into "his" farm to pick a few ears of corn for his hungry kids, and taxed the saint's days he had always observed.

Collective farms were slow to progress. On that summer day in 1978, as I was having a cold beer with Tesfu under the bright eyes of the heavenly stars, there were only a couple of dozen in existence. At their peak, there were only about forty, as the peasants put up stiff resistance. In one memorable act of defiance in early September 1979, a hundred and fifty people in the province of Sidamo were done to death by the regime for protesting against collectivization.

Other peasants managed to express their displeasure in a less risky but equally powerful way: through output. A 1983 report by the Ministry of Agriculture confirmed what we had always known, that private farms invariably outperform collective ones. Comparative yields for private and collective farms tell the whole story: for barley, private farms produced an average of 11.5 quintals per hectare while collective farms yielded just 6.48; for wheat, the comparative yield was 13.2 to 2.38; for maize, 20.2 to 11.05; for sorghum, 12.5 to 3.47; and for *teff*, the main staple food of most Ethiopians, the figure was a staggering 11.3 to 0.52.

One could easily follow the threads of famine weaving in the junta's farm policy long before it became public in 1984. Forced collectivization of the farmer; the instability of private holdings; artificially depressed prices for farm produce; and the absence of consumer goods for the peasant to aspire to purchase—encouraging him to enhance his produce—triggered the crisis, exactly one decade after the last one of similar magnitude had helped bring down the old monarchy.

State farms were the brainchild of the chairman of the junta. The experts weren't confident that the state was properly equipped to operate such an enterprise, but the chairman wouldn't hear of it. State farms were the socialist thing to do. They generated imports, alleviated food shortages, and would be impressive sites for visiting dignitaries, the chairman believed.

And so, shortly after the Land Reform Act, teams were dispatched to seek out potential state farm sites. A team consisted of agronomists, land surveyors and political cadres. The first stops this team made were at existing farms—the peasant holdings. The peasants had not yet finished celebrating their recently acquired land "ownership" when the regime came knocking at their doors.

This team visited the farms during the peak of the rainy season, when the rivers and streams overflowed their embankments, and the land was wildly alive. The fertile soil would have been nowhere visible for the verdant growth that extended from river's edge to horizon, like an emerald-coloured tapestry. The agronomists, cadres and surveyors stood on the high ground, as in some biblical drama, and envisioned the future of the land. Their words would decide what would become of the inhabitants, what the birds would sing and how the rivers would flow. Soon after, the militia would be dispatched to evict the peasants from their homes and relocate them far away—where no one knew what the land would yield, what the *Adbar* would exact. The peasants would have to find that out on their own.

In the meantime, all traces of the peasants were eradicated. Bulldozers destroyed their homes in preparation for the construction of the residences, schools and facilities required for a large-scale operation. Settlements were built for the managers, the political cadres and the proletariat, according to their Communist class distinctions. Huge equipment sheds were constructed, in anticipation of the hundreds of tractors, combine harvesters and other farm machines that would be requested. Money, however, was in very short supply. The World Bank and other international money-lending institutions actively shunned the regime. They still looked askance at the junta which had so recently confiscated foreign-owned industries and businesses without paying a cent in financial compensation. In addition, the West was not keen on state farms, and they had plenty of failures to point to in socialist Africa, Eastern Europe and the Soviet Union. But the junta would not hear of it—this wasn't a matter of mere accounting, but ideology.

Once again, the Soviet Union intervened. An open-ended line of credit was bestowed upon the regime, and thousands of tractors, combines and other farm implements were sent from the Eastern Bloc countries, primarily Russia and East Germany. Repayment of the loan was to be in coffee, at a friendly price, delivered at the ports.

Unfortunately, the new machinery did not perform half as well as the old, which had earned a reputation after years of the most demanding conditions. The new machines required frequent maintenance and broke down easily. Replacements were in short supply. Very soon, the state farms started cannibalizing one machine to get another moving. After a few planting seasons, the state farms looked like graveyards for high-tech gadgetry.

The new state farms were plagued not only by failing machinery, but declining yields as well. Every new season was overshadowed with uncertainty. As the farm managers wondered what the ground was capable of yielding season to season, the regime's quota for the farm multiplied exponentially. The original idea of improving on the achievements of the peasants by growing the same crops with better seeds, machinery and skilled labour had been a fiasco. The planners had forgotten to consult the peasants' own considerable farming lore, the result of many generations of trial and error.

As the rains kept to no man's schedule, the peasants had learned to adjust their planting season so that it would fall within the narrow band of optimal days. The primitive tools used for turning the soil were also an asset, as they disturbed only the top few inches, allowing the depths to retain their water much longer than earth that had been turned with a tractor. During the growing season, each peasant would cover his small plot with mulch, to reduce evaporation, a practice the state farms were incapable of emulating on such a large scale. All these small factors, coupled with the peasant's personal stake in success, made the small farms outshine the large state enterprises.

The junta may have won the war against its political opponents, but the failure of its entire policy had not been completely lost on it. It wasn't for me to underpin that policy, linking my arms with the high brass in office. My life needed new direction, but that would only be found in time. What I hankered after, for the moment, was a well-deserved vacation, away from rough-and-tumble politics, and for that I could think of no better place than my beloved Kuni.

In the safe retreat of Yeneta's homestead, the two-month vacation passed quite speedily. I had to prepare for school. Earlier, I had requested and received a transfer to the Alemaya College of Agriculture, which was set in a rural area twenty kilometres from Harar. I had never had any interest in agriculture. I had always wanted to be a civil engineer. But civil engineering courses were given only in Addis Ababa, and I was determined never to set foot there again. My hope was that the distance from the city, and from the paved highway, would be therapeutic—and that the cadres would have better things to do than drop by.

ECLIPSE OF THE STAR

HALF AN HOUR'S drive from the city of Harar, five kilometres from the asphalt highway, tucked between sky-blue Lake Alemaya and peasants' holdings, lay the Alemaya College of Agriculture. The vast, fertile land on which the campus had been founded was farmed, shielding from view the school buildings, the research centres and the residential villas. During the growing season, the only clue to the existence of the campus was the two three-storey apartment buildings that housed the junior staff.

There were only five departments on campus, and most of them were related to the study of agriculture. I settled for agricultural engineering.

My first year in Alemaya passed quite uneventfully, except for one major incident. One Saturday morning, at about 5 A.M., I was shocked awake as though struck by lightning. I was sweating profusely and was shaken through with tremors. I had no idea why. I hadn't had a nightmare or been ill. But I was afflicted with such a feeling of restlessness that I couldn't stay in bed any longer, so I went out for a walk.

I walked for over an hour, and when I was finally exhausted I headed for a farm run by the horticultural section of the plant sciences department. A variety of flowers, both domestic and exotic, covered the landscape like an exquisitely wrought Persian carpet. It was breathtaking to look at, even for someone like me, who was inured to the beauty of nature. I wandered from one plot to another, from greenhouse to greenhouse, before finally sitting down to let the morning sun settle into my skin, and watch the birds and insects gorge themselves on the sweet flowers.

Around ten o'clock, I returned to my dormitory to have a shower and tidy up. Then, as I stretched myself out on the bed and stared at the featureless ceiling, I heard a knock on the door. My good friend and roommate Mitiku answered it. From the pitch of the visitor's voice, I was fairly certain that it was a man employed at Students' Services. I remembered this man as loud and ill-mannered, and thought that I was mistaken in his identity, for today his voice seemed sedate, and unusually businesslike. After exchanging greetings with Mitiku, and confirming that I resided in the unit, he asked my friend to step outside to speak with him.

Mitiku returned a moment later. He was nervous and rushed me out of bed, to change, as he was already doing himself. I was told that a car was waiting for us downstairs, and that we had to get on the road, quickly. My meticulous friend, who would never cut lumber without measuring it twice, was suddenly impulsive? He refused to say what it was all about, and why he had the sudden urge for a trip. His polite ambiguousness and his refusal to look me in the eyes betrayed him. Someone close to my heart had died. I just didn't know who.

Tears ran down my cheeks, breaking free of generations of

inhibition. I wailed through the twenty-kilometre ride, which for some reason seemed to stretch to the far end of the globe. The old Peugeot rattled. Grey dust floated up into the cabin through cracks in the floor. The Adere driver, intoxicated by a night-long feast of *chat*, tried to force the little car to disengage from the shackles of gravity. He swerved wildly on the narrow asphalt road, sending highland donkeys, laden with sacks of freshly harvested *chat*, careening into open ditches.

Ages passed before the old Peugeot finally pulled into a hospital compound. I recognized Jegula Hospital immediately. It was only two years ago that Mam and I had brought the frail body of Henok here for urgent treatment.

I stumbled out of the grey car, and instinctively headed for the small group of familiar faces congregating at the gate to the hospital morgue. I was a few feet away when the group broke into an orchestra of wailing. I resumed my cries. The women beat their chests in the time-honoured Christian tradition, shedding tears that had been held in check until my arrival. The men covered their faces with colourful handkerchiefs and began their monotone dirge. I was not told who the deceased was, and didn't find out until one of the ladies called Mam's name between her sobs.

Mam had been killed by Somali rebels who had peppered the bus she was riding in with machine-gun fire. She was coming from Jijiga. She had died that very morning, before the sun had broken free of the sombre horizon.

Unknown to me, Mam had gone to Jijiga to assess the damage done to our property by the Somali enemy, and find out about the casualties sustained by our friends and relations. Now she herself was a casualty. I knew this should never have happened. Jijiga had already been retaken by Ethiopia, and the

Somalis forced back to their rightful borders. It was a time that friends and foes should have spent assessing the damage, licking their wounds, and putting the pieces of their shattered lives back together. It should have been a time for us to forgive and forget.

Mam had believed in fairy tales, in angels and spirits. She'd believed that there were spirits who were good and bad, and who were responsible for the noble things we did and for the wickedness that befell us, but that there were no good or bad people. She'd believed in the powers of the Church and its many saints, and the ancient powers of the *Adbar*. Things in our lives might go wrong, but it was nothing that a heart-to-heart conversation with the towering *Adbar* and a few humble sacrifices to Mam's favourite saints couldn't fix.

Once, when I was still a kid, Mam showed me a primitive painting done on finely beaten sheepskin. It had come from the northern highlands. There were all sorts of animals on that hide. There were lions lying next to a small water hole, watching, with neighbourly eyes, a pack of zebras quenching their thirst. There were cheetahs and gazelles rubbing shoulders in a heavenly wilderness. Vultures shedding tears over the remains of their brother rabbit.

I was captivated by the contradictions and sheer incredulity of the painting, and asked Mam about it. In her usual matter-of-fact way, she smiled at me and gave me her simple and intuitive answer: "No animal goes out of its way to exterminate his neighbour," she said. Yes, they fight one another to assert their territory; they stalk the weak from time to time, to feed their own young; but they also accept that it is everyone's right to share this world. It never occurred to me to ask if my fellow humans were so accommodating. I doubt if

Mam would have told me if she had known the truth. But on that fateful day my unasked childhood questions were vividly answered.

M<small>AM'S REMAINS HAD</small> been placed in an unvarnished wood casket, quickly thrown together by a local carpenter. The wood was pitiful and the workmanship shoddy. A famished snake could have passed through the gaps between each plank. The casket, when it was handed to us, had already been nailed shut. Three men hoisted it onto the top of a Land Rover that belonged to the son of Mam's uncle. I used to see this man on the streets of Jijiga, but our families did not often see each other socially. I thought it was nice of him to show up at such a terrible hour, to share our grief and incur the funeral expenses.

The inside of the Land Rover was quickly filled. Besides myself, there were three women and the driver, all of whom were close relations. All my siblings were in Asebe Teferi, except for my elder sister, Meselu, who still lived in a different town.

It was a memorable trip. A light rain fell. The sky was shadowed by ink-dark clouds that moved swiftly over the mountains until the wide expanse of the heavens was completely carpeted. Only a handful of people were to be seen on the streets of Harar, most wearing plastic hoods over their heads, eyes fixed on the ground. Their minds seemed to be elsewhere, and their legs led them to a land of lost dreams. A donkey stepped out of a clutch of eucalyptus trees, laden with sacks of freshly harvested *chat*. Once its feet possessed the hard ground, the animal refused to make way for passing cars. Our driver cursed it, in a low voice. He opened his window and insulted the Oromo peasant who accompanied the creature, reminding him that the road was reserved for motorized donkeys. The peasant chose to ignore him.

The road was littered with potholes, and our car hit one now and again, shaking us violently. I was becoming quite alarmed, and was afraid that the poorly built casket would fall to pieces, forcing me to stare at the bullet-riddled body of Mam. Twice during the trip, I asked the driver to stop so I could get down and check on the integrity of our precious cargo.

Grandma, the neighbours and our few relations already knew about the tragedy. When our arrival was announced, a small crowd emerged from a teetering mourning tent that had been erected for the occasion. They cried and beat their chests in a harmonious melody. Able-bodied men lined up to take a turn at the casket, carrying it at a snail's pace up the unsteady hill. The ladies intensified their wailing, jumping higher and higher, beating their chests more and more violently, until their exposed skin looked like raw meat.

The wailing continued until the elders, who stood at the periphery of the small crowd consulting the heavens, the stars, all good spirits and angels, made a solemn declaration that it was enough. They told us that any further wailing would be considered an open protest against the Almighty's decision, and would carry grave consequences for the living. The crowd quieted immediately.

Throughout the cacophony, I could see my youngest brother, Henok, standing high on the cliff watching the drama unfold at his feet. His amused five-year-old eyes could not make head or tail of the hullabaloo around him, so he didn't realize that there had been a loss in his life, and that his future no longer held that promise of warmth. Seeing me, the boy came running, glad that I had returned early from school. He hoped that I would lift him high above my head, as I always did, and tell him some good stories. That day he was disappointed.

We laid the casket on a freshly harvested bed of green grass, in the meagre shade of some tattered beige canvas. We had to give Mam's soul time to bid farewell to her last earthly home, to the *Adbar*, and to entrust the safekeeping of her kids to the good spirits in the neighbourhood. Before sunset, we carried her remains to the final resting ground.

THE ORTHODOX Christian Church had always intrigued me. The funeral rites conducted by the Lord's House reflected the status an individual held in society. Services ranged from simply covering the casket with earth to complex burial ceremonies that sometimes lasted half a day. A day-old baby would be interred without so much as a visit from an ordained priest, who argued that the baby was far too young to have committed any grievous sin. I agreed that an infant should be exempted from Original Sin. In fact, I am still a firm believer in letting everyone off for at least one sin.

At the other extreme was the burial of a feudal lord. Even the dead could tell when a feudal lord was about to join their ranks. From the moment the Church learned about the death of one such worthy soul until the time the casket was placed in the ground, the church bells rang relentlessly, and you could be sure that every priest, monk, deacon and beggar within hearing distance would come running to escort the deceased to his eternal home.

The ceremony begins in the inner chamber of the temple, before slowly moving outdoors, where holy men stand around the open grave, their ranks seven rows deep. The senior priest reads carefully chosen passages from the Holy Bible. As he pauses to take a breath, the deacons pitch in, singing hymns and clinking incense burners. They raise a wall of aromatic smoke that hides the coffin from view, and they drown out the songs of the cemetery birds with their own. Soon, the priest picks up his solemn intonations again. He grows hotter and hotter as the sun rises above him, and finds it more difficult to breathe as the smoke accumulates. He continues his prayers, peeling off layer after layer of clothes to ventilate himself, before finally rolling on the ground as the excitement of the holy message becomes completely unbearable, tearing at his hair with maniacal fury until he passes out cold.

At that moment, just as the mourners audibly sigh their relief, believing that the ceremony has finally ended, another priest picks up where the last left off. The sun takes its toll on the mourners. Slowly, one by one, they wilt. The elders faint. Young women labour in the open field giving birth to children they hadn't conceived. The men run out of patience completely. They grumble out loud, winking at the priests to express their displeasure. Having failed to interrupt the service, they whistle in protest, throwing insults at the holy men. Finally, if they are kept long enough, they will stone the priests and deacons. The holy men run indoors, only to resume their ceremony behind the protective stone walls of the compound.

At last, in anger, the crowd sends an armed man after the holy men. This man will hold them up, robbing the priests of their Bibles, prayer sticks, incense burners, crucifixes, robes and toothbrushes. He binds them up in the cellar, locking the door behind him and tossing the key in a bush. Finally, the service comes to a close as the remains of the feudal lord are unceremoniously tossed into the ground by an army of angry men.

In Ethiopia, when an event creeps along at a painfully slow pace, people often say that it has taken "as long as the burial of a feudal lord."

The Church sent out one stuttering priest and two pubescent deacons to attend to Mam's funeral. I thought the ceremony had just begun when the holy men gave the word to lower the casket into the ground.

If one could judge the type of life the deceased had led by the size of the funeral, it appeared to me that Mam had come down in the world. There were a mere handful of people at the cemetery, and all of them were blood relations. Gone were the hundreds of families who once flocked to visit us when we lived in Jijiga. Those glamorous creatures who travelled hundreds of kilometres to console Mam over the death of a family dog, or to congratulate Father on his recent promotion, had disappeared from our lives without a trace. Even the birds had joined the conspiracy. Looking up at the trees, I could see weaver birds quarrelling among themselves, or tending to their little huts, unmindful of the one worthy soul the gods had created in this universe, who was being interred in the cold, impersonal ground beneath their very feet.

We could no longer afford a headstone, so a makeshift crucifix was placed at Mam's grave. At the end of the school year, when I returned to visit her, the marker had been lost, the little earthen mound had been worn away by the highland rain, and desperate weeds had reclaimed the lot.

Now, I'd lost Mam for good.

THE HYENA'S TAIL

FINISHED SCHOOL at the end of the 1980 academic year and was employed by Addis Ababa University as an assistant lecturer for the Alemaya College of Agriculture. It was a time when every college graduate was assured of a decent job.

I welcomed the opportunity of working for the university. The pay was competitive and the position, like all other government employment, was for life. Aside from the fact that it guaranteed me an opportunity to pursue graduate studies, the university offered free accommodation for its staff in Alemaya—an indispensable benefit in those difficult days.

The year I got a position at the university, I helped my sister Meselu and her family move to Dire Dawa, a forty-five-minute drive from Alemaya. The two of us agreed that four of my siblings would stay with her and I would bear the full financial burden for raising them. It would be much easier for her to keep an eye on them, as three of them were going to enrol in the public school where Meselu would be teaching. The high school my other brother would attend was a stone's throw away from her office.

Almaz stayed behind in Asebe Teferi. The sibling rivalry that is usually apparent in large families had deepened between Meselu and Almaz into a bitter animosity. As soon as Mam was laid in the ground, they stopped talking to each other. I never quite understood what it was they fought about, but it seemed that just about anything could trigger acrimony between them. Mam used to say the only siblings God intended to be lifelong friends were cheetah cubs, and that everyone else would have to work hard at it. It was a piece of advice that went to the grave with her.

Adding four heads to her own young family was not easy on Meselu. Though her husband was quite understanding, I could sense that her own child, who was about the same age as Henok, felt neglected. I tried to help. Visiting them once a week, I brought gifts and sweets to the kids, before spending the night out with Meselu's husband. Soon I found myself not only settling sibling squabbles, but also acting as a marriage counsellor. One day, Meselu's husband asked me to dissuade her from quitting her job. "Even with both our incomes and the money that you send us, we can hardly afford to eat meat once a week," he said.

I asked Meselu why she had decided to give up her position, knowing full well the job market was as barren as the grocer's shelf, but she simply shrugged and said she'd lost interest. There is only so much one can say to a fully grown adult, so I decided not to pursue it any further. I took my leave, telling them that I would not be able to visit the following weekend.

Instead, I received a visit that next weekend from a distraught Meselu. She demanded I increase their monthly allowance. I was already spending almost half of my net income on my siblings, and could hardly afford to buy a jacket for myself after six months of scrimping. She had her own thoughts as to where I could trim my expenses. "The money that you send to Almaz is wasted," she said, "because not only has she given up school, but she has already delivered a baby out of wedlock."

I remained frozen to my seat, my eyes bulged and my temple throbbed. Beads of sweat formed on my upper lip and slowly rolled down my chin. When I looked up to the open window, I caught a glimpse of Mam in her mourning cloth and I cried. I wept for what seemed like hours, not knowing whether it was because I missed Mam or because of the endless misfortune that seemed to plague our family.

The next day, after seeing Meselu off, I took the bus to Asebe Teferi. During the four-hour ride, I asked myself how I could have failed to notice her growing belly. I had visited her no fewer than three times in the last year. Then it dawned on me; I remembered the loose-fitting dress she'd worn all that time, which, combined with a plumpish figure, had completely obscured her pregnancy.

My anger had not abated by the time I got off the bus. I'd rehearsed what I would say to her: "Neither you nor anyone else should expect me to support you for the whole of your life. I gave you a helping hand so you could stand on your own two feet." Knowing she had nowhere else to turn, I reminded myself not to be too hard on her. Almaz is terribly short-tempered; no one could predict what she might do to herself. She was also intelligent enough to realize her mistake, so I was confident she would break down in front of me and promise not to put herself in a similar position again.

What awaited me was a smiling Almaz, proudly displaying her infant in her arms. My anger quickly gave way to pity. Here was a young woman who lived in a world where even those who were well placed on the economic and political ladder found the future depressingly uncertain, yet she believed somehow that having a baby, even out of wedlock, would be a welcome distraction. I could only plead with her to go back to school while Grandma looked after the baby.

THREE YEARS HAD passed since I'd assumed the responsibilities of heading the family. My career was at a standstill. I was the only one of the original crew who remained on campus. The rest were abroad pursuing graduate studies. Scholarships from the Eastern Bloc countries were as abundant as sand. I refused to accept any of them, arguing that I didn't wish to learn a language I'd have no use for. The medium of instruction in all of these universities was the local language.

I wrote to most of the American universities and a handful of European ones, in vain; the West denied us scholarships. I'd been reminded by the college dean, more than once, that if I didn't strike out on my own by the end of the academic year, I would be sent to one of the Eastern Bloc countries. No excuse would be admissible.

I'd been brooding over my gloomy future, lost in a dazed bewilderment, when one breezy afternoon in May 1983 I got a telegram that would ultimately change my life: a long-since-forgotten application to a Western university had finally been accepted. Four hundred candidates from seventeen countries in four continents had written an entrance exam for admission into the University of Wageningen, in the Netherlands. Fifty were admitted, including myself. Moreover, I had been offered a full scholarship, including airfare.

August 3 was to be my departure date. My preparations for the trip started immediately. I arranged for my siblings to receive a monthly allowance, in my absence, from the salary that I would still be paid. My good friend Mitiku, who was also on staff at the college, agreed to watch over the young ones for me.

The departure day quickly arrived. It was rainy, and freshly hatched insects buzzed in the clean air. While waiting for my ride to the airport, a small bag in hand, I thought of the peace of mind awaiting me in Europe, and remembered a story Mam had once told me about a young Prince.

THE PRINCE IN question was very rich, and lived in the Kingdom of Gondar. But he'd taken to gambling at a fairly young age, losing all of the money he'd inherited. Only the estate remained in his hands and that was because the Church prohibited hereditary lands being put up for sale.

One night the young Prince dreamed he saw his fortune in the Kingdom of Shewa. Early the next morning, he set out for that distant empire. Before reaching his destination, bandits ambushed him, robbing him of what little money he had, taking his clothes and horse, beating him mercilessly, and leaving him for dead. Fortunately for the young Prince, a passing monk took him to a nearby monastery and nursed him back to health and vigour.

When the Prince was up and walking, the monk decided to unburden himself of the question that had weighed heavily on his mind. "I couldn't help but notice that you are not a man

used to physical labour—your delicate hands and feet are tes-
timony to that," the monk noted. "What brought you to this
part of the kingdom?"

"I had a vivid dream in which someone told me that my
lost fortune would be replenished here in your kingdom," the
Prince replied.

The monk laughed out loud until tears ran down his face.
"Your Highness, I've had no fewer than seven dreams in which
I saw wealth and fortune laid out on a piece of land in Gondar,
and you came all this way because of just one," the monk
replied. He went on to describe the field where the fortune was
hidden, which to the astonishment of the young Prince was his
own property.

The monk saddled a horse for the young Prince, a mule to
carry food for the trip back to Gondar, several bags of seeds
and a flask of water. He also gave the visitor what little money
he had, saying that when the Prince had recovered his fortune
he could give the sum to anyone who came asking for his help.
The monk helped the Prince through his difficult times. He
wanted the Prince to do the same for someone else in need.

No sooner had the young Prince arrived home than he
grabbed a hoe and shovel and set out for the field the monk had
described. For the next two months, the young Prince turned
the soil, sometimes with the help of the community, until all
fifty hectares were completely ploughed. But there was no sign
of the fortune the monk had promised. Confused and very disappointed, the young Prince looked to a local sage for an
answer to the mystery.

The young Prince told the sage the whole story, beginning
with how he'd lost his entire fortune due to his gambling affliction. The sage heard him out with patience and care before

passing judgment. "The monk is a wise man," he began, "and was right to say that there is a fortune hidden in your land. But to find it, first you must sow the seed which he gave you, then wait for seven months, before cashing it in."

And so the young Prince not only found a small fortune in farming, but also got over his gambling habit, for he was far too busy working the field to be distracted by such a sin.

I BELIEVED THAT, like the young Prince, the solutions to my problems would be found in my own backyard. While the trip abroad would give me a well-deserved hiatus, I hoped that things would have changed for the better by the time I finished school in two years, and that my homecoming would begin a new chapter in my life.

A BRIEF EPILOGUE

WHEN I LEFT Ethiopia, the junta seemed to be teetering on the brink of a long-overdue grave. Militiamen who had been sent out to fight the relentless guerrillas had been defecting at an alarming rate; the economy was in a shambles; and the farmer was refusing to toil on the co-operative farms, preferring to spend his time in the backyard garden, which aggravated the food shortage. When the long-expected famine was finally blown into the open in 1984, I believed, like many, that something would have to give in Addis Ababa. After all, the final straw that had brought the aging emperor tumbling down exactly a decade earlier was a famine of similar magnitude.

Pictures of the famine were broadcast the world over, and aid poured into the country. The junta raised $100 million and voted on how best to spend it. Their answer to the famine was to purchase crates of vintage champagne, exotic food and an assortment of gifts from Europe, and to throw a lavish party to celebrate the tenth anniversary of their coming to power. I did not think the high brass would live for long after this monumental scandal. I expected some liberal elements in the army to sense the popular discontent and remove the bigwigs from power.

But it was not to be.

As the year 1985 progressed, I started having second thoughts about returning home. But where to go? The Dutch, whom I'd come to know, are the most cultured people one could ever meet. They'd been civil to me throughout the two years, but I suspected that once I decided to overstay my welcome, my reception would be entirely different. Refugees' prospects are very limited in Europe. I had seen far too many drifters living in the streets of Amsterdam and Paris to ever contemplate setting up home on the continent. A man in my position had to look to the New World for sanctuary.

I'd been brooding over my indeterminate status when, one afternoon, I came across an article in a newspaper: Nigeria had deported ten thousand Ghanaian migrants from its territory. Well, what of it, I said to myself; if a black African country could do such a thing to its neighbours with impunity, what could I expect of a people who did not look like me? As to whether or not I would be thrown aboard the next ship home, I figured I would soon find out.

I obtained a visitor's visa to Canada. To raise money for the trip, I sold the home equipment I'd accumulated over the years, items which, like most returning African students, I had hoped to take home with me. In May of 1985, I boarded a plane to Toronto.

When my two-week visa expired, I slunk into an immigration office in Hamilton and whispered my intentions. I was shown into a small cubicle by an officer with an untamed moustache who gave me a form to fill in before he walked out, mug in hand. I realized immediately what was about to happen: I had seen the very same plot in movies. The officer would return with a colleague, the two of them would play good cop/ bad cop, ask me about my ulterior motives, punch me in the stomach, dress me in pink overalls, lock a chain around my ankles and wrists, and dispatch me to a detention centre in a windowless van.

But the officer came back alone, and smiled as he apologized for taking so long. He took my passport, giving me a slip of paper that said I was entitled to health insurance, could seek a job, and could even obtain financial assistance if I needed it. Wishing me good luck, he bade me goodbye. On the way out, I glanced at my feet, to see if I was walking on the ground.

THOSE EARLY DAYS were filled with surprises about life in a democracy, which, as a transient, I hadn't paid much attention to in Europe. The most memorable of these was an article I read in a newspaper a few days after my arrival. A man who had tortured his cat was sentenced to a three-month jail term, it shouted. This was obviously a bad joke that had found its way onto the front page through some editorial error, and I clipped the column to laugh over with some Canadian acquaintances.

It was not a joke at all.

I realized the real joke was how anyone could sanction a system that terrorized its citizens, accepted torture as a form of fact-finding and hailed murder as an effective method of exorcising government opponents. Perhaps the biggest joke of all (though some may call it an irony) was the fact that just such a government had been underpinned by a people who placed such emphasis on the rights of cats. After all, the military junta I'd left behind had received a substantial amount of financial assistance from Pierre Trudeau's administration.

Canada has been good to me from my earliest days here as a political refugee, when I spent many sweaty nights haunted by harrowing experiences from the past and often avoided human contact during the daylight hours. I have nothing but good things to say about the Canadian people. I have only wished that they, like much of the Western world, could be more considerate of the welfare of those who live in distant places.

As it seemed unlikely I would return home any time soon, I started preparing myself for the job market. In 1986 I registered for a graduate course in structural engineering at the University of Waterloo. Late in 1988, I earned my degree and was offered a position with an engineering consulting firm in Toronto.

Since leaving the Netherlands, I'd severed all contact with my friends and relations in Ethiopia, but in 1989 I made an attempt to mend fences with my siblings. I wrote a very long letter to Meselu, apologizing for my inexcusable behaviour and promising to be of help from my new station in life. Months passed without any acknowledgment, so I sent her another letter. Alas, I'd lost contact with her.

A year of frantic effort would be spent, including a great deal of footwork here in Toronto as I attempted to find an Ethiopian with relations in Dire Dawa, before I found out the status of my siblings. Meselu had thrown all four kids out when she realized I was not coming back. Henok spent months living in the streets, spending the nights at a bus terminal, before he was rescued by the "Save the Children" charity and given shelter. It was the most devastating news given to me since the death of Mam.

Henok was retrieved from the shelter by the youngest of my four sisters, who, after getting a job with an international agency in Jijiga, gathered her siblings. He'd spent years out of school, and hadn't even completed his elementary education. I urged him to make some progress in his studies before I brought him to Canada. In May 1996 I applied for him to immigrate.

Almaz had gone on to have two more kids out of wedlock. She and her children had moved to our residence in Jijiga. In 1997, Meselu and Almaz went to court, fighting over the family real estate and creating a huge scandal.

IN 1991, THE military junta that had ruled Ethiopia for over a decade was finally deposed by one of the guerrilla movements. I did not break open a bottle of champagne to celebrate the occasion, because by then I'd realized that what had happened in Ethiopia was not exceptional. To varying degrees, it had happened all over sunny Africa, and still does.

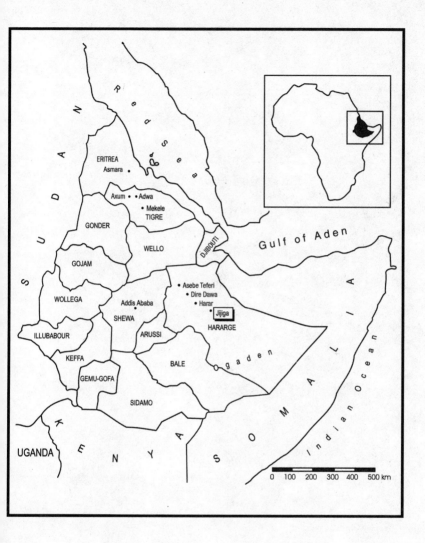

PRE-1991 MAP OF ETHIOPIA